D1561888

The Blue Planet
Informal International Police Networks and National Intelligence

Michael D. Bayer
NIU Research Fellow

NATIONAL INTELLIGENCE UNIVERSITY
WASHINGTON, DC

February 2010

NI PRESS
NATIONAL INTELLIGENCE UNIVERSITY

Michael Bayer's book *The Blue Planet* addresses the question: how can the United States engage international partners more effectively to address worldwide manifestations of destabilizing violence, often indiscriminately labeled "terrorism?" Bayer is a former chief of the Department of State's (DOS) transnational criminal investigative office. Washington, DC.

Bayer researched and wrote this book while participating in the Research Fellows Program under the Center for Strategic Intelligence Research (CSIR) at the National Intelligence University (NIU). Bayer credits former NI Press editors, Dr. William Spracher and Dr. Russell Swenson for their support and assistance while working on his book.

The goal of the NI Press is to publish high quality, valuable, and timely books on topics of concern to the Intelligence Community and the U.S. government. Books published by the NI Press undergo peer review by senior officials in the U.S. government as well as outside experts.

How to order this book. Everyone may download a free electronic copy from our website at *http://www.NI-U.edu* U.S. government employees may request a complimentary copy by contacting us at: The general public may purchase a copy from the Government Printing Office (GPO) at *http://bookstore.gpo.gov*.

Editor, NI Press
Center for Strategic Intelligence Research
National Intelligence University
Defense Intelligence Agency
Joint Base Anacostia-Bolling
Washington, DC 20340-5100

The Blue Planet

Informal International Police Networks and National Intelligence

Michael D. Bayer
NIU Research Fellow

NATIONAL INTELLIGENCE UNIVERSITY
WASHINGTON, DC

February 2010

CONTENTS

FOREWORD

Jacqueline Ross
Professor of Law
University of Illinois

Mike Bayer's book, *The Blue Planet: Informal International Police Networks and National Intelligence*, makes a powerful argument for why the United States needs to make better use of its federal law enforcement agencies abroad as an integral part of our national counterterrorism strategy. Bayer's book criticizes the primacy of the military/intelligence model in our foreign counterintelligence strategy, arguing that the counterterrorism role reserved for the FBI makes insufficient use of the global networking capabilities of our many other American law enforcement agencies abroad. Bayer's book makes an important contribution to the literature on international governmental networks, such as the work of Anne-Marie Slaughter and Kal Raustiala, describing the unique ability that informal networks of cooperating law enforcement agencies have to collect information about local conditions and local communities that may prove crucial in identifying terrorist threats and preventing terrorist attacks.

Bayer argues that such networks have proven immensely successful in investigating organized crime, but that these capabilities have been underused against international terrorist networks. By virtue of their omnipresence around the globe, police are "natural anticipatory collectors" of vast amounts of information. They are for that reason well-placed to detect suspicious activities—particularly given the overlap between terrorist cells and criminal networks. Law enforcement personnel have a unique ability to draw on trust and a common culture with their counterparts in other countries, resulting in a regular informal interchange of useful information. Building on the work of Mathieu Deflem, Bayer recognizes the particular advantage that the police enjoy by virtue of their professional autonomy and relative independence from the centers of political decision-making. The same forces that insulate them politically facilitate close, albeit informal, cooperation between law enforcement agencies from such vastly different legal systems as those of the United States, Cuba, China, and Indonesia. Informal police cooperation thrives because it benefits not only powerful countries like the United States, which depend on information flows from a large variety of cooperating countries, but also relatively weak police entities seeking to increase their professionalism and autonomy from their own political centers. Given their special access to sources of intelligence not easily exploitable by the intelligence establishment, law enforcement agencies could play a much more important role than they currently do as full partners in a comprehensive American counterterrorism strategy.

Embedded in Bayer's argument about the power of international law enforcement networks is a powerful critique of the intelligence establishment and its approach to countering terrorism. Bayer identifies the mismatch of an intelligence strategy that is founded on a Cold War model which fails to distinguish security risks posed by states from threats posed by terrorists. Here Bayer builds on the work of Richard Posner and Melvin Goodman. One symptom of this mismatch is the over-reliance of the American intelligence community on the classification of intelligence, and its tendency to overvalue secret sources of information, in contrast with the relatively unfettered flow of information among cooperating law enforcement agencies. Bayer sees the tendency to over-classify intelligence as a form of turf protection by military and intelligence agencies, aimed to forestall feared encroachments by law enforcement agencies. Ironically, however, classified intelligence may be particularly prone to exploitation and manipulation by those with personal agendas, and more prone to leaks—in part because intelligence agencies enjoy less autonomy from political pressure compared to the relatively less centralized American law enforcement agencies. Thus, Bayer argues that consignment to less sensitive categories of classification may actually make intelligence safer, as evidenced by the success of the Witness Security Program, the security of which has never been breached, or the achievements of the Drug Enforcement Administration, based largely on informal, trust-based networks of international contacts. By contrast, classification of intelligence tends to defeat the free flow of information and impede its critical evaluation. Bayer illustrates these points with striking examples of successful law enforcement cooperation that depended on the confidential exchange of unclassified but sensitive information.

Like Deflem, Bayer argues for the importance of building international cooperation around a vision of terrorism as primarily a criminal phenomenon, closely linked to organized crime. Thus he questions the tendency to treat terrorism information as national security intelligence rather than crime data. Law enforcement networks enjoy unique advantages as investigators by virtue of their access to a variety of law enforcement databases, such as records of criminal histories and border crossing information. Their international presence makes law enforcement agencies ideally suited to play a leadership role in the investigation and prevention of terrorism. Using examples drawn from his own wealth of experience with the State Department and Diplomatic Security, Bayer illustrates and documents his claim that terrorism is not only itself a crime but also draws support from criminal networks and a range of criminal activities, including credit card fraud, visa fraud, arms smuggling, human trafficking, extortion, and bribery. Terrorists draw on criminal networks for their infrastructure and logistical support, and they also commit crimes to fund their terrorist activities.

In this vein Bayer builds on the work of Jones and Libicki as well as Ludo Block, Rob McKusker, and Tamara Makarenko in criticizing the artificial distinction between terrorism and organized crime. Law enforcement agencies have special techniques in detecting and countering these types of activities. They also have a greater local presence, better local knowledge, a special ability to generate cooperation by doing favors for locals (including national law enforcement agencies), and greater transparency and accountability than intelligence agencies, making it more likely they will gather information in formats and through procedures that render it usable as evidence in a criminal prosecution. The author argues that the U.S. government can and should make much more routine use of its own overseas law enforcement capabilities to combat international terrorism and to assess the criminal activities that support terrorist activity.

Bayer backs these arguments up with impressive examples of successful law enforcement cooperation that resulted in the arrest of a notorious arms dealer (by the DEA) and of Indonesian terrorists (by Diplomatic Security). Each of these examples involved the investigation of crimes such as visa fraud and arms trafficking that are typically associated with organized crime, but that led to the identification and arrest of terrorists. At the same time, Bayer shows that law enforcement agencies have investigative skills which transcend their expertise in making criminal cases, to wit, an expertise in conducting surveillance that has permitted American law enforcement agencies overseas to anticipate and prevent terrorist attacks on U.S. embassies and diplomatic personnel. Precisely because of their local implementation, law enforcement agencies can obtain intelligence in less targeted ways than their counterparts in the intelligence community, identifying persons of interests and a wealth of other preventive information (or "actionable intelligence"). For Bayer, informal links with national police abroad are the basis of this local presence, and the access it affords American law enforcement to information provided by cooperating law enforcement agencies' own informant base. Once police agencies have started to cooperate on common enemies such as counterfeiters, arms smugglers, and manufacturers of false documents, law enforcement has laid the foundation for successful cooperation against terrorists as well—particularly given the dependence of terrorists on weapons dealers, forgers, and other members of organized crime.

COMMENTARY

Monica den Boer
Academic Dean, Police Academy of The Netherlands
Professor of the International Police Function
VU University Amsterdam

Under the shield of *The Blue Planet*, law enforcement professionals and academics will discover an intricate web of arguments and cases concerning the continuing need for informal international police networks. On the basis of his rich experience, Mike Bayer argues in an authoritative and persuasive manner that the control of transnational organised crime and terrorism can only be successful if informal information exchange is acknowledged as a necessary asset which can complement formal law enforcement bureaucracies. Notwithstanding current developments in the direction of intelligence-led policing, Mike Bayer observes persistent myopia when it concerns conceptions about the separation between information and intelligence. The latter field of activity is steadily being cultivated as typically belonging to the realm of intelligence agencies and secret services. Hence, intelligence is often labeled as "classified" and not capable of being disclosed.

As police officials have their grassroots in the local communities, they are in the position to sensor information which may be decisive when it concerns structural signs of embedded crime or ideological radicalization. Hence, by using the potential of community-based police officers, more effective and efficient use can be made of a huge reservoir of live information. Even in countries where intelligence-led policing has become part and parcel of the daily law enforcement routine, creeping controversies thrive and turf battles are fought over intelligence priorities and protocols. Now that several Western European countries are heading for a multilateral style of policing—which embraces the idea that several public and private agencies should cooperate in order to maximize their effectiveness—the question is whether hitherto erected firewalls between police and secret services will eventually be torn down.

To underpin his argument about the need for more appreciation of international law enforcement networks, the author has found inspiration in recent theories concerning transnational governance, most of which emphasize the vast capacity for the formation of flexible epistemic and information networks. Notwithstanding the value of international law enforcement bureaucracies—such as Interpol and Europol—informal networks remain essential for the daily business of transnational crime control. Future research will have to be devoted to questions concerning the good governance of international law enforcement networks: despite their practical value, are they sufficiently accountable and do they generate reliable information that will lead to solid evidence in court? Can we make sure that police liaison officers who work in a foreign jurisdiction abide by the rules of that jurisdiction? Are judges in national courts in the position to verify the sources of information that has been generated by informal networking? These are pressing questions which are frequently expressed by citizens and their parliamentary representatives.

Polities like the European Union have discovered the rich potential of cross-border law enforcement networks and seek to encourage and facilitate direct information exchange between police officers through the principle of mutual recognition. While the prevailing practice is that nation-states continue to claim sovereignty rights over international intelligence exchange, they realize they have to consider new avenues for settling their uncomfortable relationship with networked law enforcement cooperation. Very promising are the new networked type of intelligence architectures, in which intelligence from a range of agencies is shared, validated, and operationalized, under the regime of a joint protocol. Gradually, this may lead to the establishment of a series of good practices, which can be exchanged between law enforcement cultures across the "blue planet." Bayer's valuable book tickles and invites interested parties to reflect on future perspectives on the governance of international police networks.

COMMENTARY

Mathieu Deflem
Associate Professor
Department of Sociology
University of South Carolina

The contemporary dynamics of international cooperation in the areas of intelligence and policing work have historical origins that trace back to well into the 19th century. To be sure, the era of globalization that we experience today is unprecedented in intensity and scale, but it would also not be wise to view law enforcement from a historical viewpoint that would disregard the gains and pains in the development of law enforcement. Thus, Michael Bayer's observations on the relevance of informal networks in international policing are all the more to be taken seriously because they are thoroughly rooted in the history of law enforcement and related security and intelligence agencies. Indeed, the development of a professional police culture, in which law enforcement is conceived in terms of efficiency considerations, may count among the most critical aspects of the historical transformation of policing. Informalism in police work, therefore, is not just something to be taken at will; on the contrary, it is framed in a long history of development.

The role of informalism in international law enforcement activities is heightened at times when international crime problems have moved to the foreground. Since the events of September 11, 2001, our world cannot be thought of outside the concerns posed by terrorist organizations and individuals. In this fight against terrorism, which is no doubt to be approached from various perspectives, it is clear that the role of law enforcement has grown considerably in recent years. It is, however, equally to be observed that the part played by law enforcement institutions in the broad constellation of counterterrorism has not yet been sufficiently analyzed and understood. This relative neglect of the police function in counterterrorism is not only intellectually puzzling, but also shortsighted from a policy-oriented viewpoint that seeks to establish sound and effective strategies against terrorism.

Institutionally, it is clear that the previous years of the "war on terror" have primarily involved a de-metaphorization to bolster the military approach to counterterrorism at the expense of other and alternative methods, including those devised by law enforcement. As the careful and sensitive study of Michael

Bayer shows, however, law enforcement institutions are not only useful but oftentimes indispensible in countering the terrorist threat of today. Unhindered by the restrictions that can mark formal collaboration across borders, informal international police networks can be most effective. At the same time, as civilian institutions, they also forego an enemy-oriented wartime approach in favor of a more permanent methodology aimed at tracking suspects. In view of the enduring nature of the terrorist threat, international police networks are no mere sideshow, but ought to be recognized as an invaluable resource.

AUTHOR'S PREFACE

A fundamental doctrine of the United States is the system of checks and balances, a system wherein political power is dispersed among various governmental elements so that no particular interests or segments can dominate the government—or the people. One of the most strident criticisms of the former Bush-Cheney administration has been that in the time of crisis and immediately after, and in the years following the 9/11 terror attacks, executive (presidential) authority had been greatly expanded during the strategic response to those attacks and was, according to some, abused—thereby skewing our revered system of checks and balances.

Certain segments of governments are acknowledged to be tools of political power—particularly subject to political influences. In the United States the military is exceptionally susceptible to the political designs of the President and the administration because he is their direct-line Commander in Chief. It is also widely acknowledged that intelligence services are part of the political epicenter of governments, because they too are a vitally important direct-line tool of national leadership. As it happened, these are the two segments of our government that benefited most, in terms of power, mission, and funding, from the prosecution of the United States' Global War on Terrorism. In fact, it had been asserted by former Vice President Cheney on U.S. national television (*FOX*) that the war on terrorism was an effort to be waged by the U.S. military and the U.S. intelligence services and *not* law enforcement.

This book maps out how bureaucratic maneuvering in the aftermath of 9/11 led to the U.S. military/intelligence apparatus assuming primacy and garnering near exclusivity in the international aspect of U.S. counterterrorism policy. This ultimately resulted in the fundamental exclusion of some of the most powerful components of the vast international resources at the fingertips of U.S. law enforcement.

The book argues that allowing this to happen was a big mistake—and an unnecessary one at that. The existing networks of international law enforcement are powerful in their own right, but globalization and concomitant worldwide reconfiguration of national sovereignty have greatly empowered inter-governmental networks (such as those of international law enforcement). This book asserts that law enforcement is especially conducive to the advantages afforded to international networks because the "culture of the badge" provides an immediate basis of trust and commonality to build upon—a commonality that can transcend borders, politics, religion, ethnicity, and other categories of segregation. Furthermore, some international policing scholarship asserts that law enforcement entities seek their own autonomy away from centers of political power by striving to find better, more efficient ways to serve the state and the public (corruption influences notwithstanding) and in so doing are given the leeway to do so. One way they do this is by engaging in informal means of doing business—seeking one-on-one interaction with foreign counterparts rather than going through multiple layers of bureaucracy and government. Those who work in international law enforcement understand implicitly and explicitly that using informal networks is how *most* international police business is accomplished—especially in this day and age of e-mail and cell phones.

But it is not the power of the network alone that brings value added to transnational policing. It is the sheer volume of numbers of police that are dispersed throughout nearly every nation in the world—and who live and work at all levels of societies, from the back alleys and villages from where terrorism breeds to the wealthiest levels, from where political/religious terrorism is financed. It is the numbers of police combined with their mandates to gather and acquire information—whether for investigative or public security purposes. Police have always had a vested interest in gathering and tracking information about local troublemakers and criminal activity in order to maintain public order and, as such, are a natural resource of acquiring terrorism information—particularly in regard to cells which might be financing or otherwise supporting operations through criminal activity. It is the ability to conduct their business among multiple levels of societies and within populations at large which makes international law enforcement very likely the largest and most potent counterterrorism network on the face of the earth. Hence, the title of this work—*The Blue Planet.*

The worldwide network of police is a formidable asset—made even more formidable by the investigative and arrest authorities bestowed upon U.S. law enforcement and its foreign counterparts. This book will demonstrate that the willful disregard of such a spectacularly valuable asset was not only foolhardy, but also served to deny the American public the measure of national security they would have been entitled had the process been honestly brokered and strategically considered. Instead, in spite of the best of intentions, the parochial interests of the most powerful agencies prevailed at the expense of our own citizens.

Police can and do cooperate with one another internationally to combat transnational crime. Organizations such as Interpol and Europol exist for this purpose—but those organizations, while valuable, bring with them the burdens and inefficiencies of their own diplomatic formalities, rules, regulations, and procedures along with the accompanying bureaucracies of participating member governments. Informal policing has been around for even longer than formal arrangements, and evolved as an efficient means to deal with the internationalization of crime. Transnational terrorism is an extreme form of international crime, but it is very often supported by other types of organized criminal activity such as drug trafficking, weapons trading, and document fraud.

One of the main objections from abroad of the U.S.'s conduct of the war on terrorism has been the perceived disregard for the "rule of law," particularly among our European allies. While some critics might find the worldwide unification of law enforcement cause for concern, this work will argue that the potential for human rights abuses are far more likely under war conditions and intelligence operations than by globally enabled police. While the potential for human rights abuses certainly exists, national law enforcement elements respecting their own "rule of law" and the laws of counterpart nations will find the means to cooperate within existing legal frameworks. This work will also argue that international police cooperation is one way that weak nations can serve to build their own governmental infrastructures and contribute in a positive way to international relations.

There will be those who will assert that the current manner in which the United States deals with gathering terrorism information from our present intelligence posture provides adequate worldwide coverage of the problem. But even a cursory analysis of the numbers of sources available to worldwide police networks versus rational estimates of intelligence assets will show those assertions to be implausible.

There are also those who might argue that international police interaction is problematic because police are an instrument of force and are endowed with powers that can be abused. This concern is valid in that abuse of police powers can readily impact human rights. The idea of informal international police relationships that are unregulated and therefore lack accountability can seem a slippery slope. However, the trend since 9/11 has been to attempt to integrate law enforcement with functions of intelligence services—as what occurred in the United States with the FBI. This linkage is gaining acceptance and is being implemented throughout Europe but it is implicitly far more slippery. The intelligence service/law enforcement dichotomy is primarily one of legal versus extra-legal constructs. Intelligence services are extra-legal forces unconstrained by legality and matters of sovereignty—and they too can be, and often are, instruments of force. When the two are integrated, the idea of rule of law becomes moot because of the extra-legal prerogatives of intelligence services—"poisoning" the law enforcement function and therefore the rule of law. It is no coincidence that one of the hallmarks of a police state is the convergence of the legal policing and extra-legal intelligence functions.

Law enforcement, on the other hand, is legally sanctioned and generally permitted to exercise its authorities for the benefit of the greater good. This work advocates solely for the legal and legitimate exercise of the rule of law through international police cooperation, whether through formal channels or through the much more powerful and effective informal networking. If a nation's laws forbid informal police cooperation, so be it. But national governments should recognize the positive role that international police cooperation can serve—not the least of which is serving the right of the people (or the people of other nations) not to be exploited, molested, or harmed by external criminal forces.

This book was not written with ill will toward any agency or governmental community. The people who work in our traditional power agencies are, by and large, dedicated public servants and are true believers in their ability to combat challenges to our national security. I am proud to call them friends and colleagues. The problem, however, lies in the nature of bureaucracies, the quest for funding and influence, and over-affiliation with organizational cultures that foster a misguided sense of competition and exclusivism. This tendency, when combined with over-reliance on time-honored ways of doing business, organizational structures designed for different times and circumstances, unimaginative strategic policy and leadership fixated on popular myths of what intelligence agencies are capable of, makes for a deadly combination—especially when confronted by a strategically adept enemy that takes advantage of the rapid changes associated with globalization and advancements in technology and applies that knowledge toward attacking national infrastructure vulnerabilities.

Eight years later we are still experiencing the after-effects of the 9/11 attacks. When the consequences can be nuclear, biological, or chemical, especially in these precarious times, can we afford to deny our public the benefits of such a powerful instrument of counterterrorism—the informal networks made available to U.S. law enforcement?

DEDICATION

To my lovely wife Suzanne, for evenings forsaken. To my son Gus, for games of catch foregone. To my daughter Ingrid, for stories unread and board games unplayed. To our Border Collie Gracie, for Frisbee throws untossed…

ACKNOWLEDGMENTS

My heartfelt thanks to those who made this book possible: To Dr. Russell Swenson for your guidance, wisdom, and tireless hard work. To Dr. Paul Swallow for your mentoring and friendship. To Dr. Jacqueline Ross for your expertise, solid help, and sound judgment. To Dr. Monica den Boer and Dr. Mathieu Deflem for your pioneering works and thoughtful support. To Dr. Phil Williams for some excellent advice. To Dr. William Spracher for your dedication and perseverance when the going grew difficult. And to all the good cops and special agents out there who help make the world a better place…

CHAPTER 1
An Orbital View of the Blue Planet

As the tragic events of 11 September 2001 recede into history, we are fortunate that since that day there has not been a significant attack on the United States, many of the original al-Qaeda hierarchy (and thousands of extremists) have been killed and captured, and terrorist plots in the United States, Europe, Asia, and Africa have been discovered and thwarted. Yet glaring uncertainties endure. Al-Qaeda remains active and, worse, many of the same problems and conditions that afflict the U.S. intelligence and security enterprise remain stubbornly entrenched.[1]

In their haste to respond to the events of 9/11, the Bush administration and Congress acted quickly, creating in the process a jury-rigged, massive new Department of Homeland Security (DHS) and accompanying counterterrorism strategic policy mishmash.[2] Under those challenging circumstances, it is not surprising that some viable strategies were pushed aside or inadequately considered. This study shows how one viable strategy—the law enforcement community's use of its informal international intelligence networks to anticipate, identify, and respond to counterterrorism threats in a detailed and tailored fashion—has been undersold and, in the end, neglected.

A War of Words

In the view of key observers, the U.S. government's post-9/11 "Global War on Terror" has conferred primacy to its military/intelligence apparatus.[3]

---

[1] "Today, we are still vulnerable to attack because—as on 9/11—we are still not able to connect the dots." The Markle Foundation Task Force on National Security in the Information Age, Nation At Risk: Policy Makers Need Better Information to Protect the Country (March 2009), 5. Also see: Amy Zegart, Spying Blind (Princeton, NJ: Princeton University Press, 2008), 13.

[2] James B. Steinberg, Erasing the Seams: An Integrated, International Strategy to Combat Terrorism (Washington, DC: Brookings Institution, 3 May 2006), 1; Melvin A. Goodman, Failure of Intelligence: The Decline and Fall of the CIA (Lanham, MD: Rowman and Littlefield, 2008), 215; Zegart, Spying Blind, 172-175, 177. For a detailed critique of the convoluted formation of the Department of Homeland Security, see Richard A. Clarke, Your Government Failed You: Breaking the Cycle of National Security Disasters (New York, Harper Collins Publishers, 2009), 203-260.

[3] Philip B. Heymann, Terrorism, Freedom and Security: Winning without War (Cambridge, MA: The MIT Press, 2003), 28. Heymann does not claim that intelligence is part of the concept of military primacy. The present author has developed the term "military/intelligence apparatus" from his interpretation of the work of Conetta, Goodman, and Flournoy and Brimley, whose works are cited below.

The present study begins from the position that this primacy has had the effect of limiting the formal U.S. federal law enforcement role in counterterrorism to what amounts to domestic security. U.S. federal law enforcement does play a significant international counterterrorism role, but primarily through border control systems, and formal protocols such as mutual legal assistance treaties (MLATs), memoranda of understanding (MOUs), letters rogatory, diplomatic notes, and agreements with international entities like Interpol and Europol. The Federal Bureau of Investigation (FBI) has taken a pro-active role internationally but bills itself as a hybrid intelligence and law enforcement agency and indeed it is a formal member of the Intelligence Community.[4] This approach has some clear benefits in that it enables the FBI to officially interact with foreign intelligence entities, but it also has some drawbacks in that certain foreign law enforcement elements now identify the FBI as a full-fledged intelligence agency and harbor a strong reluctance to coordinate with it for that reason.[5] Regardless, as the FBI has aligned itself with the Intelligence Community, and as that Community has asserted primacy on the international counterterrorism front, it will be clear from the present study that other U.S. law enforcement assets have been dissuaded from international activity—to the detriment of U.S. national security.

This study will explain how this unfortunate state of affairs has come about, and how circumstance, earnest intent, agency power plays, and pre-existing legislation have combined to slow the development of one of the most powerful and readily exploitable of counterterrorism resources: the relationships and networks of the international law enforcement community.

Since 9/11, the U.S. government has been trying to reinvent itself to cope with the problem of global terrorism (or global insurgency) as a threat to its national security and as a direct menace to its citizenry. In response to the attacks, and as a means to contain what they perceived to be a growing threat, the administration and Congress created the Department of Homeland Security, enacted the USA PATRIOT Act and related legislation, instituted some intelligence reforms, moved to enhance security at U.S. facilities abroad, drove the Taliban from Afghanistan, and invaded Iraq. The government also outlined its national counterterrorism strategy in a series of formal publications.

---

[4] Federal Bureau of Investigation, National Security Branch, available at http://www.fbi. gov/hq/nsb/nsb_integrating.htm. See also, Richard Gid Powers, Broken: The Troubled Past and Uncertain Future of the FBI (New York: Free Press), 429; original citation, FBI, The FBI's Counterterrorism Program Since September, 2001, Report to the National Commission on Terrorist Attacks upon the United States, 14 April 2004, 14, 37.

[5] This discomfort has been articulated to me on numerous occasions by foreign police contacts and by other U.S. federal law enforcement officials as I have carried out duties as criminal investigator and Regional Security Officer.

All of these measures, collectively, reflect national security policy. However, some powerful national agencies have managed to retain traditional positions of prominence when a fresh approach to international security relationships might prove more appropriate. A critical observer notes that, overall, the post-9/11 division of labor among government agencies largely perpetuated the allocation of powers and authorities that had evolved after World War II to wage the Cold War.[6]

The first order of U.S. post-9/11 business abroad, the initially successful rout of the Taliban in Afghanistan, set the stage for the preeminence of the military/intelligence apparatus in counterterrorism strategy.[7] The PATRIOT Act (2001) was designed to equip law enforcement (particularly the FBI) to deal with domestic threats – after all, the nineteen 9/11 hijackers had been living and plotting against us in our own backyard. The PATRIOT Act was also supposed to help break down the barrier between law enforcement and intelligence by dismantling the so-called "wall" that had long restricted law enforcement use of classified, intelligence-derived information for domestic criminal investigation or prosecution. But other factors operated to keep the wall standing in some areas. The Posse Comitatus Act (1867) effectively prevents U.S. military entities from engaging in domestic law enforcement. The National Security Act of 1947, which created the CIA, along with the Foreign Intelligence Surveillance Act of 1978, the Church/Pike Committee hearings, the Levi Guidelines, and United States Signals Intelligence Directives all effectively preclude intelligence agencies from conducting intelligence activities in the United States or targeting U.S. citizens.[8] The implementation of these laws has, in effect, demarcated the line between foreign and domestic intelligence—and has led intelligence and military agencies to think of the foreign domain as their "turf" because they are fundamentally precluded from serving a domestic role. At the same time, law enforcement agencies have been restricted to the domestic arena.

In the immediate aftermath of 9/11, U.S. military and intelligence services were invigorated and eager to contribute their particular talents toward the newest threat to our collective well-being—international terrorism waged within our borders. The nation's "Global War on Terrorism" (GWOT) strategy was crafted to redirect the U.S. military's resources toward the international

---

6 Amy Zegart, Spying Blind, 65.

7 James B. Steinberg, Erasing the Seams: An Integrated, International Strategy to Combat Terrorism (Washington, DC: Brookings Institution, 3 May 2006), 7, available at http://www.brookings.edu/papers/2006/0503terrorism_steinberg.aspx.

8 Richard A. Best, Jr., Intelligence and Law Enforcement: Countering Transnational Threats to the U.S., CRS Report for Congress RL30252 (Washington, DC: The Library of Congress, 16 January 2001), 9.

terrorism threat, which came to be described in terms of a global Islamist insurgency.[9] This counterterrorism "war" led to heavy military deployments in Afghanistan and Iraq, and had the positive effect of engaging the military intelligence apparatus on a massive scale. But it also had the negative consequence of misdirecting some resources that could have been better used elsewhere. This view was articulated in a 2006 assessment of the War on Terror: "The absence of an effective counterterrorism strategy has led to an over-utilization of military and covert action tools and a notable under-utilization of other instruments of national power that are vital to success against a dangerous ideology."[10] A 2008 RAND Corporation Report put it more succinctly, "After 11 September 2001, the U.S. strategy against al-Qaeda centered on the use of military force. Indeed, U.S. policymakers and key national security documents referred to operations against al-Qaeda as the War on Terrorism. Other instruments were also used, such as cutting off terrorist financing, providing foreign assistance, engaging in diplomacy, and sharing information with foreign governments. But military force was the primary instrument."[11]

While it has been famously documented that the Department of Defense and the Central Intelligence Agency were at odds over how best to wage the war on terrorism, they both had—and continue to have—significant roles in the effort, each with its share of successes and failures. Even as infighting continues, these two entities have become increasingly interdependent, mainly because the Department of Defense controls over 80 percent of the Intelligence Community's budget. In the bid for primacy, the military and intelligence communities are inextricably tied together in their new global war.[12]

As former CIA analyst Melvin Goodman points out, "The appointment of general officers (Hayden, McConnell, and Clapper) to the three most important Intelligence Community positions [respectively, Director of the Central Intelligence Agency, Director of National Intelligence, and Under Secretary of Defense for Intelligence] points to the militarization of overall

---

[9] Steinberg, Erasing the Seams, 7.

[10] Michele Flournoy and Shawn Brimley, "U.S. Strategy and Capabilities for Winning the Long War," in Five Years after 9/11: An Assessment of America's War on Terror, Julianne Smith and Thomas Sanderson, eds. (Washington, DC: The CSIS Press, 2006), 43.

[11] Philip B. Heymann, Terrorism, Freedom and Security, 9-10. Noting the limitations of international law enforcement, "The President responded by expanding the notion of international war, previously limited almost exclusively to conflict among states, to reach foreign non-state groups that wanted to harm the United States—and invoking the expanded use of the term 'war.'"

[12] Melvin A. Goodman, Failure of Intelligence: The Decline and Fall of the CIA (Lanham, MD: Rowman and Littlefield, 2008), 331-332.

national security policy.[13] The trend toward militarization began in the Clinton administration when the President's lack of military service and wartime experience led to great deference toward the military and was fully realized in the Bush administration's designation of the Global War on Terror."[14] On a similar note, Carl Conetta of the Project on Defense Alternatives notes that:

> The 9/11 attacks may have stupefied the US policy debate, rendering it narrow, reactive, and timid—but there is a more fundamental and longer-standing problem. Since the end of the Cold War, much of the US policy community has been mesmerized by the advent of US military primacy and the advantages it supposedly conveys. This circumstance seemed to provide the leverage with which the United States might further enhance its security, extend its position of world leadership, and advance an American vision of world order—a "new rule set." The 1997 *Quadrennial Defense Review* and US *National Security Strategy* went a step further, construing military primacy as essential to US global leadership and security—not just a fortuitous thing, but a necessary one. Thus, primacy became a security end in its own right and the cornerstone of our global policy.[15]

Former Deputy Attorney General Philip Heymann argues that defining the situation we face as "war" strongly suggests that our primary reliance will continue to be on military force, even after our military victories in Afghanistan and Iraq. If use of the military was in fact the most promising avenue to deal with the variety of forms of terrorism that threaten us, there would be nothing really misleading (although nothing very helpful) about describing the situation we face as "war." However, the term strongly implies the primacy of military force. According to former National Security Advisor Lieutenant General (Ret) Brent Scowcroft, U.S. Government leadership declared a "war" on terrorism to invoke the resources of the military in counterterrorism efforts, "but it had the effect of fundamentally removing expansion of our international law enforcement options from the equation."[16] Homeland security commentator Donald Reid likewise states the following: "In labeling its post-9/11 efforts the 'war' on terror, the United States invoked

---

[13] President Obama appears to be continuing this trend with the designation of Admiral Dennis Blair as Director of National Intelligence and General (Ret) James Jones as National Security Advisor. The appointment of Leon Panetta as Director of the Central Intelligence Agency could also be construed as a testament to the political foundation and role of intelligence services. This will be an important point—to be addressed further in chapter 3.

[14] Goodman, Failure of Intelligence, 335.

[15] Carl Conetta, "A Prisoner to Primacy," Project on Defense Alternatives, Briefing Memo #43, 5 February 2008, 3.

[16] Interview of Lieutenant General (Ret) Brent Scowcroft by the author in Washington, DC, 10 July 2007.

a specific metaphor to galvanize the national effort. In doing so it has tied success or failure to the doctrinal rules of war."[17] Reid maintains that this choice of terminology is problematic because, although

> it allows national leaders the flexibility to define and redefine success in ways that suit political purposes, it also has potential drawbacks. From an operational perspective, it potentially leads to lack of clarity and understanding, and thus lack of focused national effort along with its attendant risk of failure. The very phrase "war on terror" lacks definition, and therefore presents the United States with a strategic issue that inhibits its efforts to prosecute the war effectively. As multiple sources have indicated, "terror" is not the enemy. In the "war" on terror, neither terror nor terrorism can be defeated since terror is a method and terrorism is a tactic. From this perspective, neither terror nor terrorism takes on the characteristics of entities that can be defeated in the traditional sense.[18]

For much of the history of the United States, we have turned to our military to address grave dangers. In the Cold War, when nuclear war threatened, we relied more heavily on intelligence, through a predominantly military/intelligence apparatus, for security.[19] If the preponderant flow of resources to the military instrument of power continues undiminished, the demand for military transformation to fight this "war of words"—war predicated on semantics—will grow.[20] Already, with military and intelligence institutions essentially conjoined, there seems to have been no better place to invest in security. Although we have always relied on law enforcement to provide domestic security, we have increasingly come to rely on the military intelligence structure to protect us from external threats, and this appears to have been the direction of thinking behind the formulation of our present counterterrorism strategy.[21] Noted scholar James Sheptycki refers to the U.S. military and other secret institutions as representing the dominant intelligence paradigm of U.S. national security since before the Cold War—a dominance now seen by critics as an overly persistent doctrinal and operational approach.[22]

---

[17] Donald Reed, "Why Strategy Matters," Homeland Security Affairs 2, no. 3 (October 2006), 6 http://www.hsaj.org/?article=2.3.10.

[18] Reed, "Why Strategy Matters," 6.

[19] Michael Herman, Intelligence Power in Peace and War (Cambridge University Press, 1996) and Intelligence Services in the Information Age (London: Taylor and Francis, 2001), especially Chapter 9, "The Cold War: Did Intelligence Make a Difference?" 159-163.

[20] Bruce Berkowitz, The New Face of War: How War Will Be Fought in the 21st Century (New York: The Free Press, 2003).

[21] Heymann, Terrorism, Freedom and Security, 28.

[22] James Sheptycki, "Policing, Intelligence Theory and the New Human Security Paradigm: Some Lessons From the Field," in Intelligence Theory: Key Questions and Debates, Peter Gill, Stephen Marrin, and Mark Pythian, eds. (Routledge: New York, 2009), 166-185.

Military and Intelligence Primacy in U.S. Counterterrorism Policy and Strategy: A Marriage of Convenience

In *The Secret History of the CIA and the Bush Administration*, *New York Times* reporter James Risen asserts that the Bush administration simply rejected the capabilities of law enforcement and favored the Intelligence Community, particularly the CIA, to prosecute the "Global War on Terror."[23] Dana Priest of the *Washington Post* asserted that the CIA had taken the lead on counterterrorism operations worldwide."[24] Former senior CIA analyst Goodman declared that, after 9/11, "the Bush administration boasted of a 'marriage' between the Pentagon and the CIA, which indicates its support for an intelligence community subordinated to Pentagon priorities."[25] According to GAO in its 2003 interagency report, "While the level of funding for intelligence activities is classified—and included with DOD funding to prevent the disclosure of classified data—recent unclassified statements by the Director of Central Intelligence provide information on the magnitude of increases in intelligence programs related to terrorism. According to the Director, intelligence funding to combat terrorism tripled between fiscal years 1990 and 1999. The Director also said that the percent of the CIA's budget dedicated to combating terrorism increased from less than 4 percent in fiscal year 1994 to almost 10 percent in fiscal year 2002."[26] These circumstances lead to the obvious conclusion that there exists a clear primacy assigned to the military and intelligence community that extended directly from the White House. In the chapters to come, this work will refer to this primacy as the (presidential) military/intelligence apparatus.

Enduring Dichotomies: Foreign vs. Domestic/Intelligence vs. Law Enforcement/Classified vs. Unclassified/Covert vs. Overt

The division of labor between intelligence and law enforcement, having evolved over time from policy, habit, legislation, and interagency maneuvering, dictated that "intelligence" is foreign and "law enforcement"

---

[23] James Risen, State of War, The Secret History of the CIA and the Bush Administration (New York: The Free Press, 2006), 3.

[24] Dana Priest, "Bush's War on Terror Comes to a Sudden End," Washington Post, 23 January 2009, A1. http://www.washingtonpost.com/wp-dyn/content/article/2009/01/22/AR2009012203929_pf.html1.

[25] Goodman, Failure of Intelligence, 331.

[26] General Accountability Office, "Combating Terrorism: Interagency Framework and Agency Programs to Address the Overseas Threat," May 2003.

is domestic. This evolution seems likely to have been exacerbated by the establishment of military/intelligence primacy in the post-9/11 era—in light of comments from some of the most prominent subject matter experts on national security. The dichotomies of foreign versus domestic, and intelligence versus law enforcement, were declared unnecessary and obsolete as early as 1995 in a seminal book, *U.S. Intelligence at a Crossroads*.[27] Likewise, former Deputy National Security Advisor and current Deputy Secretary of State James Steinberg observed that: "In 2002, the Congressional Joint Inquiry into intelligence community activities detailed in a report the problems of the 'wall' between various agencies, stating that it 'was not a single barrier, but a series of restrictions between and within agencies constructed over sixty years as a result of legal, policy, institutional, and personal factors.' Walls separate foreign from domestic activities, foreign intelligence from law enforcement operations, the FBI from the CIA, communications intelligence from other types of intelligence, the Intelligence Community from other federal agencies, and national security information from other forms of evidence."[28] A 2001 Congressional Report echoed Steinberg: "Closely coordinating the efforts of law enforcement agencies and the Intelligence Community (alongside the State and Defense Departments) presents … significant challenges. As three knowledgeable observers have written: "The law enforcement/national security divide is especially significant, carved deeply into the topography of American government."[29] Steinberg, too, recently wrote that "efforts to date have not adequately redressed one of the most serious flaws of U.S. counterterrorism strategy: its bifurcation into *domestic* and *foreign* components," and "The problem of disconnect between foreign and domestic intelligence collection and analysis has been the heart of post 9/11 analyses of 'what went wrong.'"[30] The 9/11 Report also follows this line of reasoning—that the foreign/domestic divide must be overcome if we are going to defeat the threat of transnational terrorism.[31]

The separation between law enforcement and national security institutions and procedures, evident from before 9/11, and targeted for elimination by the PATRIOT Act, lives on. In March 2002, the U.S. Department of Justice (USDOJ), in coordination with the International Association of Chiefs of Police (IACP), convened a Criminal Intelligence Sharing Summit

---

[27] U.S. Intelligence at a Crossroads, Roy Godson and others, eds. (Washington, DC: Brassey's, 1995).

[28] Steinberg, Erasing the Seams, 8.

[29] Ashton Carter, John Deutch, and Phillip Zelikow, "Catastrophic Terrorism: Tackling the New Danger," Foreign Affairs (November/December 1998), 82.

[30] Steinberg, Erasing the Seams, 6.

[31] 9/11 Commission, The 9/11 Commission Report (2004), 400.

that called for the creation of a nationally coordinated criminal intelligence effort.[32] In the words of Jim Sullivan, the former Director of the U.S. National Central Bureau (USNCB) of Interpol,[33] that pivotal meeting set the tone for U.S. federal and domestic counterterrorism law enforcement.[34] According to some prominent attendees, the original intention of the meeting was to discuss *all* sources of information, to include the coordination of international law enforcement information, inclusive of that obtained from police sources overseas, but enthusiasm for that prospect waned as the conference narrowed its focus to U.S. *domestic* distribution of terrorism and criminal intelligence information to law enforcement.[35] Participants speculated that this orientation was due to the influence of the CIA and/or the FBI, which ostensibly wanted to maintain control of overseas sources of information.[36] From this convocation of federal, state, and tribal law enforcement, the National Criminal Intelligence Sharing (NCIS) Plan was formed.[37] The goal of the NCIS was to provide a means for all levels of U.S. law enforcement elements to share terrorism-related information in order to protect the U.S. general public.[38] The aim was to have a coherent means of coordinating and disseminating criminal intelligence information on a national scale. What was overlooked was the role of international law enforcement as a source of criminal information and information related to terrorism—along with a means to coordinate such data.

Some at the DOJ event had spoken grandly of a Global Intelligence Information Sharing Initiative, but one that would be strictly and firmly grounded in *domestic* U.S. law enforcement. However, no mention is made of international police coordination in the final report of that meeting, nor in the 2005 revised version of the NCIS Plan, despite the event being co-sponsored by the *International* Association of Chiefs of Police. Naturally, after 9/11 it was critical that the U.S. achieve coordination among its diverse domestic law enforcement population and the intelligence and national security apparatus, but to have done so with the conspicuous omission of a potentially valuable asset seems misguided.

---

[32] International Association of Chiefs of Police, Criminal Intelligence Sharing: A National Plan for Intelligence-Led Policing at the Local, State and Federal Levels (Alexandria, VA: IACP, 2002), i.

[33] Interpol is administered through "national central bureaus" of Interpol member countries. The U.S. National Central Bureau is at this time administered through a joint agreement between the U.S. Department of Justice and the U.S. Department of Homeland Security.

[34] Telephone interview with Jim Sullivan, U.S. Marshall, U.S. Virgin Islands, 23 May 2008.

[35] Sullivan interview.

[36] Sullivan interview.

[37] Bureau of Justice Assistance, United States Department of Justice, in collaboration with the Global Justice Information Sharing Initiative, The National Criminal Intelligence Sharing Plan (Washington, DC: Bureau of Justice Assistance, revised June 2005).

[38] Bureau of Justice Assistance, The National Criminal Intelligence Sharing Plan.

In a May 2007 interview with the author, the President's former National Security Advisor for Counterterrorism and Homeland Security, Frances Townsend, acknowledged as much: "In the post 9/11 period, by any measure, we've done pretty well—but we've had to be careful. This was a new kind of threat we were facing and there was a fear of unintended consequences. We have derived enormous benefit from how we do things, but now we are at a point where we can ask, 'How can we get more out of the system?'"[39]

Most Wanted Terrorists and Rewards Offered for Their Capture.
Source: State Department, with permission.

U.S. Federal Law Enforcement Loses Out on the "War," but the FBI Gets Its Due

In 2003, as part of the National Strategy for Combating Terrorism, the President directed that U.S. law enforcement entities "expand and improve

---

[39] Interview with Frances Fragos Townsend, former National Security Advisor to the President for Counterterrorism and Homeland Security, Washington, DC, 7 June 2007.

their relations with their foreign counterparts."[40] Apparently, however, this Presidential Directive went largely unheeded, because in May 2007 a General Accountability Office (GAO) report found, from even before 9/11, a general lack of guidance for U.S. federal law enforcement engagement with foreign counterparts in combating terrorism. Specifically, the GAO report found that: "with the exception of the FBI, U.S. law enforcement agencies (LEAs) have not been given clear guidance; they lacked clearly defined roles and responsibilities on helping foreign nations identify, disrupt, and prosecute terrorists."[41] The GAO further explained that although the President issued a series of national strategies providing broad direction for overseas U.S. law enforcement efforts toward counterterrorism, "most LEAs have not been provided clear directives. They generally lacked (1) clearly articulated roles and responsibilities to assist foreign nations; (2) guidance on setting funding priorities and providing resources; (3) performance monitoring systems to assess LEA progress; (4) formal structures to coordinate LEA operational and technical assistance to foreign nation LEAs; and (5) comprehensive country needs assessments to tailor LEA technical and operational assistance to specific foreign nation needs."[42]

Similarly, in 2005, the GAO submitted a report to Congress stating that the United States lacked a strategic plan to deliver counterterrorism financing training and technical assistance abroad.[43] Then, in March 2006, the GAO published a report critical of the federal government's information-sharing policies between intelligence and law enforcement.[44] This report cited six previous reports that had addressed the challenges associated with information sharing within the federal government.[45] Likewise, in April 2008, DOJ set out a detailed strategy to marshal combined U.S. LEA resources to combat

---

[40] This was to be done alongside similar efforts of the U.S. Intelligence Community. See National Strategy for Combating Terrorism (Washington, DC: White House, 2003), 16-17. http://www.whitehouse.gov/nsc/nsct/2006/nsct2006.pdf.

[41] General Accountability Office (GAO), "Combating Terrorism, Law Enforcement Agencies Lack Directives to Assist Foreign Nations to Identify, Disrupt, and Prosecute Terrorists," GAO Highlights, May 2007.

[42] GAO, "Combating Terrorism," May 2007, 3.

[43] GAO, "Combating Terrorism," May 2007, 2.

[44] GAO, Information Sharing: The Federal Government Needs to Establish Policies and Processes for Sharing Terrorism-Related and Sensitive but Unclassified Information (Washington, DC: GAO, 2 March 2006), 11-13.

[45] In May 2008, the White House issued a Presidential memorandum, Memorandum for the Heads of Executive Departments and Agencies, Subject: Designation and Sharing of Controlled Unclassified Information, available at http://www.whitehouse.gov/news/releases/2008/05/20080509-6.html, providing guidelines for sharing "sensitive but unclassified" information. Although the program does put in place a means for sharing unclassified information, it does not address the problem of over-classification. That issue will be addressed in the fourth chapter of the present work.

international organized crime, yet no strategy exists for LEAs to combat transnational terrorism.[46] Despite Presidential Directives and GAO criticisms, the low level of non-FBI, U.S. federal law enforcement participation in overseas counterterrorism coordination indicates, at the very least, its low priority in Washington.[47] The responsibility for this unhelpful approach can be assigned to the "military-intelligence apparatus of the United States."[48] In this context, the "wall" between the law enforcement and national security communities is still very much in place.

Further evidence of the primacy of the military/intelligence apparatus over the "foreign" domain and the relegation of non-FBI, U.S. law enforcement assets to a domestic role lies in what is, and *what is not*, included in other publications designed for public consumption. *The National Strategy for Information Sharing* (2007) seems carefully worded to avoid the mention of international law enforcement agency sharing of information among themselves.[49] While some attention is given the international sharing of information between governments, sharing of information between foreign and U.S. law enforcement agencies is not directly mentioned (although Interpol is obliquely referenced).

What is mentioned as a "foundational element" in the text, however, is essentially a declaration of the primacy of the Intelligence Community over the foreign information-sharing spectrum and over U.S federal law enforcement assets:

---

[46] U.S. Department of Justice, Overview of the Law Enforcement Strategy to Combat International Organized Crime (Washington, DC: DOJ, April 2008). Also see GAO, "Combating Terrorism, Law Enforcement Agencies Lack Directives..." The DOJ report incidentally identifies international crime as a support mechanism for terrorism.

[47] U.S. law enforcement does participate in the fight against terrorism in the sense that law enforcement mechanisms, particularly border control instruments, criminal databases, and warrant notice systems, are routinely employed. However, the GAO report in particular points out how the contribution of U.S. law enforcement to counterterrorism has been hamstrung in the international arena.

[48] It is perfectly understandable that any competent agency or instrument of power would defend what it perceives to be its turf. It is also perfectly understandable for the military/intelligence establishment to believe that the foreign information and intelligence arena is its "turf," especially given the long history of animosity between U.S. federal law enforcement and the U.S. intelligence services, and that U.S. legislation effectively precludes the military/intelligence apparatus from participating in domestic security. For a comprehensive account of the history of FBI/CIA antagonism, see Mark Riebling, Wedge: From Pearl Harbor to 9/11: How the Secret War between the FBI and CIA Has Endangered National Security (New York: Alfred A. Knopf, 1994). Also see John Miller and others, The Cell: Inside the 9/11 Plot, and Why the FBI and CIA Failed to Stop It (New York: Hyperion, 2002). For practitioner perspectives, see Improving the Law Enforcement-Intelligence Community Relationship: Can't We All Just Get Along? Timothy Christenson, ed. (Washington, DC: NDIC Press, 2007), available at http://www.ndic.edu/press/5463.htm.

[49] The White House, National Strategy on Information Sharing: Successes and Challenges In Improving Terrorism-Related Information Sharing (October, 2007), 3.

The instruments of our national power have long depended on the capabilities of the Intelligence Community to collect, process, analyze, and disseminate intelligence regarding our adversaries and enemies. Our efforts to combat terrorism depend on enhancing those intelligence capabilities, while enabling other Federal departments and agencies responsible for protecting the United States and its interests to regularly share information and intelligence with other public and private entities in support of mission critical activities. Information sharing at the Federal level has improved significantly since September 11, but challenges still remain that must be addressed before our strategic vision is realized.[50]

Translated, this means that the Intelligence Community will collect terrorism information from overseas, and the U.S. law enforcement community may disseminate it (appropriately, of course, after it is sanitized and declassified). To drive this point home, this 40-page national strategy document mentions law enforcement domestic dissemination of information (through state, local, and tribal channels) over 220 times but mentions international law enforcement sharing of information only once—and then only in the context of engaging Interpol. On the other hand, a 2008 DOJ strategy for combating international organized crime speaks freely and openly about interagency cooperation and coordination with its own foreign partners to combat transnational organized crime.[51] Ironically, many academics and other experts consider transnational terrorism a form of international organized crime. Clearly, there are factors and interests at work that have superseded common sense and overlooked the logic of employing the full range of counterterrorism tools to carry out U.S. strategic counterterrorism policy.

The Blue Planet

"We Are the World…"

Commissionaire Emile Perez, of the French National Police and current Chairman of the Board of the College of European Policing (CEPOL), estimates that between ten and fifteen million law enforcement officers serve worldwide.[52] Nearly every country on earth has a police force of some kind or another. The United States has nearly one million police officers; India,

---

[50] National Strategy on Information Sharing, 6.

[51] U.S. DOJ, Overview of the Law Enforcement Strategy to Combat International Organized Crime, 12.

[52] Interview in Paris with Commissionaire Emile Perez, French National Police, 7 March 2008.

1.2 million; China, 1.5 million; and although the numbers in many other countries are difficult to know with certainty, they are likely quite large.[53] The world over, police are ubiquitous and are very often powerful elements of the governments and societies they serve. In referring to U.S. law enforcement, criminal intelligence analyst Deborah Osborne points out that "local law enforcement officers, given their numbers, collect an enormous amount of information. Untold, untapped quantities of information exist within their reports that, if analyzed, could help solve many crimes, help direct efforts to prevent crime, and possibly help find and/or connect some of the dots to help prevent terrorist acts in the United States."[54] When all the nations of the world are factored in, the value of international police cooperation will be enormous.[55] The sheer numbers of police in the world, with the information they hold, with the contacts they have, is a mind-boggling resource. Osborne continued with this irrefutable logic: "The more people you know outside of your agency, the more access you have to information. In brief, it is not only who you know, but as important, who they know."[56]

Because police and other branches of law enforcement hold "prerogatives for the legitimate use of force," and hold authorities for investigation, search, detention, and arrest, they are entrusted by society and governments to wield these powers judiciously. These authorities make the police a powerful component of a nation's security. Police, because they are so entrusted, use their powers to protect the general public. Their powers provide police and law enforcement access to the most sensitive information in their home societies, including insight into the lifestyle and conduct of private citizens. Unquestionably, great care needs to be taken in using such powers, but the greater sin, from the perspective of national strategic interests, would be in *not* using these powers to full, legal advantage against so clearly a universal problem as transnational terrorism. Law enforcement agencies have long exercised the ability to coordinate with their international counterparts on a variety of criminal enforcement issues, including international organized crime, drug trafficking, human smuggling, illegal arms trading, and fugitive location, to name but a few.

---

[53] U.S. Department of Justice, Bureau of Justice Statistics, World Factbook of Criminal Justice Systems, http://www.ojp.usdoj.gov/bjs/abstract/wfcj.htm.

[54] Deborah Osborne, Out of Bounds: Innovation and Change in Law Enforcement Intelligence Analysis (Washington, DC: Joint Military Intelligence College, now National Defense Intelligence College, 2006), 2. Available at http://www.ndic.edu/press/2201.htm.

[55] Malcolm Anderson, Policing the World: Interpol and the Politics of International Police Cooperation (Oxford: Clarendon Press, 1989), briefly addresses the relationship of national intelligence agencies to respective national police institutions.

[56] Osborne, Out of Bounds, 58.

Police and law enforcement elements inhabit virtually every sector of government and society. In any given country, there may be federal or national police, state or provincial police, local and municipal police, sheriffs, marshals or their equivalent, border and immigration police, customs police, coastal and river police, military police, inspectors general, gendarmerie, tax and revenue police, narcotics police, fish and wildlife police, park rangers, constables, gaming and gambling police, traffic police, highway police, parking police, transportation police, religious police, counterterrorism police, vice police, court police, agricultural police, beach patrols, campus police, diplomatic police, presidential police, security police, facility police, prison police and guards, postal police, aviation police, treasury police, mint police, securities police, tourism police, consumer protection police, animal control police, crossing guards, high police, low police, and an unending variety of regulatory police with quasi-law enforcement powers.

Police and law enforcement therefore are present in villages, back alleys, and other areas in which rural and urban terrorists operate—and they are often present in large numbers.[57] By the nature of their work, police elements are often intimately in tune with what is going on in their neighborhoods, precincts, districts, and patrol routes. As noted in a RAND report,

> Local police, in particular, live with the community and tend to remain in local areas, unlike military units that, in many countries, are recruited throughout the nation and move frequently, which in turn inhibits their ability to develop intimate knowledge of local conditions. The police tend to be permanently located in specific areas. They have the opportunity to learn who the "bad actors" are in a region—including which groups may be politically motivated terrorists as opposed to common criminals.[58]

Law Enforcement as Intelligence Source and Resource

Contrary to the apparent thinking of pundits and experts, police and other law enforcement entities do *not* restrict their professional activities to ongoing or open criminal investigations only. In fact, police are among the most natural, anticipatory collectors of information of their surroundings,

---

[57] Richard Clarke advocates an increased level of support for community-based policing on an international scale—to be piloted by the U.S. State Department through its international police assistance programs. See Clarke, Your Government Failed You, 196-197.

[58] David C. Gompert and John Gordon IV, War by Other Means: Complete and Balanced Capabilities for Counterinsurgency (Washington, DC: RAND, 2008), 186. Available at http://www.rand.org/pubs/monographs/MG595.2/.

and are, by far, the best suited for recognizing suspicious activity.[59] Further, in the words of former CIA analyst Paul Pillar,

> [S]ome of the most unquestioning cooperators with the United States on counterterrorism are the less developed countries. They often worry less about procedural niceties than do counterparts in more developed states and are more inclined to work quickly with less red tape. They are also likely to have acquired less of the institutional baggage that often accumulates in larger and older liaison relationships and that sometimes impedes cooperation between even close allies.[60]

Gathering information about what is happening in their own areas of responsibility is what police do as a function of professionalism—it is their job to know what is going on, and who is doing what, even if it is merely a suspicion.[61] Even corrupt and inept police understand the value of gathering local information. For this reason, police are the consummate and original collectors of intelligence—not "spy" intelligence or classified intelligence, but local information that can become the basis for criminal intelligence and national security intelligence—especially when the information pertains to terrorist cell activity.[62] Long-term observers note the considerable overlap between criminality and terrorist cells:[63]

> Both crime syndicates and terrorist groups thrive in the same subterranean world of black markets and laundered money, relying on shifting networks and secret cells to accomplish their objectives. Both groups have similar needs: weapons, false documentation and safe houses.[64]

Terrorist activity stretches across a bewildering variety of cultures, loca-

---

[59] Gombert and Gordon, War by Other Means, 189.

[60] Paul Pillar, Terrorism and Foreign Policy (Washington, DC: Brookings, 2003), 186.

[61] Policing scholar James Sheptycki avers that intelligence (information gathering) in the police sector is of long standing and is used for a variety of strategic purposes separate from the direct investigation of crime. Sheptycki, "Policing, Intelligence Theory and the New Human Security Paradigm," 167.

[62] Within the last several years, the term "intelligence-led policing" has become ubiquitous. The New Jersey State Police defines intelligence-led policing as "a collaborative philosophy that starts with information gathered at all levels of the organization that is analyzed to create useful intelligence and an improved understanding of the operational environment." See New Jersey State Police, Practical Guide to Intelligence-Led Policing (Center for Intelligence-Led Policing at the Manhattan Institute, September 2006), 3. Available at: http://www.cpt-mi.org/pdf/NJPoliceGuide.pdf.

[63] For example, see Siobhan O'Neil, Terrorist Precursor Crimes: Issues and Options for Congress, CRS Report for Congress, RL34014 (Washington, DC: Congressional Research Service, 24 May 2007). Available at http://www.fas.org/sgp/crs/terror/RL34014.pdf.

[64] David Kaplan, "Paying For Terror," U.S. News & World Report, 5 December 2005.

tions, languages, criminal linkages, support networks, and financing mechanisms.[65]

The Culture of the Badge…

Law enforcement, like many other vocations, has a culture all its own. To those in the business, it is the "culture of the badge," "the thin blue line" or, in the context of this work, "The Blue Planet." The influence of this culture of the badge is well documented, although often in its negative sense, as in the popular dramas "Serpico" or "Prince of the City." The positive side of police culture can be seen in a professional attitude of wanting to do the right thing, of public service, of a desire to do good, of wanting to help those in trouble or those who have been wronged.[66] Another positive aspect is the unity implied by the culture:

> Cultures can support both positive and negative dynamics in organizational behavior. For instance, the culture of police fraternity, where police officers across the profession view each other as a family of comrades, can be a powerful element for creating unity.[67]

Policing sociologist Deflem refers to this phenomenon as "the quest for professionalism" and cites it as a driving force behind international police cooperation.[68]

The international culture of police fraternity, according to policing scholar Anthony Balzer, is primarily based on a heightened world consciousness within law enforcement, punctuated by the notion of police the world over "fighting a common enemy" and in that finding a common cause for which to cooperate.[69] It is this quality, the culture of the badge,

---

[65] Thomas Sanderson and Mary Beth Nikitin, "International Cooperation," in Five Years After 9/11: An Assessment of America's War on Terror, Julianne Smith and Thomas Sanderson, eds. (Washington, DC: The CSIS Press, 2006), 33.

[66] Mathieu Deflem, Policing World Society: Historical Foundations of International Police Cooperation (New York: Oxford University Press, Inc., 2002), 96, quotes criminologist Cyrille Fijnaut: "An international brotherhood of police was formed that developed into 'a fraternity,' which felt it had a moral purpose, a mission to fulfill for the good of society."

[67] A.R. (Rod) Gehl, "Multiagency Teams: A Leadership Challenge" The Police Chief 71, no. 10 (October 2004), 142, available at http://www.policechiefmagazine.org/magazine/index.cfm?fuseaction+display_arch&article_id+1395&issue_id+102004.

[68] Mathieu Deflem, "Bureaucratization and Social Control: Historical Foundations of International Police Cooperation," Law and Society Review 34, no. 3 (2000), 616. Article available at http://www.cas.sc.edu/socy/faculty/deflem/zinsoco.htm.

[69] Anthony J. Balzer, "International Police Cooperation: Opportunities and Obstacles," in Policing in Central Asia and Eastern Europe: Comparing Firsthand Knowledge with Experience from the West (Slovenia: College of Police and Security Studies, 1996). Available at http://www.ncjrs.gov/policing/int63.htm.

that gives international law enforcement a benefit not available to other governmental counterterrorism instruments. Those of us in law enforcement, particularly in international law enforcement, know very well—intuitively—that the culture of the badge transcends borders, nationalism, ethnicity, race, politics, religion, and even blood-tie familial bonds. As Anthony Cordesman notes,

> This kind of cooperation has value at all levels, but particularly when it cuts across religions, cultures and political systems. It builds trust and effectiveness at a very different level from the public, but this kind of trust is just as important.[70]

Trust is very real among law enforcement and it contributes to the power of police relationships and networks. Naturally, police and other law enforcement entities rely on one another for support in dangerous circumstances. Although trust at one level is a matter of self-preservation, it also serves to advance professional interests. As the author's friend, Klaus Heil, a senior international liaison official with the German *Bundeskrimalimt* (BKA, the German equivalent of our FBI), declares, "the badge gets you in the door; the trust you have to earn," suggesting that although there is a certain amount of trust implicit in holding the badge, the really good, productive relationships come later after delivering on requests.

This trust among police elements also holds value for national intelligence services. Trust is not known as a virtue/asset/benefit in the intelligence or spying profession. In contrast, trust plays a major role in the effectiveness of international policing, and its value for intelligence lies in providing a means and a basis for verification and as an incentive to deliver on a request. Based on 20+ years of international law enforcement experience, the author suggests that a willingness to cooperate, predicated upon the symbol of the badge, and a common culture that provides access to the informal networks and relationships of the international police community, can yield great dividends in the realm of both internal and international security.

Perhaps more than any other counterterrorism tool, the trust and common culture that law enforcement personnel bring to the international stage can open a path to real cooperation in the battle against terrorism. As valuable as formal institutions may be for carrying out the counterterrorism mission, informal, expert collaboration actually occurs at a distance from conventional diplomats, political figures, and contracted experts who are the key players in formal liaison relationships.

---

[70] Anthony Cordesman, "The Lessons of International Cooperation in Counterterrorism," Address to the RUSI Conference on Transnational Terrorism, A Global Approach, 18 January 2006, 5.

Formal Relationships Are Helpful; Informal Relationships Are Powerful

Those who work in international law enforcement know that informal police relationships are the primary means of facilitating international police business. Business is accomplished through phone calls or e-mail and occasionally through a mutually acquainted third party. Formal pathways like mutual legal assistance treaties (MLATs), Interpol, Europol, and intergovernmental letters rogatory (formal requests between governments for law enforcement assistance) are the last resort for those professionals who wish to get their work done expeditiously—especially if they are on a hot case.

Formal, bureaucratic channels require days or weeks, as requests are written, then cleared by supervisors and attorneys, stamped and approved by other officials, transmitted, received, considered, discussed, debated, examined, parsed, approved or disapproved, and *if* approved, the request carried out. If a police facilitating agency such as Interpol or Europol is involved, then the process can take even longer as *those* bureaucracies are encumbered with their own procedures, levels of vetting and approvals, and other sorts of red tape. Because police often need to work quickly, to move before a trail goes cold or before a suspect harms someone, the preferred method of communication is through a phone call, often lasting less than ten minutes. In the words of the German Klaus Heil: "There is no substitute for the efficiencies that cop to cop interaction can bring about in the international law enforcement community." He added, "I can get more done with one phone call, than a legion of diplomats could armed with a mutual legal assistance treaty."[71] Unless specifically prohibited by national laws, police can and do communicate with one another routinely on an informal basis. In the author's experience as chief of Diplomatic Security's international criminal investigative liaison section, we were seldom engaged by our foreign counterparts through formal procedures and channels. We generally received and gave assistance as requested. The places generating the most resistance to informal requests were those with the most highly developed bureaucracies (or existing MLAT treaties) in Western Europe, along with former British colonies of the Far East, and the heavily regulated societies like Saudi Arabia and other monarchies in the Arabian and Persian Gulfs. Most surprising were our successes with places not normally seen as friendly to the United States or as open to cooperation, such as Cuba, Vietnam, Cambodia, Tunisia, and China.

---

[71] Interview with Klaus Heil and Stephan Krause, German Embassy BKA Liaison Representatives, 31 July 2007, Washington, DC.

Most of our successes did come from places where police are relatively autonomous—South and Central America, Africa, and Asia. Some of these locations host terrorist-related criminal enterprises, which, ironically, seldom attract attention from international law enforcement, let alone from Western intelligence services. Even among tightly regulated governments, police agencies generally rely on informal methods to accomplish their goals and revert to formal pathways only when absolutely necessary or when legal proceedings (collection and establishment of a chain of evidence, conduct of formal interviews, validation of documents for court records and administration, and the like) become a factor. My own experience in the successful exploitation of informal international police relationships parallels those spelled out by international policing scholar Mathieu Deflem.

Author's Professional Observation Supported by Scholarship

Deflem argues that police almost anywhere, through effective and efficient performance of their mission, can earn a significant measure of autonomy from their central government.[72] My own experience indicates that informal international police networks and relationships can be astonishingly effective precisely because of the relative autonomy enjoyed by particular national police entities, to include those in the U.S. Because informal methods are much more efficient than formal methods, autonomous, effective policing naturally favors informal pathways. Clearly, greater efficiency leads to greater effectiveness. The author will present cases that showcase the versatility and efficiency of informal policing. In extending Deflem's findings, these cases will show that police not only become more effective but also more autonomous as a function of efficient policing. Dean Anne-Marie Slaughter of Princeton University comments repeatedly on the efficiencies provided by government networks, particularly regulatory networks, of which law enforcement is a big part.[73]

First, national police entities often need to improve and overcome their own weaknesses and deficiencies. According to the May 2003 GAO report, already cited, institutional shortcomings in foreign countries hin-

---

[72] Mathieu Deflem, "Europol and the Policing of International Terrorism: Counter-Terrorism in a Global Perspective," Justice Quarterly 23, no. 3 (2006), 338-339. Available at http://www.cas.sc.edu/socy/faculty/deflem/zeuroterror.htm.

[73] Anne-Marie Slaughter, "Government Networks: The Heart of the Liberal Democratic Order," in Democratic Governance and International Law, Gregory H. Fox, ed. (Cambridge, UK: Cambridge University Press, May, 2000), 214, 217, 223-225. Also see Anne-Marie Slaughter, "Governing the Global Economy through Government Networks," in Role of Law in International Politics, Michael Byers, ed. (Oxford, UK: Oxford University Press, 2000), 179-180.

der federal efforts to combat the spread of international terrorism and other transnational crimes. Local police and the judicial systems in many countries in which terrorists and terrorist organizations operate are ineffective. They lack adequate resources, have limited investigative authorities, or are plagued by corruption. The working group reported that many countries have outdated or even nonexistent laws involving extradition, immigration, asset seizure, anti-money laundering, computers, and antiterrorism. According to the interagency working group,

> many countries simply do not have adequate resources, training, equipment, expertise, or the political will to carry out complex, sustained investigations of international terrorism or to conduct counterterrorism operations. Terrorists and terrorist organizations take advantage of these institutional limitations and weaknesses to find and establish sanctuaries, while governments and law enforcement remain constrained by national boundaries."[74]

If Deflem and Slaughter are correct, then weak police entities can increase their overall professionalism, competence, and efficiency by virtue of coordinating with international police counterparts. In this manner, U.S. and international law enforcement elements can bolster national and international counterterrorism security efforts. In short, international police collaboration can serve respective national interests, and the international interests of counterterrorism. Even as weak national police entities and their governments can benefit from participating in international police cooperative networks, so strong nation-states, under siege from random acts of terrorism that can emanate from sanctuaries anywhere, can also benefit from a widespread network of international contacts and influence. Furthermore, Slaughter notes that informal international governmental networks can bypass "a great deal of cumbersome and formal international negotiating procedures."[75] International law scholar Kal Raustiala borrows a concept from economic theory as he refers to the *network effect* phenomenon, whereby networks serve to augment and build upon themselves as they multiply and flourish.[76]

Policing authority Monica den Boer goes so far as to say that international policing is *dependent* on informal relationships: "Law enforcement

---

[74] GAO, Combating Terrorism: Interagency Framework and Agency Programs to Address the Overseas Threat for Combating Terrorism, May 2003, 28.

[75] Anne-Marie Slaughter, "Governing the Global Economy through Government Networks," 180.

[76] Network effect—the phenomenon whereby a service becomes more valuable as more people use it, thereby incorporating ever-increasing numbers of adopters. See http://www.marketingterms.com/dictionary/network_effect/. See also Kal Raustiala, "The Architecture of International Cooperation: Transgovernmental Networks and the Future of International Law," Virginia Journal of International Law 43, no. 1 (Fall 2002), 9, 63-64.

agencies view information and intelligence as a precious commodity." Trust and reciprocity are thus essential for success in cross-border investigations. Studies in the field of international police cooperation show that informality is a prerequisite for trust: "without the consolidation of an informal network, police cooperation will not succeed."[77] Intelligence-led policing scholar, former Assistant U.S. Attorney, and University of Illinois law professor Jacqueline Ross adds:

> Police also have abilities in dealing with locals that extend far beyond the abilities of the intelligence world... The fact is that terrorists tend to be very wary of including outsiders (infiltrators) in their networks, but they do have to deal with outsiders—often members of organized crime—when financing their activities (e.g., through drug sales), laundering the funds, or even purchasing arms. Thus, police access to methods previously associated with intelligence agencies, and their greater effectiveness in using them to penetrate networks that interact with terrorists, is one of the advantages of using informal police networks against terrorists.[78]

Finally, and ironically, international policing critics Peter Andreas and Ethan Nadelmann powerfully tie together the efficiency of informal policing with the efficacy of the "culture of the badge" in their landmark book:

> One significant outcome of the regularization of law enforcement relations across borders has been the emergence of an international law enforcement community, with its own distinct expertise, understandings, and subculture. The common sentiment that a cop is a cop, no matter whose badge is worn, and a criminal a criminal regardless of citizenship or where the crime was committed, serves as a sort of transnational value system that can override both political differences and formal procedures. It provides the oil and glue of international law enforcement.[79]

Although these authors intended to portray this sort of international cooperation as a vice, they very effectively substantiate the advantages that international police cooperation can convey. The concept of an international law enforcement community and subculture exists as a tailor-made tool in law enforcement's counterterrorism arsenal.

---

[77] Monica den Boer, "Law Enforcement Cooperation and Transnational Organized Crime in Europe," in Transnational Organized Crime & International Security, Mats Berdal and Monica Serrano, eds. (Boulder, CO: Lynne Rienner, 2002), 111. Den Boer adds that informal methods need to be supported by accountability. She adds that, because police are allowed the application of force, their standards of conduct should be higher than other governmental entities. Den Boer-Bayer e-mail, 22 February 2009.

[78] Jacqueline Ross, e-mail interview, March 2008.

[79] Ethan Nadelmann and Peter Andreas, Policing the Globe: Criminalization and Crime Control in International Relations (New York: Oxford University Press, 2006), 232.

Formality Is All Well and Good, *but…*

Invariably, the U.S. government, like every government, has institutionalized formality and displays a reflexive propensity toward formalization to address its problems. Formalization, institutionalization, and rule-making, after all, are basic governmental functions—especially in the international realm.[80] U.S. international outreach in the law enforcement realm has depended on formalized processes, agreements, and relationships. The 2003 GAO report documents this tendency:

> The Department of State negotiates formal bilateral agreements to strengthen law enforcement cooperation with other individual countries. For example, there are a number of law enforcement-related treaties negotiated by the Department of State, in conjunction with the Department of Justice, related to legal assistance and extradition. These agreements promote increased cooperation with foreign law enforcement authorities for the exchange of evidence and apprehension of terrorist suspects.[81]

"Real" Work Is Done Informally

Much of the counterterrorism literature, even work mainly done for the federal government, springs from individuals who harbor too little familiarity with the law enforcement frame of reference. Respected commentators such as former DOJ official Philip Heymann, federal Judge Richard Posner, and former CIA officials Michael Scheuer, Paul Pillar, Elizabeth Rindskopf, and Henry Crumpton all erroneously characterize international law enforcement as oriented solely toward a legal process, whose protagonists are hamstrung by a concern for carefully orchestrated criminal investigation and prosecution.[82] None of these commentators is a law enforcement officer, and thus none has an adequate frame of experience on which to base these claims.

---

[80] Slaughter, "Governing the Global Economy," 189-192.

[81] GAO, Combating Terrorism: Interagency Framework and Agency Programs to Address the Overseas Threat for Combating Terrorism, 129.

[82] Examples of this unfortunate form of groupthink can be found in Philip Heymann, Terrorism, Freedom and Security: Winning without War (Cambridge, MA: The MIT Press, 2003), 64-65; Richard Posner, Preventing Surprise Attacks: Intelligence Reform in the Wake of 9/11 (New York: Rowman and Littlefield Publishers, 2005), 173-180; Henry Crumpton, "Intelligence and Homeland Defense," in Transforming U.S. Intelligence, Jennifer L. Sims and others, eds. (Washington, DC: Georgetown University Press, 2005), 207-210; Michael Scheuer in Imperial Hubris: Why the West is Losing the War on Terror (Washington, DC: Potomac Books, 2004), 197-199; and Paul Pillar, in Terrorism and U.S. Foreign Policy (Washington, DC: Brookings Institution Press, 2001), 79-92.

The present author, on the other hand, with over twenty years as a U.S. federal law enforcement officer in the Foreign Service, thinks and operates primarily from the law enforcement frame of reference. Not once has the author been prohibited from discussing or obtaining criminal, security, or counterterrorism information from foreign counterparts for any reason. Even the normally rigid FBI and its Legal Attaché network understand that liaison relationships become subject to legal process concerns only as necessary for the procedural requirements of individual casework. Casework represents only a small portion of international law enforcement interaction. Law enforcement elements are adept at gathering information and intelligence for security purposes, for criminal investigation, but also for acquiring criminal intelligence information, to include the crime of terrorism and we are not limited to discussing these matters in the context of casework and criminal investigations. Because police operate all over the world, the military and intelligence communities would be better served not to view police and other law enforcement elements as competitors, or even as restricted partners, but rather as potentially powerful partners with access to important, overt sources of unexploited intelligence.

The BIG Question

This work therefore poses the question: How can the United States engage international partners more effectively to address the worldwide manifestations of destabilizing violence, which is often indiscriminately labeled "terrorism"? In view of this principal question, can we overcome the entrenched parochial interests of the most powerful agencies (law enforcement, intelligence, and military) to bring greater coordination to the task of combating this violence and thus bring to bear the benefits and advantages of individual agencies and local police departments? And, especially, how can U.S. law enforcement effectively harness the power of international informal police networks without destroying them by adopting formalized procedures?[83]

---

[83] Formalization involves governmental processes that can introduce political influences into the equation—to include those with territorial or parochial interests in asserting control over policing entities.

CHAPTER 2
The Co-Evolution of Transnational Crime, Terrorism, and Policing: A Brief Pre-History of the Blue Planet

Terrorism relies on violence and fear for advantage and power. Alan Dershowitz argues that, since 1968, when the Palestine Liberation Organization hijacked an Israeli airliner, international terrorism's success is undeniable and monumental.[84] What methods or approaches have been adopted in recent years to confer tactical advantage to such groups?

Al-Qaeda brought terrorism to a new tactical sophistication by incorporating knowledge gleaned from 1,400 years of violent conflict.[85] Bernard Lewis observes that after the decline of Islam, for the Islamic leadership, the question arose—is it permissible to imitate the infidels? The answer of the religious authorities was that it is permissible in order to more effectively fight against them.[86] Lewis' thesis explains Islamist embrace of technology in their grand strategy, as he notes, "Even the most extreme and most anti-Western fundamentalists nowadays accept the need to modernize and indeed to make the fullest use of modern technology, especially the technologies of warfare and propaganda."[87] Prominent authorities on al-Qaeda agree on the point.[88] Former CIA analyst Michael Scheuer suggests that al-Qaeda's most important action since the 11 September attacks has been its expansion into the Internet,[89] and terrorism authority Bruce Hoffman makes clear that al-Qaeda does use the Internet for intelligence gathering purposes and targeting.[90] The Internet is not the only tool of the technological revolution adopted by terrorists, according to

---

[84] Alan M. Dershowitz, Why Terrorism Works: Understanding the Threat, Responding to the Challenge (New Haven, CT: Yale University Press, 2002), 36.

[85] Rohan Gunaratna, Inside Al Qaeda: Global Network of Terror (New York: Columbia University Press, 2002), 6.

[86] Bernard Lewis, What Went Wrong: Western Impact and Middle Eastern Response (New York and London: Oxford University Press, 2001), 43.

[87] Lewis, 73.

[88] Louise Shelly, "Organized Crime, Terrorism and Cybercrime," in Security Sector Reform: Institutions, Society and Good Governance, Alan Bryden and Phillip Fluri, eds. (Baden Baden, Germany: Nomos Verlagsgeleelschaft, 2003), 302-312; Brynjar Lia, Globalisation and the Future of Terrorism: Patterns and Predictions (New York: Routledge, 2005), 175.

[89] Michael Scheuer, Imperial Hubris: Why the West is Losing the War on Terror (Washington, DC: Brassey's Inc. 2004), 78.

[90] Bruce Hoffman, Inside Terrorism (New York, NY: Columbia University Press, 2006), 175.

Peter Bergen: "The head of the secretive U.S. National Security Agency said that bin Laden has better technology for communications than the United States. The Saudi militant's followers communicate by fax, satellite phone, and e-mail. They encrypt memos in their Macintosh and Toshiba computers."[91] Al-Qaeda messages are downloaded to cell phones and MP3 players.[92] In June 2008, as the *Washington Post's* Craig Whitlock observed:

> The war against terrorism has evolved into a war of ideas and propaganda, a struggle for hearts and minds fought on television and the Internet. On these fronts, al-Qaeda's voice has grown much more powerful in recent years. Taking advantage of new technology and mistakes by its adversaries, al-Qaeda's core leadership has built an increasingly prolific propaganda operation, enabling it to communicate constantly, securely and in numerous languages with loyalists and potential recruits worldwide.

He continues, "Some U.S. officials acknowledge that they missed early opportunities to disrupt al-Qaeda's communications operations, whose internal security has since been upgraded to the point where analysts say it is nearly bulletproof."[93] Their video producers are "outfitted with some of the best technology available. They use ultra light laptops and top-end video cameras. Files are protected using PGP, or Pretty Good Privacy, a virtually unbreakable form of encryption software that is also used by intelligence agencies around the world."[94]

Al-Qaeda fully embraces other aspects of globalization. Al-Qaeda in Europe allegedly finances operations through credit card fraud, obtaining up to $1 million a month. They access and copy information from the magnetic strips on stolen cards, and have purchased credit card manufacturing machines.[95] Gunaratna maintains that al-Qaeda has adopted the more legitimate aspects of globalization as well, involving themselves in importing-exporting, construction, manufacturing, banking, and charities. Bergen characterizes al-Qaeda as a multinational corporation ideally suited for international conflict and Osama bin Laden as the epitome of a very capable globalized CEO (chief executive officer) of terror.[96] As Hoffman says, "Clearly,

---

[91] Peter Bergen, Holy War, Inc. (New York, NY: The Free Press, 2001), 28.

[92] Associated Press, "Al Qaeda Deploys Cell Phone Video Downloads," 6 January 2008. Available at: http://www.msnbc.msn.com/id/22526746/.

[93] Craig Whitlock, "Al Qaeda's Growing Online Offensive," Washington Post, 24 June 2008, A01.

[94] Whitlock, A01.

[95] Gunaratna, 87.

[96] Bergen, 30-31.

terrorism and the media are bound together in an inherently symbiotic relationship, each feeding off and exploiting the other for its own purposes."[97] It is ironic that a society that created Madison Avenue and invented media manipulation and subliminal seduction remains unable to turn the psychological warfare tables against homicidal religious zealots.[98] Former Director of the CIA and current Secretary of Defense Robert Gates has declared, "We are miserable at communicating to the rest of the world what we are about as a society and a culture. It is just plain embarrassing that al-Qaeda is better at communicating its message on the Internet than America."[99] In a statement that mirrored Gates, the State Department's then-incoming chief of public diplomacy, James Glassman, said, "Our enemies are eating our lunch in terms of getting the word out in digital technology."[100] Bruce Hofmann (quoting media trendsetter Tina Brown) says, "The conjunction of 21st century Internet speed and 12th century fanaticism has turned our world into a tinderbox."[101] We can ask whether Lenin's aphorism, "Capitalism will sell us the rope with which we will hang them," now applies to Islamist extremists.

Globalization Begets *Smart* Globalized Terrorists

How can we hope to counter the well-educated and technically proficient terrorists of al-Qaeda? The question's importance is reinforced by the idea that A.Q. Khan, the father of Pakistan's nuclear bomb and central figure in its proliferation to other states, remains at least a tacit ally of al-Qaeda and the Taliban, and like them, subscribes to pan-Islamist beliefs. Former CIA Director George Tenet allegedly said that Khan was "at least as dangerous as Osama bin Laden."[102]

Just as al-Qaeda exhibits good understanding of shock tactics, calculated attacks for maximum damage, and media manipulation, it also possesses a strategic understanding of the power of networks and the resultant attributes of globalization.[103] This notion resonates with Gombert and Gordon:

---

[97] Hoffman, 183.

[98] In the words of Scheuer, is it "Arrogance (or is it racism?) because the elites cannot believe a polyglot bunch of Arabs wearing robes, sporting scraggly beards, and squatting around campfires in Afghan deserts and mountains could pose a mortal threat to the United States," Imperial Hubris, 198.

[99] Ann Scott Tyson, "Gates Urges Increased Funding for Diplomacy," Washington Post, 27 November 2007.

[100] Charley Keyes, "U.S. Enemies Eating Our Lunch Online," http://www.conn.com/2008/POLITICS/01/30/internet.pr.failure/index.html.

[101] Hoffman, 198.

[102] David Albright and Corey Hinderson, "Unraveling the A.Q. Khan and Future Proliferation Networks," The Washington Quarterly 28, no. 2 (Spring 2005), 112.

[103] John Arquilla, "It Takes a Network," Los Angeles Times, 25 August 2002.

Groups and persons who are dissatisfied with the nation-states in which they live identify with transnational communities, such as the global Muslim "nation of one billion," or *Ummah*. Globalization can give insurgents extended reach and access to destructive know-how and materials, enabling them to directly threaten those they blame for the suffering of the people they claim to be defending. The spread of jihadism, the speed with which it can acquire energy in a given country, and the dispersal of inspirational messages, fighters, money, and methods are facilitated by global connectivity and mobility.[104]

In contrast, a 2007 GAO report asserts that in its current form the U.S. *National Strategy for Homeland Security* and the other national strategies do not provide authority for directing the various federal agencies to work in synchronization in prosecuting the war on terror,[105] making it difficult to adopt a network-based approach to combating the globalized opponent. Can the vast, globalized, and networked resources of international law enforcement confront al-Qaeda in its own arena of expertise and innovation? Law enforcement has been adapting and adjusting to the habits of international crime for a long time—and terrorist organizations use the same pathways and methods of operation as do criminal enterprises.

Globalization Also Begets Transnational Crime and Globalized Police

In many ways, the internationalization of crime foreshadowed, or at least mirrored, what we have now come to know as globalization. Piracy evolved along with the establishment of trade routes and has been around for at least 3,000 years.[106] Transnational organized crime has followed immigration patterns. Lia notes that ethnic groups brought particular licit and illicit talents to lands in which they settled, and continued to maintain old traditions and close contacts with their countries of origin. In this way, smuggling routes to new lands emerged, and from that the development of the usual repertoire of services attributed to organized crime—black markets, extortion, protection rackets, prostitution, hijacking, burglary, gambling, and so on. As these activities became entrenched, they grew to be accepted and adopted into the host societies and associated with specialized, ethnic-based, organized crime

---

[104] Gombert and Gordon, War by Other Means, xxviii.

[105] GAO, Information Sharing.

[106] H.A. Ormerod, Piracy in the Ancient World (Liverpool, UK: University of Liverpool Press, 1978). Originally published in 1924. Pirate historian Douglas Burgess interestingly has equated piracy with terrorism. See Douglass R. Burgess, Jr., "Piracy is Terrorism," International Herald Tribune, 6-7 December 2008, 8.

groups. New pathways were created as alliances between various ethnic criminal groups were formed and connected back to the old countries.[107] Deflem affirms that technological developments in the early part of the 20th century, particularly improvements in transportation (trains and automobiles), created opportunities for criminals to seek refuge in foreign countries beyond the jurisdictions of national police forces.[108] In the post-Cold War era, transnational organized crime prospered as globalization gained momentum. Just as earlier technological advances enabled the first major steps toward the internationalization of crime, the changes brought on by rapid globalization of the past twenty years provided impetus for traditional organized crime groups to modernize their weapons trafficking and drug trafficking in the new world order.[109]

Evolving alongside globalization are troubling new incarnations of long-established or nearly extinct crimes that can be attributed to the technological revolution. Identity theft and Internet scams like phishing and "419" schemes are reinventions of confidence crimes, and computer viruses exist as a form of e-vandalism.[110] Over the centuries, as crime internationalized, so too did the police, or their equivalent. Mathieu Deflem traces the origins of organized international policing to the mid-19th century, when the German territories of Prussia, Sachsen, Hanover, Baden, Wurttemberg, and Bavaria consolidated into the Police Union of German States in 1851. In 1883, the Russian Government established headquarters for its "vast" police networks with a police Foreign Bureau in Paris—to counter revolutionary activity against the Russian Empire.[111] Interestingly, according to Deflem, even in those early days of established international police cooperation, terrorism was a concern. The International Association of Chiefs of Police was founded in 1893 as the world's first informal international police network.[112] In 1898, an antiterrorism conference took place—the International Conference of Rome for the Social Defense against Anarchists—with delegates from 21 countries. In 1901, Germany, Austria-Hungary, and Denmark agreed on a "Secret Protocol for the International War on Anarchism."[113]

---

[107] Brynjar Lia, Globalization and the Future of Terrorism (New York: Routledge, 2005), 126-127.

[108] Deflem, Policing World Society, 95.

[109] Jonah Alexander, ed., Combating Terrorism: Strategies of Ten Countries (Ann Arbor: University of Michigan Press, 2002), 5-6.

[110] Peter Andreas and Ethan Nadelmann, Policing the Globe (London: Oxford University Press, 2006), 57.

[111] Deflem, Policing World Society, 64.

[112] Deflem, Policing World Society, 100-101.

[113] Deflem, Policing World Society, 64-68.

Soon, the International Criminal Police Commission was established in 1923 at the International Police Congress in Vienna. Later it was renamed The International Criminal Police Organization (ICPO-Interpol) in 1956.[114] Today, Interpol comprises 186 member countries and is dedicated to facilitating international police, cross-border cooperation. A similar organization, Europol, was established in 1992 to deal with the specific needs of the European constituency.

Deflem maintains that the development of criminal identification systems, such as the bertillonage system from which information could be transmitted by telephone or telegraph, and the advancement of fingerprinting techniques which could by broken down into numeric expression and transmitted by telegraph, have been central to the development of international police cooperation from the middle of the 19th century.[115] Over time, international police cooperation expanded to the level it holds today. Andreas and Nadelmann credit advances in technology and the creation of criminal databases as the most important factors contributing to the internationalization of law enforcement.[116] Appendix A shows some of the databases available to the worldwide counterterrorism and international police community.

Many other countries have comparable databases and many of these can also be shared with Interpol. Generally, almost every country has arrest reports and records that can be made available to law enforcement for investigative purposes. All over the world, border and passport control databases are shared with Interpol computer systems and are set up to flag transnational fugitives and terrorists in transit.[117] According to criminologist James Sheptycki, "the great concentration of databases on criminals and criminal activity has come about out of a perceived need to build in economies of scale and to facilitate transnational communication."[118]

As technology has expanded the geographical reach of transnational crime and terrorism, it has also made the world a much smaller place for the police. The advent of computer databases and the ability for these databases to interface on an international scale is a principal example of the globalization and successful technological innovation of transnational policing. The near future holds even more

---

[114] Deflem, Policing World Society, 124-152.

[115] The bertillonage system was developed by French anthropologist Alphonse Bertillon which "classified the identification of criminals on the basis of certain measurements of parts of their head and body and the color of their eyes, hair, and skin." See Deflem, Policing World Society, 67-68, 93-94, 108-109.

[116] Nadelmann and Andreas maintain that crime transnationalized itself as a result of technological advancements as well. See Nadelmann and Andreas, Policing the Globe, 125-126.

[117] Some systems, of course, are better than others.

[118] James Sheptycki, "Transnational Policing and the Makings of a Postmodern State," British Journal of Criminology 35, no. 4 (Autumn 1995), 629-630.

significant promise. The *Washington Post* recently reported the FBI's plan to introduce a vast database of biometrics called Next Generation Identification, which will hold digital images of faces, fingerprints, palm patterns, and will eventually contain iris patterns and face shape data. According to the report, "if all goes as planned, a police officer making a traffic stop or a border agent at an airport could run a 10-fingerprint check on a suspect and within seconds know if the person is on a database of the most wanted criminals and terrorists. An analyst could take palm prints lifted from a crime scene and run them against the expanded database. Intelligence agents could exchange biometric information worldwide."[119]

The FBI system is being designed to standards shared by Great Britain, Canada, Australia, and New Zealand and will interface with the National Criminal Identification Center (NCIC) database. The U.S. Department of Justice has in development an integration of databases of the FBI, the Drug Enforcement Administration, the U.S. Marshals Service, the Bureau of Prisons, and the Bureau of Alcohol, Tobacco, Firearms, and Explosives.[120] Interpol, too, recognizes the importance of information technology and is positioning itself as a central clearinghouse for police data. It has databases designed to interface with those of member countries for international terrorism, fingerprints, DNA profiles, lost and stolen travel documents, child sexual abuse images, stolen works of art, and stolen motor vehicles. Interpol also plans to employ a system that will incorporate biometric information into all of the above databases. Systems, databases, and controls now in place, and the more advanced ones being developed, constitute a worldwide, networked "dragnet," designed to capture or positively identify persons of interest, fugitives, terrorists, and their associates. Dragnets, as a police tactic, are designed to cast as wide a net as possible and winnow out those who are of interest to law enforcement. It does not matter if those persons are international jewel thieves, serial killers, organized crime figures, or terrorists. The systems are designed to ensnare and identify suspicious persons.

The dragnet approach has resulted in an increase in issuances of Interpol notices for wanted individuals and persons of interest. The Interpol website as of December 2007 shows 4,556 wanted notices in 2006, a 60 percent increase from 2005; for 2007, 5,146 total issuances were recorded, a 13 percent increase from the previous year. Likewise, Interpol notes an increase in 2006 in arrests of criminals who were the subjects of notices, up 20 percent from the previous year. Similar increases have appeared in the number of U.S. Marshals and Diplomatic Security Service overseas fugitive "locates, apprehensions and returns" from overseas.[121]

---

[119] Ellen Nakashima, "FBI Prepares Vast Database of Biometrics," Washington Post, 22 December 2007.

[120] Dan Eggen, "Justice Dept. Database Stirs Privacy Fears," Washington Post, 26 December 2006.

[121] Professional files of the author.

Incarceration rates in the United States have been rising at an increasing rate for the past three decades—attributable to improvements in policing.[122]

Interpol Notice Procedures.

Source: Interpol, with permission.

[122] Stephen D. Levitt and Stephen J. Dubner, Freakanomics: A Rogue Economist Explores the Hidden Side of Everything (New York: Harper Collins, 2006), 123.

All notices are published on INTERPOL's secure website for authorised law enforcement users. In addition, extracts of notices may also be published on the Organization's public website if the requesting entity agrees. Public knowledge of an arrest warrant is often of great value to law enforcement agencies in their efforts to obtain important police information.

In accordance with INTERPOL's rules, the General Secretariat can only publish a notice if it is satisfied that all the conditions for processing the information have been fulfilled. For example, a notice will not be published if it violates Article 3 of the Constitution, which forbids the Organization from undertaking any intervention or activities of a political, military, religious or racial character. In addition, the General Secretariat retains the right to refuse to publish a notice that it considers unadvisable, or a risk to international police co-operation, the Organization, its staff, or its member countries.

Key figures

The General Secretariat published 4,596 notices in 2008:

Red	Blue	Green	Yellow	Black	INTERPOL -UN	Orange
3,126	304	664	385	91	26	7

Another frequently used tool is a 'diffusion', a message sent by an NCB to some or all member countries through INTERPOL's I-24/7 global police communications system requesting the arrest or location of an individual or additional information in relation to a police investigation. In 2008, 13,339 diffusions were registered in INTERPOL's nominal database.

There were 23,898 notices and 41,460 diffusions in circulation at the end of 2008. The number of people arrested on the basis of a notice or diffusion since the year 2000 reached 27,630.

The INTERPOL-UN Security Council Special Notice

The INTERPOL-United Nations Security Council Special Notice was created in 2005 in response to UN Security Council Resolution 1617, to provide better tools to help the UN Security Council's 1267 Committee carry out its mandate regarding the freezing of assets, travel bans and arms embargos aimed at individuals and entities associated or belonging to Al Qaeda and the Taliban.

The Red Notice

The legal basis for a Red Notice is an arrest warrant or court order issued by the judicial authorities in the country concerned. Many of INTERPOL's member countries consider a Red Notice to be a valid request for provisional arrest. Furthermore, INTERPOL is recognized as an official channel for transmitting requests for provisional arrest in a number of bilateral and multilateral extradition treaties, including the European Convention on Extradition, the Economic Community of West African States (ECOWAS) Convention on Extradition and the United Nations Model Treaty on Extradition.

www.interpol.int

Contact information
E-mail info@interpol.int
For matters relating to specific crime cases, please contact your local police or the Interpol National Central Bureau in your country.

Interpol Notice Procedures.
Source: Interpol, with permission.

International policing in the globalized age is not just about databases. Forensic investigation techniques, the introduction of DNA matching as evidence, application of link analysis, state-of-the-art surveillance equipment, electronic sensing equipment for explosives and drugs, advanced, secure communications networks, Regional Information Sharing Systems (RISS), and the like are in play. Just as transnational criminals and terrorists can use the Internet to exploit the unwary and advance their goals, law enforcement can exploit the policing of cyberspace.[123] As al-Qaeda has used video to propagandize the Islamic world, police have used video surveillance to identify and capture al-Qaeda-associated perpetrators of the London subway bombings.[124] *Policing the Globe* describes the use of surveillance planes and advanced radar systems to counter narcotics traffickers, and of sophisticated X-ray technology to examine cargo trucks and containers. Presently, the U.S. Department of Justice is working on fast-capture fingerprint technology that can obtain full-palm and ten-finger prints in a matter of seconds. In what might be the ultimate level of civilian law enforcement use of military systems, the U.S. Customs and Border Patrol has acquired squadrons of Predator B unmanned drone aircraft.[125]

Although law enforcement plays an integral role in U.S. and world counterterrorism actions, for the United States the intelligence and military apparatus remains the primary actor, and law enforcement has been restricted to what amounts to a domestic security role.[126] As a result, what may be one of the most potent tools in the counterterrorism arsenal, the worldwide network of police, has been largely overlooked as a resource for the execution of U.S. counterterrorism strategy.

The Power of Networks

Ummah—"The Network of the Faithful"

Globalization abets the power and importance of international networks. These networks are not limited to computer and communications networks; they include banking and financial networks, professional, corporate, and trade networks. All of these networks are facilitated and empowered by the Web, and many have been expressly engendered by Internet technology. According to a recent

---

[123] Andreas and Nadelmann, Policing the Globe, 172-173. See also Sheptycki, 628.

[124] Letta Tayler and Colby Itkowitz, "Names Put to Video Faces," Newsday, 26 July 2005.

[125] Jeff Wise, "Civilian UAVs: No Pilot, No Problem," Popular Mechanics, April 2007.

[126] Brent Scowcroft, Lieutenant General (Ret), interviewed by the author on 10 July 2007, thinks "We made a big mistake in calling this a 'war' on terrorism. Sure we did that so we could invoke the resources of the military—but it had the effect of fundamentally removing expansion of our international law enforcement options from the equation. It also harmed us in our intelligence relationships. Countries that did not like our actions in Iraq made life difficult for our intelligence assets. This happened even in countries that we consider to be our allies." Also see GAO, Combating Terrorism: Law Enforcement Agencies Lack Directives to Assist Foreign Nations to Identify, Disrupt and Prosecute Terrorists, GAO-07-697, 4 October 2007. Available at: http://www.gao.gov/new.items/d08144t.pdf.

RAND study, "insurgencies are increasingly skilled on higher planes; information and cognition. Using Western network technology and infrastructure, they can operate and influence effectively while remaining distributed and slippery."[127]

Islam holds as one of its central precepts the concept of *Ummah*—the worldwide community of Muslims or "The Community of the Faithful."[128] As presented by the Embassy of Saudi Arabia in Washington, DC: "Islam is at once a religion and a total way of life. It prescribes order for individual societies and governments and codifies law, family relationships, matters of business, etiquette, dress, food, hygiene, and much more. The *Ummah*, or community of believers, is unified across national boundaries by its conscious acceptance of the oneness of God and its dedication to the teachings of Islam."[129] In a sense, Islam is a religion whose foundation is predicated upon its own absolute network. In effect, Islam itself is a network—a religious *network* of the faithful, and inclined to spawning networks. For instance, the culturally embedded, ancient Hawala banking system acts as a networked extension of the Islamic sense of community. The Hawala system (originally Chinese) is based on trust, and is designed to transfer money. It remains unregulated by government and accountable only to the parties involved. According to Rohan Gunaratna, the Hawala system is responsible for the influx of $2.5 to $3 billion into Pakistan each year versus only $1 billion by formal banking mechanisms.[130] Al-Qaeda uses Hawala extensively to transfer funds for operations.[131]

Gombert and Gordon in quoting John Mackinlay and Alison al-Baddawy make the point that military primacy in combating an enemy that perverts the Ummah is counter-intuitive: "The existence of a global Muslim community that has a personality in the world arena challenges the U.S. strategic concept of a war on terror that narrowly seeks military outcomes while ignoring the hostility it may engender in that larger community."[132] They continue: "The jihadist formula of selling the story of Muslims under attack while also provoking attack is brilliant. Because the story has been globalized—spanning the *Ummah*—an attack on Muslims anywhere can

---

127 David C. Gompert and John Gordon IV, War by Other Means: Building Complete and Balanced Capabilities for Counterinsurgency (Washington, DC: RAND, 2008), xxxv.

128 Gunaratna, Inside Al Qaeda, 127.

129 www.saudiembassy.net/Country/Islam/IslDetail3.asp. Accessed 11 September 2008.

130 Gunaratna, Inside Al Qaeda, 84. He attributes this number to a CIA estimate, but does not cite the source of the information.

131 Gunaratna, Inside Al Qaeda, 84.

132 David C. Gompert and John Gordon IV, War by Other Means, 8, quoting John Mackinlay and Alison al-Baddawy, Rethinking Counterinsurgency—A British Perspective: RAND Counterinsurgency Study Paper 5 (Santa Monica, CA: RAND Corporation, OP-177-OSD, forthcoming).

both justify global jihad and bolster the commitment of local insurgents continents away."[133]

Osama bin Ladin and Ayman al-Zawahiri attempt to unite all Muslims to rise against the West under their tutelage. In al-Zawahiri's words, "the battle is not the battle of a group or organization, but is the battle of the entire Ummah. Therefore, it is imperative that we break the chains of partisanship to the groups, parties, and organizations which stand between the sincere ones and their effective participation in the fighting against the trespasser enemies of Islam, and that we rush before the opportunity passes us by, to stand in the column of Jihad against the Zionist-Crusader aggression."[134] Gunaratna characterizes bin Ladin's global jihadist philosophy in terms of pan-Islamism, tracing it back to bin-Ladin's mentor, Abdullah Azzam, stating that "it was Azzam who steered toward creating a multinational organization based on the idea of uniting the vanguard of the believers, irrespective of their geographic origin."[135] Michael Scheuer attests to the relative success of this strategy: "[T]he oppression of Muslims outside the Arab heartland—in Kashmir, Chechnya, India, and Xinjiang—has become a gut issue for Muslims thanks to bin Laden's rhetoric and even more, the pervasive presence of real-time Muslim-owned satellite television."[136]

In my role as a federal law enforcement officer (special agent) with the Diplomatic Security Service, I can attest to the intense networking environment among Muslims, and to the international manifestation of that networking.[137] In my experience as a (non-Muslim) criminal investigator and Regional Security Officer, I have had a number of devout and not-so-devout Muslims as informants and contacts in the United States and abroad (i.e., informants for criminal investigations in the United States; professional contacts, acquaintances, and friends—but no informants—overseas). In my investigations, I have spent a great deal of time with Muslims whom sociologists would consider examples of the disaffected masses of Islam. I have gone to their homes, shared meals, joked among them and had long talks with them, as well as with their friends and relatives. I have held their children on my lap, argued with them, and come to regard many of them with a great deal of affection and

---

[133] Gompert and Gordon, War by Other Means, 65.

[134] Ayman al-Zawahiri, "Realities of the Conflict Between Islam and Unbelief," available at: http://www.lauramansfield.com/j/zawahiri_12206.asp.

[135] Gunaratna, Inside Al Qaeda, 116.

[136] Scheuer, Imperial Hubris, 212.

[137] For example, investigations of one incident can quickly involve leads in widespread locations such as Togo, Senegal, Egypt, and Mali. For a recent analysis of Muslim behavior in "natural" (familial) and "imagined" communities (p. 42), see Olivier Roy, Globalized Islam: The Search for a New Ummah (New York: Columbia University Press, 2006).

admiration. I have seen the community of Islam come to life before me, and it has been a fascinating thing to behold—something I envied in a way, wishing I could be part of something so *"friendly."* With due respect to scholars and experts who offer various insights into the world of Islam, I would like to add a thought of my own: Among Muslims, the concept of community manifests itself, in some ways, in a fashion close to what we Americans and Western-ers might call *"hanging out."* The Muslims with whom I have come into con-tact, a representative cross-section of the Islamic world, visit and *"hang out"* with one another—a lot. They drop in on one another, usually unannounced and uninvited, and are always welcomed. By all appearances, they like and appreciate one another in ways very distinct from those in the West. From sub-Saharan West Africa to Pakistan to Turkey, for me, this phenomenon has been nearly universal. I think I was relatively successful as an investigator in these cases because "hanging out" is something that I find comfortable doing. Normally, I would not endorse hanging out as an investigative technique, but for a white, Roman Catholic federal agent dealing with West African and pan-Asian Muslim informants, it seems to have worked pretty well.

Policing Networks: The "Ummah" of the Cops

It takes networks to fight networks. Governments that want to defend against netwar may have to adopt organizational designs and strategies like those of their adversaries. This does not mean mirroring the adver-sary, but rather learning to draw on the same design principles that he has already learned about the rise of network forms in the information age. These principles depend to some extent on technological innovation, but mainly on a willingness to innovate organizationally and doctrinally, per-haps especially by building new mechanisms for interagency and multi-jurisdictional cooperation.[138]

As suggested here, the international law enforcement community is also an enormous network bound together by a common culture and a common mission. In many ways, it is an "ummah" itself and, because of its networked nature and the "brotherhood of the badge," it has the ability to transcend nationalism, borders, ethnicity, and religion. Like Islam, it has for-mal and informal components and, furthermore, the informal aspects are by far the most powerful. The difference is that our strategically inclined adver-saries have discovered the power of the informal networks—and we have yet to do so. According to Gombert and Gordon of RAND, "The U.S. government has not adopted the requisite principles, practices, skills, reforms, and culture

---

[138] John Arquilla and David Ronfeldt, Networks and NetWars: The Future of Terror, Crime, and Militancy (Washington, DC: RAND Corporation, 2001), 16.

to exploit networking and … the U.S. counterterrorism/counter-insurgency efforts are not organized to take advantage of networking."[139] They add that the more prompt and capable the United States is in using civil means [that is, law enforcement] the more likely local security services will be adequate and obviate the need for U.S. deadly force. Their recommended reengagement strategy for U.S. federal law enforcement assets overseas, and exploitation of potential, informal networks, reinforces the theme of the present work.

Deflem highlights the importance of international policing as a counterterrorism instrument, emphasizing the efficiency of existing and potential international police cooperation, which is a function of international police culture—the "Blue Planet." He argues that the evolution of a common police culture fosters counterterrorism policing that is based on professionalism, expertise, and cooperation, and is significantly removed from the political motivations that beset the military and other branches of government.[140] Deflem characterizes international police organizations as a collaborative network among police of different nations which establish systems of communication and information exchange and create other institutions of cooperation, such as central headquarters, through which information can be routed. By this measure, police agencies of nation-states are "affirmed as partners of cooperation."[141] While acknowledging the deficiencies of Interpol, Deflem also extols its values: "A central advantage is that Interpol has managed to attract cooperation from police agencies that are ideologically very diverse and not always on friendly terms politically," and further suggests that available "evidence shows that the fostering of internal cooperation primarily takes place by establishing direct means of communication among police."[142]

Law Enforcement: Part of a Wider International Governmental Community

Anne-Marie Slaughter, Dean of the Woodrow Wilson School of Public and International Affairs at Princeton University, has written extensively

---

[139] Gompert and Gordon, War by Other Means, summary, iv, 42.

[140] Mathieu Deflem, "Social Control and the Policing of Terrorism: Foundations for a Sociology of Counter-Terrorism," The American Sociologist 35, no. 2, 84.

[141] Mathieu Deflem, "Police and Counter-Terrorism: A Sociological Theory of International Cooperation" paper presented at Bilkent University, Ankara, Turkey, 6-8 December 2007, 13, forthcoming as a chapter in a book on intelligence sharing.

[142] Deflem, "Police and Counter-Terrorism," 16.

on the proliferation of governmental networks.[143] She argues that the information-technology revolution and the related phenomenon of globalization empower individuals (within government) and is steering government toward decentralization and the diminishing of its centralized authority. She maintains that these circumstances are creating opportunities and incentives for individuals at working levels to create their own professional networks, domestically, internationally, and at the sub- and supra-state levels.[144] She also suggests that trans-governmentalization now exists as a mode of international governance and that "dissaggregated institutions acting quasi-autonomously with their counterparts abroad are generating a growing body of rules and understandings that stand outside traditional international law but that nevertheless constitute a dense web of obligations recognized as binding in fact. The result is a new generation of international law—transgovernmental law."[145] Like Slaughter and Deflem, policing scholar Anthony Balzer comments on the importance of a "common enemy" in international police cooperation: "Would-be leaders such as athletic coaches, politicians, and labor officials have long employed the 'syncretism' principle—that is, the threat of a common enemy and the focus of a shared goal—to unify and motivate groups of people. Transnational crime appears to be assuming the role of a common enemy to the whole world."[146] Deflem goes further in defining law enforcement's unifying common enemy: "Legal and moral considerations aside, [even] a vague conception of terrorism becomes a powerful and highly consequential basis for police work."[147]

Slaughter even proposes that international networks can overcome the foreign versus domestic divide that continues to plague intergovernmental cooperation (in the United States):

---

[143] Anne-Marie Slaughter, "Government Networks: The Heart of the Liberal Democratic Order." Also see Anne-Marie Slaughter, "Breaking Out: The Proliferation of Actors in the International System," in Global Prescriptions: The Production, Exploration, and Importation of a New State Orthodoxy, Yves Dezalay and Bryant G. Garth, eds. (Ann Arbor: University of Michigan Press, 2002) and her "Governing the Global Economy through Government Networks," in Role of Law in International Politics, M. Beyers, ed. (Oxford, UK: Oxford University Press, 2000) and, finally, Anne-Marie Slaughter and David Zaring, "Networking Goes International: An Update," in Annual Review of Law and Social Science 2 (December 2006), 211-229, available at http://arjournals.annualreviews.org.

[144] Anne-Marie Slaughter, "Government Networks," 200; Mathieu Deflem, "Bureaucratization and Social Control: Historical Foundations of International Police Cooperation," in Law and Society Review 34, no. 3, 601-640. Deflem would refer to this as equivalent to the quest for professionalism and expertise in policing.

[145] Slaughter, "Government Networks," 201.

[146] Anthony J. Balzer, "International Police Cooperation: Opportunities and Obstacles," in Policing in Central Asia and Eastern Europe: Comparing Firsthand Knowledge with Experience from the West (Slovenia: College of Police and Security Studies, 1995), 4. See http://www.ncjrs.gov/policing/int63.htm.

[147] Deflem, "Social Control and the Policing of Terrorism," 86.

The unifying framework that has emerged to understand all these entities is the network. Although defined differently depending on the writer and the context, networks may be understood as informal institutions linking actors across national boundaries and carrying transgovernmental form. These networks exhibit "patterns of regular and purposive relations among like government units working across the borders that divide countries from one another and that demarcate the domestic from the international sphere." They allow domestic officials to interact with their foreign counterparts directly without much supervision by foreign offices or senior executive branch officials, and feature "loosely-structured, peer-to-peer ties developed through frequent interaction rather than formal negotiation."[148]

It's the Network, Stupid

Counternetwar may thus require very effective interagency approaches, which by their nature involve networked structures. It is not necessary, desirable, or even possible to replace all hierarchies with networks in governments. Rather, the challenge will be to blend these two forms skillfully, while retaining enough core authority to encourage and enforce adherence to networked processes. By creating effective hybrids, governments may become better prepared to confront the new threats and challenges emerging in the information age, whether generated by ethnonationalists, terrorists, militias, criminals, or other actors.[149]

As a network, international law enforcement has numerous advantages over current, militarized counterterrorism instruments. Military force has rarely been the primary reason that the reign of specific terrorist groups comes to an end.[150] This suggests that, where terrorist groups cannot or will not make a transition to nonviolence, policing is usually most effective in defeating them.

Of indigenous security services, none is more critical than police. By maintaining neighborhood safety and enforcing the rule of law with minimal necessary force, police can be both more effective and more legitimate than combat troops, especially if combined with fair, efficient, and transparent justice and penal systems. Even if they are not enamored with the state itself, Muslims who are concerned about family security, as most surely are, may accept and even cooperate with well-trained,

---

[148] Slaughter and Zaring, "Networking Goes International," 215.

[149] Arquilla and Ronfeldt, Networks and NetWars, 16.

[150] Seth Jones and Martin Libicki, How Terrorist Groups End: Lessons for Countering al Qa'ida, (Washington, DC: RAND Corporation, 2008), 31-32.

well-led, well-behaved, and even-handed police. In comparison, military force, being inherently clumsier and more lethal, may intimidate more than reassure the population, especially when insurgents are hidden in urban areas, as is often the case in Islamist insurgency.[151]

The advantages that greater reliance on law enforcement sources of operational intelligence confer over military, technical sources to address counterterrorism and counterinsurgency are summed up by Donald Reed:

> The emerging information age paradigm is a network-centric approach based on the premise that a fundamental shift in power has occurred from industry to information. It is rooted in information-age concepts that focus on nonconventional, asymmetrical threats and responses, and non-hierarchical command and control. It expands beyond the geographical base of territory and space. Its standard for defending the United States against both internal and external threats is a universally networked defense across the operational domains that comprise the information-age global commons—the physical, information, cognitive, and social domains. Network-centric operations seek to create an information advantage and translate it into an operational advantage. This approach accepts that military force, while essential, may be neither the first nor the most significant line of defense.[152]

If law enforcement: represents a superior source of human-source intelligence (HUMINT), especially in the realm of counterterrorism and counterinsurgency; offers an exemplary worldwide networking instrument; has worldwide population coverage; enjoys legal access to registration, criminal history and border crossing databases; enjoys legal (regulated) access to personal information; and taps the supportive culture required for effective network exploitation, why would it *not* be used to its fullest potential? That story is the subject of the following chapter.

---

[151] Gompert and Gordon, War by Other Means, 81.

[152] Donald Reed, "Why Strategy Matters," Homeland Security Affairs 2, no. 3 (October 2006), 17. Available at http://www.hsaj.org/?article=2.3.10.

CHAPTER 3
Analyzing Impediments:
A Core Sample of the Blue Planet

The terrorists exploited deep institutional failings within our government.
—The 9/11 Commission Report (p. 265)

For many Americans, the 9/11 attacks were personal. The attacks were so utterly evil that those of us in public service wanted to be a part of the good fight to set things right. We *all* wanted to be the one to catch bin Laden. It became more than just a cause; it was a calling.

In the chaos and confusion that followed 9/11, our leaders did not want to rely on new strategies, or depart radically from proven practices (although the tried and true had already apparently failed us). According to Amy Zegart, "decision makers operate in a world where rationality is limited or bounded. Confronted with an unknown future, incomplete information, and cognitive constraints, organizational leaders do the best they can, settling for options that appear "good enough" but may in fact be nowhere close."[153]

We have visited Mathieu Deflem's argument that law enforcement enjoys some unique benefits as a function of its culture, its political independence, its "us versus them" group mentality, its ability to transcend borders and barriers (in politics, ethnicity, and religion), and its professional proficiency. We can also judge from Anne-Marie Slaughter's work that other segments of government, not just law enforcement, aim toward professionalism at the international level. Although professional expertise and efficiency are of course generally positive aspects of bureaucracy, they may also have a negative effect on the implementation of some strategic counterterrorism tools.

Human Nature as Impediment

Michael Turner refers to a phenomenon that placed some powerful agencies in the Intelligence Community in positions of prominence in the post-9/11 power realignment. Consistent with their emphasis on expertise and professionalism, "Intelligence officials reinforce their absolute faith in the exceptionalism of intelligence with a "can-do" attitude. This view, that

---

[153] Zegart, Spying Blind, 51.

U.S. intelligence can accomplish any task successfully, is a reflection of the broader American cultural ideal of Americans as doers who can accomplish any task set before them better than anyone else. This attitude also derives from the assumption that imagination, daring, and persistence will yield useful intelligence about national security threats.[154] But this "can-do" attitude, though a positive quality, can be insidious. As Wilson notes: "Ideally, a government bureau would like to be the only organization in town curing cancer [or catching Bin Laden] and would like to have no limitations on how it goes about achieving that cure."[155] Although Wilson maintains that there is no evidence that bureaucracies universally seek to expand and grow, there is a universal sense in government that separate bureaucracies are *all* competing for *funding*.[156]

Federal government employees are evaluated, and judge themselves in relation to their peers, on the monetary size of the programs they control. The reality of competition for funding, and "can-do" bravado, appears in the strategic response to the 1998 U.S. embassy bombings in Kenya and Tanzania. In the 9/11 Commission report, James Pavitt, the head of the CIA's Directorate of Operations, said, "if there's going to be money spent on going after Bin Laden, it should be given to him…My view Richard Clarke's, was that he had had a lot of money to do it and a long time to do it and I didn't want to put good money after bad."[157] The CIA was, and still is of course, not the only agency looking for terrorism funding. The FBI received a boost in funding despite significant failings: "FBI Director Robert Mueller … heard sharp complaints from lawmakers about the bureau's past failures, but found no opposition to plans for a big budget increase."[158] Conventional wisdom in the federal government, especially among non-FBI federal agents, is that whenever there is a significant newsworthy event, the FBI asks for, and receives, massive additional funding—seemingly without fail. And the story is the same for the IC's budget, which after 9/11, "has been increased to match the increases in the defense budget. The State Department's entire current budget is smaller than the CIA's."[159]

---

[154] Michael A. Turner, Why Secret Intelligence Fails (Washington, DC: Potomac Books, Inc., 2006), 45.

[155] James Q. Wilson, Bureaucracy: What Government Agencies Do and Why They Do It (Basic Books, 1989), 181.

[156] Wilson, Bureaucracy, 180.

[157] 9/11 Commission, The 9/11 Commission Report (2004), 184.

[158] Terry Frieden, CNN, 1 April 2008 http://www.cnn.com/2008/POLITICS/04/01/fbi.counterterrorism/index.html.

[159] Goodman, Failure of Intelligence, 272. Goodman also points out that the State Department's budget has been steadily reduced in recent years.

In the same manner that many of us in public service felt a strong desire or calling to participate in the fight against terrorism, it is only natural to presume that those in positions of power and authority in the "premier" security agencies felt the same way. It is not good bureaucratic practice to point out to Congress, or to the President, that "others" (in smaller, less well represented agencies) "are doing pretty good work—let's give some money to them!" It has not gone unnoticed that the bravado of agency culture and associated "lack of imagination" have contributed to an ineffectual strategic response to the threat of transnational terrorism.[160] These factors continue to inhibit innovation in how we respond to any crisis.

"Bureau*crazy*"—Organizational Pathologies as an Impediment to Engaging Worldwide, Informal Networks of Law Enforcement

The premier counterterrorism agencies are easy to identify. They are the ones we hear about on the news—the FBI, the CIA, and the Department of Defense. A General Accountability Office report reinforces the idea:

> The Department of Justice has the *lead* in law enforcement and criminal matters related to terrorism—both domestically and overseas"; and "the FBI *leads* Department of Justice efforts to investigate international terrorism. Specifically, the FBI is responsible for the apprehension and rendition of foreign terrorists who are suspected of violating U.S. statutes. According to the FBI, it also has the *primary* responsibility to collect foreign intelligence and counterintelligence information, including that related to terrorism, within the United States."

GAO's report continues: "DOD Department of Defense is the *lead* agency for military operations against terrorist organizations and states that sponsor them"; and "the CIA has the *lead* for gathering, analyzing, and disseminating intelligence on foreign terrorist organizations."[161]

In the U.S. federal universe, the term "lead" connotes "turf"—a powerful word, and a synonym for "funding." Wilson devotes an entire chapter to the subject.[162] Even U.S. presidents cannot override this bureaucratic power.[163] Agencies have carved out niches for themselves, and no agency wants

---

160 9/11 Commission, The 9/11 Commission Report, 344.

161 United States Government Accountability Office, Report to Congressional Requesters, COMBATING TERRORISM: Interagency Framework and Agency Programs to Address the Overseas Threat (Washington, DC: May 2003), 55-56, 58-60. Upper case in title added by the author.

162 Wilson, Bureaucracy, 179-195.

163 Zegart, Spying Blind, 57.

to cede turf to any other agency. The author has been, and to a degree still is, an active and exuberant participant in turf battles of every sort, at a variety of levels. Certainly, turf wars can be exhilarating, especially when one "wins."[164] Wilson maintains that organizations crave and strive for autonomy, which means "undisputed jurisdiction,"[165] an even stronger concept than "turf." Wilson further says that, in the quest for autonomy, "the best a government agency executive can do is minimize the number of rivals and constraints."[166]

Wilson's concepts explain why non-FBI U.S. federal law enforcement agencies have not been able to use their resources and contacts as a source of overt counterterrorism information. Again, a GAO report supports this assertion.[167] Bureaucratic temperament explains how and why nominally "international" and "global" counterterrorism law enforcement conferences can focus exclusively on *domestic* U.S. counterterrorism coordination issues. Undisputed jurisdiction means that lead agencies will not share the stage with other agencies. This situation perseveres despite the guidance provided by the 2003 National Strategy for Counterterrorism.[168]

In the author's experience, the most contentious arena among U.S. counterterror agencies is within the foreign domain[169]—perhaps because of the implications for foreign relations. Typically, U.S. state or local agencies do not play at all in this arena.[170] At the same time, and problematically, by exerting control over information from the foreign arena, our premier national

---

[164] My impressions stem from experience in the past ten "terrorism" years, after the Nairobi and Dar es Salaam Embassy bombings, and on through 9/11. An embassy's Regional Security Office only rarely loses a security dispute—even against formidable counterparts. No embassy executives want to be called to testify before Congress to explain why they disregarded the guidance of the security officer. Embassy management will generally defer to their instinct for self-preservation and rule in favor of caution—with a nod toward security.

[165] Wilson, Bureaucracy, footnote on p. 183.

[166] Wilson, Bureaucracy, 188.

[167] U.S. GAO, Combating Terrorism: Law Enforcement Agencies Lack Directives to Assist Foreign Nations to Identify, Disrupt, and Prosecute Terrorists, GO 07-697 (Washington, 2007). http://www.gao.gov/new.items/d07697.pdf.

[168] National Strategy for Combating Terrorism, 2003, 16-17. "Our regional partners are often better poised than the United States to gain access to information and intelligence. Therefore, the intelligence and law enforcement communities will continue to expand and improve their relations with their foreign counterparts in an effort to take better advantage of their source reporting."

[169] The author once had a disagreement at a U.S. embassy overseas in which a U.S. agency chief asserted control over all foreign sources of information—including those cultivated by the author in his role as chief of embassy security. The author strongly objected to this assertion and the matter was adjudicated in the author's favor by the Ambassador.

[170] Although some city-level U.S. law enforcement agencies, notably the New York City Police Department, have an overseas presence for coordination purposes, domestic police departments overwhelmingly maintain a predominantly domestic focus. See Brian Nussbaum, "Protecting Global Cities: New York, London, and the Internationalization of Municipal Policing for Counter-Terrorism," in Global Crime 8, no. 3 (August 2007), 228.

agencies can control the actions of domestic agencies and departments that receive the information and which are charged with acting on it.

Organizational theory asserts that bureaucracies resist change; Wilson similarly argues that organizations resist innovation.[171] But only innovation will allow us to deal with the threat of transnational terrorism. The 9/11 Commission Report emphasizes: "It is therefore crucial to find a way of routinizing, even bureaucratizing, the exercise of imagination."[172] Even the turf master himself, Donald Rumsfeld, said "improving our efforts will likely mean embracing new institutions to engage people around the world," and "we need to consider the possibility of new organizations and programs that can serve a similarly valuable role in the war on terror."[173] Given bureaucracy's tendency to resist change, in the period of adjustment after 9/11, it would certainly have been innovative to include all of the instruments of governmental power in our nation's strategic counterterrorism response, not only those of the premier agencies.[174] To paraphrase National Security Advisor Frances Townsend—we went with what we were familiar with at the time, "because we had a fear of unintended consequences."[175]

The FBI and CIA have in common a strong sense of mission.[176] They are also renowned for their pursuit of "unrestricted jurisdiction"; that is, they share a reputation for being militantly turf-conscious.[177] In a chapter on "Fighting Osama One Bureaucrat at a Time," Amy Zegart writes: "The CIA faced a number of cultural pathologies, chief among them were a debilitating sense of agency parochialism, resistance to change, and a belief in the overriding importance of security, captured by the phrase 'need to know.'"[178] She continues:

> [The CIA] was built and designed to operate in secret, with strict rules governing contact between individuals, even those within the agency, a

---

[171] Zegart, Spying Blind, 45; Wilson, Bureaucracy, 221.

[172] 9/11 Report, 344.

[173] Brian Michael Jenkins, Unconquerable Nation: Knowing Our Enemy, Strengthening Ourselves (Santa Monica, CA: RAND Corporation, 2006), 122. Original source: Donald Rumsfeld, "War in the Information Age," Los Angeles Times, 23 February 2006.

[174] Hence the 9/11 Commission's plea to include all instruments of governmental power in the fight against international terrorism. The 9/11 Commission Report, 401.

[175] Interview with Frances Fragos Townsend, Washington, DC, 7 June 2007: "This was a new kind of threat we were facing and there was a fear of unintended consequences. We have derived enormous benefit from how we do things, but now we are at a point where we can ask, "How can we get more out of the system?"

[176] For the FBI, see Wilson, Bureaucracy, 107. For the CIA, see Michael Turner, Why Secret Intelligence Fails, 45 and, Victor Marchetti and John D. Marks, The CIA and the Cult of Intelligence (New York, NY: Alfred A. Knopf, 1974).

[177] Mark Riebling, Wedge.

[178] Zegart, Spying Blind, 67

classification system designed to protect information rather than share it, and a host of other security measures separating the agency from the rest of the outside world. This isolation not only made oversight and learning difficult, it made internal social norms, habits and cultural values all the more important in daily agency life. Left alone, agency officials grew more attached to the internal bonds that kept them working together.

Time, finally, made everything worse. For any organization, change becomes harder with time, as habits and policies and cultures become ingrained. For the CIA, the demand for change came after 40 years—an entire organizational lifetime—of fighting the same enemy.[179]

As for the FBI, Zegart maintains that it was incapable of transforming its culture. She notes that, after 9/11, the nature of organizations, rational self-interest, and the fragmented structure of the federal government made adaptation to the challenge of international terrorism all but impossible for the FBI.[180] If, as Wilson, Zegart, and others claim, institutions are resistant to change, there is little reason to presume that any of these agencies have changed even eight years after 9/11.[181]

The 9/11 attacks were perpetrated by a new, ruthless, strategically oriented, thoroughly networked, intelligent adversary that demanded, and continues to demand, innovative and creative new ideas and methods of countering it. The United States needs the capability to combat a new adversary in a completely new arena. However, if we continue to shoehorn the problem of international terrorism to suit the bureaucratic intransigence of our most powerful agencies, then the very disturbing implication is that our strategic counterterrorism policy is hostage to bureaucratic and organizational *pathology*.

Resistance to Organizational Change

Riebling examines how the FBI and CIA structured themselves in response to the Soviet threat and their interagency, cultural war.[182] Zegart adds that "When the cold war ended, the CIA did not emerge a blank slate. Its legislative origins had lasting effects, crippling the agency's ability to manage

---

[179] Zegart, Spying Blind, 90.

[180] Zegart, Spying Blind, 155.

[181] For a historical account of the FBI's tendency to view other intelligence and law enforcement agencies as rivals and their reluctance to cooperate as a still-applicable defining characteristic, please see Powers, Broken, 97-100.

[182] In the Borzoi edition of Mark Riebling's Wedge (1994), an editor notes that "Over the past two decades there have been eleven White House reform directives attempting to correct the unhealthy and destructive relations between CIA and FBI." Wedge places the fervent counterintelligence debate in a historical context and vividly describes the fascinating and disturbing world of American espionage.

an expanding set of intelligence agencies, and erecting jurisdictional boundaries, particularly between domestic and foreign intelligence, that hardened with time.[183] The FBI, in her view, suffers from a similar history:

- For the CIA, adapting to terrorism meant doing the job differently. For the FBI it meant doing a different job entirely. Like the CIA, the FBI did not succeed;

- Like the Central Intelligence Agency, the FBI was hobbled by weaknesses in organizational structure, culture and incentives;

- [For the FBI] "the problem came when the Cold War ended and counterterrorism required a radically different approach;"

- By 1991, the Bureau's law enforcement mission, procedures, career incentive, and culture had set like stone.[184]

As for the Intelligence Community as a whole:

- Six years after the World Trade Center and Pentagon attacks, the U.S. Intelligence Community's worst problems endure. Although legislative, executive, and internal agency initiatives have made many changes to U.S. intelligence agencies, most have created halting progress. Some have made matters worse;

- We believe that many within those agencies do not accept the conclusion that…the Community needs fundamental change if it is to confront the challenges of the 21st century;

- It is fair to say U.S. intelligence agencies since 9/11 have made more headlines than progress;

- It is now sixteen years since the end of the Cold War and the U.S. Intelligence Community is still struggling to develop the rudimentary building blocks to combat terrorism;

- Although al Qaeda has not attacked the U.S. homeland since 9/11, there is little evidence to suggest that effective intelligence is the reason. As one Congressional Intelligence Committee lawmaker noted in the fall of 2005, "We still stink at collecting. We still stink at analysis…all the problems we set out to correct are still there."

- The CIA and FBI failed to adapt before 9/11…effective intelligence is unlikely even now, years after the terrorist attacks. The nature of organizations, rational self interest, and the structure of the American government are not going anywhere anytime soon.[185]

---

[183] Zegart, Spying Blind, 69.
[184] Zegart, Spying Blind, 120, 121, 125, 148.
[185] Zegart, Spying Blind, 182. 182, 193, 195, 197, 44.

Resistance to Procedural Change

It is not only organizationally related, cultural attributes that continue to reflect a Cold War mentality. Procedural areas, where one might reasonably expect more rapid change to occur, have not seen that change. According to former Congressman Lee H. Hamilton, "Current classification policy was set in 1982 by President Reagan."[186] This procedural guidance was a creature of the Cold War.

Chief among the negative effects of using Cold War practices in the United States' conduct of the war on terror is the over-reliance on and abuse of procedures for the classification of information. Although protection of information, sources, and methods is absolutely critical to national security, a classification system designed nearly seventy years ago and growing out of military and wartime necessity[187] clearly appears inappropriate for a problem perpetrated primarily by stateless actors in the criminal arena.

The U.S. government exhibits an almost universal tendency to over-classify information. As an embassy Regional Security Officer (RSO), and thus the custodian and protector of the classified information held in embassies, the author saw evidence of this phenomenon every day—particularly with respect to terrorism information. U.S. Court of Appeals Judge Richard A. Posner notes that "Critics contend plausibly that the intelligence community, and government generally, have a fetish for secrecy."[188] Riebling refers to the attraction of "Everyman's fascination with forbidden knowledge, a will to know what no one else knows."[189] Jennifer Sims concludes that, because for most of their existence U.S. intelligence agencies worked against the Soviet Union, a particularly secretive state, it is not surprising that secret sources are even now almost instinctively the most prized.[190] A fixation on secret sources now amounts to a debilitating cognitive bias. A number of U.S. adversaries are less secretive than the Soviet Union was, and Sims suggests that they do not necessarily know how to keep their actions out of the public eye.

---

[186] Hon. Lee H. Hamilton, "Government Secrecy after the Cold War," Congressional Record, 1 April 1992. Available at http://fas.org/irp/congress/1992_cr/h920401-spy.html.

[187] Timothy L. Ericson, "Building Our Own 'Iron Curtain': The Emergence of Secrecy in American Government," American Archivist 68 (Spring/Summer 2005), 18-52. He finds that "Executive Order 8381, signed by Franklin Roosevelt on March 22, 1940, probably marks the beginning of the modern executive order era as related to classification of government information." Available at: http://www.archivists.org/governance/presidential/ericson.asp.

[188] Richard A. Posner, Uncertain Shield: The U.S. Intelligence System in the Throes of Reform (Lanham, MD: Rowan & Littlefield Publishers, Inc., 2006), 16.

[189] Reibling, Wedge, 382.

[190] Jennifer Sims, "Understanding Ourselves," in Transforming U.S. Intelligence (Washington, DC: Georgetown University Press, 2005), 37.

Al-Qaeda is not the Soviet Union. Treating terrorism information, best thought of as criminal intelligence information—the domain of the police, as a state secret defies common sense. However, defining terrorism in terms of national security can confer primacy on both the presidential and military/intelligence domain. Posner argues that "the problem of over-classification is exacerbated by a failure to distinguish between the different security risks presented by foreign states and by terrorists. Foreign states have their own intelligence agencies that can steal secrets by pooling and analyzing scattered bits of information obtained from leaks or moles. Terrorist groups have a much less elaborate intelligence apparatus."[191]

Those defending the current classification guidelines might argue that terrorism is an exceptionally violent and risky business, and that sources and providers of information are at an extremely elevated risk of being harmed. Under the national security classification guidelines, information classified as "Confidential" would cause damage to national security if disclosed; information classified as "Secret" would cause serious damage to national security if disclosed; and information classified as "Top Secret" would cause grave danger to national security if disclosed.[192] It is difficult to imagine a scenario in which information disclosing a source on a criminal terrorist action could damage national security, unless the source were part of a network that could thwart an attack on the U.S.—for example, if a source were about to uncover information on an impending catastrophic attack on the United States and was suddenly exposed and thereby rendered useless.

---

[191] Posner, Uncertain Shield, 215.

[192] While the standard classification guidelines call for foreign information and protection of sources to be "considered" for classification, the classifying individual has discretion over the level of classification or whether to classify at all. The White House, Executive Order Further Amendment to Executive Order 12958, as Amended, Classified National Security Information, http://www.archives.gov/isoo/policy-documents/eo-12958-amendment.html.

The U.S. Foreign Service's *Foreign Affairs Manual* (FAM) provides guidelines for the use of Sensitive But Unclassified (SBU) information.[193] This guidance cites as an example of SBU information: *law enforcement information or information regarding ongoing investigations.*[194] This designation is intentional—law enforcement information often needs to be shared—with other law enforcement elements, with prosecuting and defense attorneys at trial, or, in some cases, to pass along for public safety purposes. As shown below, the *Foreign Affairs Manual* also provides standards for the classification of information, in so doing tacitly confirming that classification abuse does take place, and in what form the abuse takes place.[195]

---

12 FAM 516 STANDARDS

12 FAM 516.1 Classification

c. Do not classify information unless its disclosure reasonably could be expected to cause damage to the national security. Information may not be classified to:

(1) Conceal violations of law, inefficiency, or administrative error;

(2) Prevent embarrassment to a person, organization, or agency;

(3) Restrain competition; or

(4) Prevent or delay the release of information that does not require protection in the interest of national security.

Abuse and misuse of the classification system is not new.[196] Melvin Goodman, a former intelligence professional, alleges: "One of the greatest

---

[193] Sensitive But Unclassified (SBU) information is information that is not classified for national security reasons, but that warrants/requires administrative control and protection from public or other unauthorized disclosure for other reasons. SBU should meet one or more of the criteria for exemption from public disclosure under the Freedom of Information Act (FOIA), which also exempts information protected under other statutes, 5 U.S.C. 552, or should be protected by the Privacy Act, 5 U.S.C. 552a. Foreign Affairs Manual, 12 FAM 540, SENSITIVE BUT UNCLASSIFIED INFORMATION (SBU), 12FAM 54, Scope note.

[194] Foreign Affairs Manual, 12 FAM 540, SENSITIVE BUT UNCLASSIFIED INFORMATION (SBU), 12FAM 541, Scope note.

[195] Foreign Affairs Manual, 12 FAM 516 STANDARDS, 12 FAM 516.1, Classification.

[196] Turner, Why Secret Intelligence Fails, 102.

scandals within the intelligence community is the over-classification of government documents in order to keep important information out of the hands of the American people… documents are often classified to hide embarrassing political information, not secrets."[197] Even more insidious reasons exist to over-classify: reasons associated with protecting turf and neutralizing erstwhile competitors. Considering terrorism information in national security terms, rather than as crime data, allows the premier military and intelligence agencies to assert control over an extended domain.

Protecting turf, concealing mistakes and embarrassments, and minimizing rivals represent expected bureaucratic behavior.[198] French National Police *Commissionaire* Emil Perez agrees matter-of-factly with this assessment: "Information does not get classified to protect information; it gets classified to keep out the competition."[199] The author's own published view is that: "Law enforcement and the IC have repeatedly stymied one another. Law enforcement invokes privacy concerns and investigative case secrecy to protect its information. The IC invokes 'sources and methods' to protect its capabilities… There are good reasons to maintain case control and protect sources; but there are many occasions when cooperation can work around these issues."[200] Cooperation between the IC and national law enforcement agencies is not unknown, but remains unusual. The combination of organizational turf wars and procedural problems with classification contribute to the negative inertia that might support cooperation, and to an explanation for how and why the instruments and capabilities of international law enforcement have been excluded from the Global War on Terror.

Can the Problems Get Worse?

De facto politicization, combined with the abuse and inherent weaknesses of the classification system, endangers sources more than it protects them. Classification is typically a political decision and not a technical action.[201] Harry Howe Ransom's conclusion is compelling: "Intelligence is subject, object and instrument of power politics."[202] Georgetown University's

---

197 Melvin A. Goodman, Failure of Intelligence, 345.

198 Posner, Uncertain Shield, 16.

199 Interview with Commissionaire Emile Perez, Paris, France, 7 March 2008.

200 Mike Bayer, "Commentary," in Improving the Law Enforcement-Intelligence Community Relationship: Can't We All Just Get Along? viii, available at http://www.ndic.edu/press/5463.htm.

201 Goodman, Failure of Intelligence, 345.

202 Harry Howe Ransom, "The Politicization of Intelligence," in Intelligence and Intelligence Policy in a Democratic Society, Stephen J. Cimbala, ed. (United States: Transnational Publishers, Inc., 1987), 23.

resident intelligence expert, Jennifer Sims, is equally forceful: "The influence of American political culture on U.S. Intelligence is pervasive."[203]

Politicization of intelligence, paired with the lust for the secret and forbidden, makes for a deadly combination. Politicization circumvents the fundamental and basic precepts of classification by providing those who do not necessarily "need to know" with the ability to access and manipulate classified information.[204] The reverence for the secret, the quest for forbidden knowledge, and the idea that "knowledge is power" attract the attention of those in positions of authority and those who are well-connected. These individuals include those who have security clearances and who work in the White House and Congress, as well as political appointees who reside in any and all agencies. Sims alleges that "confusion of the sensitivity of the source or method with the quality or importance of the information is subtly reinforced by the intelligence community's inclination to prioritize the dissemination of its most highly classified information according to the recipients' respective ranks and prior clearances rather than on the basis of their respective needs…"[205]

Selective leaks of sensitive or classified information to satisfy other political or ideological ambitions are one manifestation of politicization. The alleged CIA "secret prison leaks" were supposedly ideologically or morally motivated, but may have been perpetrated in an effort to damage the Bush administration.[206] The *Washington Post* speculated that "bitterness within the agency the CIA about allegations that the administration misused intelligence resources and reports in connection with the war" may have been a motivation for the alleged leaker. Leaks about illegal NSA monitoring also purportedly resulted from moral and ideological differences—but with strong overtones of political motivation. Thomas Tamm, the Justice Department attorney who allegedly divulged information about the NSA program, was quoted in *Newsweek* saying that he was "pissed off" at the Bush administration, and that he contributed money to the Democratic National Committee in 2004—the year he allegedly leaked the story. Tamm concedes he was also motivated by his anger at other Bush administration policies at the Justice Department, including its aggressive pursuit of death penalty cases and the legal justifications for "enhanced" interrogation techniques that many believe are tantamount to

---

203 Jennifer Sims, "Understanding Ourselves," in Transforming U.S. Intelligence, 40.

204 As what allegedly occurred in the justifications to wage the war in Iraq.

205 Jennifer Sims, "Understanding Ourselves," 39.

206 R. Jeffrey Smith and Dafina Linzer, "CIA Officer's Job Made Any Leaks More Delicate," Washington Post, 23 April 2006, A01.

torture.[207] The "anonymous" author of *Imperial Hubris*, former CIA terrorism analyst Michael Scheuer, writes, "Leaking classified intelligence to journalists, even the most highly classified, has long been common among senior U.S. government officials, politicians, civil servants and senior military officers."[208] Scheuer goes on to say:

> Leaks are a major factor limiting the effectiveness of U.S. efforts to defeat Osama bin Laden, et al. The first serious leak about al Qaeda was in the *Washington Times* after the 20 August 1998 U.S. cruise missile attack near Kwost, Afghanistan. The attack was in response to the bombing of our embassies in Kenya and Tanzania thirteen days earlier. In the 24 August *Times* article, "senior" U.S. Department of Defense officials revealed that precise U.S. targeting of the camps was based on electronically intercepting bin Laden's conversations. "In the two weeks following the Aug. 7 attacks, against the U.S. embassies in Kenya and Tanzania," Ernest Balzer wrote in his "Inside the Ring" column, "the United States reaped an intelligence bonanza from intercepted terrorists' radio and telephone calls." The senior leaker told Balzer they had not leaked sooner because "it was hoped that terrorists would again use their compromised networks to rally in the wake of the Tomahawk [cruise missile] attacks. Said one U.S. official: 'We want to see who is still using the same cell phone numbers.'" Apparently these genius leakers had decided it was time to make sure the terrorists would not use the phone again. Well, as night follows day, the intelligence community lost this priceless advantage when bin Laden and his men stopped using the phones. A direct trail leads from the leak that caused the loss of access to bin Laden's planning conversations to the surprise attack on 11 September 2001.[209]

Many individuals in federal law enforcement, the author included, consider classification an inadequate means of protecting sources and methods and, in fact, consider classification of our case information to be a complicating factor in protecting sensitive information because it provides an avenue for exploitation and manipulation by those with personal agendas. Some years ago, the author was the lead investigative agent for a major human trafficking case that involved Eastern European (Czech), Russian, and Italian organized crime groups. The case centered around a Czech organized

---

207 Michael Isikoff, "The Fed Who Blew the Whistle: Is He a Hero or a Criminal?" Newsweek, 22 December 2008. http://www.newsweek.com/id/174601; and Greg Simmons, NSA Spy Story Could Lead to New Leak Probe, FoxNews.com, 29 December 2005. http://www.foxnews.com/story/0,2933,180149,00.html.

208 Anonymous (Michael Scheuer), Imperial Hubris, 192.

209 Anonymous (Scheuer), Imperial Hubris, 193-194.

crime gang that contrived to lure young jobless Eastern European women into the New York City illicit sex industry with the promise of legitimate work as waitresses and models—but in reality the women were forced to work as peepshow dancers and prostitutes. The case coincided with a major White House/State Department/Department of Justice initiative to combat trafficking in women and children.[210] As I was preparing to take the case into its final stages with search warrant-backed raids on the peepshows, business offices, and homes of the principal subjects, I began receiving calls from the Department of Justice informing me that there was high-level interest in the case that extended to the White House and that then-Attorney General Janet Reno was requesting daily updates on the progress of the case. The evening before the raids I received a phone call from a senior executive in my own organization informing me that there was high-level interest in the case and that I should consider allowing press to be on-site to film the arrests and raids—which I respectfully declined. On the day of the raids, as we walked out of the building with bags of evidence, documents, cash, and our material witnesses and subjects in tow, we were nearly blinded by the lights of the television crews filming the proceedings. I still do not know who leaked the information to the press about the raids.

While this case did not involve classified information, it is indicative of what can happen when political interests come into play. In my case the press attention ultimately did not negatively affect the outcome of the case— although it easily could have. For example, as part of the case strategy, we knew that many of the women were being held and forced to work against their will, and that many of them would be willing to testify against the gang's ringleaders—the principal subjects. Indeed, we "flipped" about fifteen potential witnesses. Upon their arraignment, the arrested women (witnesses) were released of their own accord. On the day of the arrests, we also arrested one of the gang's ringleaders but other gang leaders could not be immediately located. Because the press cameras filmed the arrests of the trafficked women, the remaining organized crime gang leaders knew who the potential witnesses against them would be. Sure enough, in short order two of our primary witnesses called, complaining of harassment and death threats. Soon thereafter, my two prime witnesses disappeared. It is difficult to describe the state

---

[210] The raids occurred on 12 March 1998. The day before, President Clinton issued an Executive Memorandum on "Steps to Combat Violence Against Women and Trafficking in Women and Girls," ordering DOJ and the State Department to focus their resources to combat the trafficking of women and children—with emphasis on the sex industry. See The White House, Executive Memorandum: Steps to Combat Violence Against Women and Trafficking in Women and Girls, 11 March 1998, available at The American Presidency Project, http://www.presidency.ucsb.edu/ws/indx.php?pid=55607.

of panic that accompanies the realization that two witnesses, for whom you are responsible, might be dead—and that this development would soon need to be explained (through channels) to the Attorney General and probably also to the President of the United States. My concern for the young women was equaled (or surpassed) by my concern for my own career and well-being. As it turned out, however, the two witnesses had wisely gone underground for self-preservation purposes, and resurfaced shortly thereafter. Upon reestablishing contact, we placed them immediately into protective custody. Subsequently, we turned the tables on the gang hierarchy by enlisting one of the threat-ened witnesses to "wear a wire" and meet with the subjects who had been the source of the death threats. This operation was also successful, and we arrested four more gang members for witness tampering, as well as the gang's ringleader. A year later, a U.S. Marshal and I re-arrested the gang's boss after he had gone fugitive. In the end, my agency, the Diplomatic Security Service (DSS), and the White House's "trafficking in women and children" initiative received some positive press coverage. After the case was resolved, and with the principals in jail, it was featured on television's *America's Most Wanted* and was the subject of a major story in New York's *Newsday*.[211]

Deflem argues that politicization of law enforcement information occurs far less often than that associated with the national intelligence services. The reason, he suggests, is that law enforcement remains for the most part less centralized than national intelligence, and enjoys greater autonomy.[212] The human trafficking case outlined here represents an anomaly because the tim-ing coincided with a political interest on the part of the White House.

Although every system and mode of protecting information have advantages and disadvantages, none is perfect. The very act of classifying information compounds the problem in a number of ways—not the least of which is that classified information attracts those who seek to exploit it— hence the preponderance of spy cases and the problems associated with polit-ical interference.[213] Nor should classification be considered an ideal vehicle

---

[211] Graham Raymond, "Stripped of Their Dignity," Newsday, 21 March 1999. After-the-fact press coverage is generally acceptable and even desirable, but press presence and coverage during case operations can be disastrous. The case was also reported in the New York Times, Chicago Times, Los Angeles Times, and the Prague Post the day after the arrests.

[212] Mathieu Deflem, "Global Rule of Law or Global Rule of Law Enforcement? International Police Cooperation and Counter-Terrorism," The Annals of the American Academy of Political and Social Science, vol. 603 (2006), 240-252. Also see Deflem, Policing World Society and "Bureau-cratization and Social Control."

[213] Alleged State Department spy Kendall Meyers is said to have been directed by the Cuban government to seek positions that would give him access to classified information—at higher and higher classified clearance levels. Associated Press, "Couple Accused of Spying for Cuba," Washington Observer-Reporter," 6 June 2009. Available at: http://www.observer-reporter.com/OR/StoryAP/06-06-CUBA-SPY-CHARGE-7.

for protecting sources and methods at the tactical level. How many lives have been lost in connection with recent U.S. spy cases is incalculable but, by way of example, CIA spy Aldrich Ames is thought to be responsible for up to two dozen deaths of American intelligence assets in the Soviet Union.[214] FBI traitor Robert Hanssen is widely considered to have been responsible for at least three executions of American spies in the former USSR, the exposure of nine Soviet officials recruited to spy for the United States, and for making available to foreign agents information on at least five Soviet defectors to the United States.[215] According to an Office of the Inspector General (OIG) report, "Hanssen liked working in the Soviet Analytical Unit in FBI Headquarters because he found it, 'overwhelmingly attractive' because of the extremely broad access to sensitive information it offered."[216] CIA renegade Phillip Agee is said to have been responsible for exposing up to 250 covert CIA officers with several deaths attributable to him—including an alleged CIA Station Chief in Athens, Greece.[217] In what might be the first infiltration into the U.S. intelligence system by a terrorist-related group, illegal alien Nada Prouty, who worked for both the FBI as a Special Agent *and* the CIA—she had obtained a security clearance and FBI Special Agent credentials, was caught illegally accessing classified files and information on Hezbollah. Prouty's own ties to Hezbollah, and what she may have compromised, continue to be the subject of speculation.[218]

In what might be considered a twist of irony, many of us in U.S. federal law enforcement consider the use of less sensitive categories of classification, such as Sensitive But Unclassified or Law Enforcement Sensitive, to be a superior means of protecting sensitive information, sources, and methods. First, use of unclassified/sensitive designations encourages the use of opera-

214 Tim Weiner, "Betrayer's Tale—A Special Report: A Decade as a Turncoat: Aldrich Ames's Own Story," New York Times, 28 July 1994. Also in The International Spy Museum, Aldrich Ames—Dozens Exposed, www.spymuseum.com/pages/agent-ames-aldrich-html.

215 Glen A. Fine, Office of the Inspector General (OIG), A Review of the FBI's Performance in Deterring, Detecting, and Investigating the Espionage Activities of Robert Philip Hanssen, 14 August 2003. Available at http://www.fas.org/irp/agency/doj/oig/hanssen.html.

216 Fine, A Review of the FBI's Performance in Deterring, Detecting, and Investigating the Espionage Activities of Robert Philip Hanssen.

217 Jamie Glazer, "Symposium, the Death of a Traitor," Front Page Magazine.com, 29 February 2008. Available at http://frontpagemagazine.com/Articles/Read.asp.aspx.

218 Clark, Your Government Failed You, 148.

tional (or operations) security[219]—which is what really protects information and discourages the false sense of security imparted by over-classification.[220] Second, unclassified but sensitive categories convey responsibility to the individual case agents for whom the best interests of protecting information prevail—no law enforcement officer wants to have a case blown to which months and sometimes years of work have been dedicated (or that might result in harm to a valued informant). This is why law enforcement officers strive to exercise stringent case control and zealously guard case and law enforcement information. Third, law enforcement information is protected under the umbrella of the law by the Privacy Act, making public disclosure of personal information a crime. Fourth, most federal law enforcement cases are prosecuted using the grand jury process as a powerful investigative tool. The grand jury process is even more highly protected under the law, and violations of grand jury secrecy mandates are much easier to prove than unauthorized disclosures of classified information. A case in point: Lewis "Scooter" Libby was neither charged nor convicted for disclosing the (alleged) classified "secret" identity of CIA officer Valerie Plame—he was convicted of perjury (lying to a grand jury), obstruction (of justice), and lying to the FBI (false statements).[221]

A shining example of the efficacy of law enforcement effectively protecting its own information—information that is highly coveted by many with ruthless dispositions and virtually unlimited resources—is the U.S. Marshals Service's Witness Security Program (WitSec). The Service's Witness Protection Program (WPP) has kept secret the identities of over 18,000 high-risk federal witnesses and their families—to include those who have testified

---

[219] The Interagency Support OPSEC Support Staff defines "operations security" as: 1. A systematic, proven process by which a government, organization, or individual can identify, control, and protect generally unclassified information about an operation/activity and thus deny or mitigate an adversary's/competitor's ability to compromise or interrupt said operation/activity (NSC 1988). 2. OPSEC is a process of identifying critical information and subsequently analyzing friendly actions attendant to military operations and other activities to (a) identify those actions that can be observed by adversary intelligence systems, (b) determine indicators adversary intelligence systems might obtain that could be interpreted or pieced together to derive critical information in time to be useful to adversaries, and (c) select and execute measures that eliminate or reduce to an acceptable level the vulnerabilities of friendly actions to adversary exploitation (DOD JP 1994; JCS 1997), available at http://www.ioss.gov/docs/definitions.html#o.

[220] The U.S. classification system is essentially a procedural security exercise, supported by physical security in the form of building access controls, physically secure storage areas such as Controlled Access Areas (CAAs), secure containers (such as safes), and computer security systems. It is highly dependent on those with access not to discuss classified information outside of secure areas, to remove documents from secure areas, or to transfer classified material over non-secure computer systems.

[221] Al Shapiro, "Lewis 'Scooter' Libby Found Guilty of Lying," All Things Considered, National Public Radio (NPR), 6 March 2007. Available at http://www.npr.org/templates/story/story.php?storyid=7738465.

against traditional, extremely violent organized crime enterprises (such as the Italian "Mafia," Russian and Eastern European organized criminal outfits), drug cartels, transnational gangs (Asian and Latino), and terrorist and narco-terrorist groups.[222] In over 30 years of operation, the Marshal's Witness Protection Program has not lost a single witness.[223] With a record like that, those in the Intelligence Community might presume such sensitive information that might endanger some of the most high-risk subjects in the world would need to be highly classified in order to properly protect it. Such is not the case; WitSec information remains unclassified and under the information handling caveat of "Law Enforcement Sensitive."[224]

Few agencies are more heavily protective of sources and methods, because of direct, dangerous, and life-threatening consequences, than the DEA.[225] Few agencies are more effective at doing so. Yet DEA chooses not to classify its most sensitive information.[226] DEA is primarily a law enforcement agency and requires that information be "developed" to a level of acceptability for courtroom use.[227] Like national security intelligence agencies, DEA relies heavily on informant information—or what would be known to the Intelligence Community as human intelligence, or HUMINT. The drug business is extremely dangerous and informants can and do occasionally get hurt or killed. However, DEA has managed to be successful despite the dangers. DEA, in coordination with international partners, dismantled the Medellin, Cali,

---

[222] In April 2009, a Deputy U.S. Marshal serving on the WitSec program was convicted for leaking information about a witness to an alleged organized crime associate. According to press reporting, the incident did not result in any harm to the witness and a consensus among the U.S. Marshals is that the Deputy was more careless than malicious. See Mike Robinson, "Deputy US Marshal, Guilty of Leaking Secrets to Mob," Associated Press, 28 April 2009. Available at http://abcnews.go.com/US/wireStory?id=7452819.

[223] The caveat restricting the applicability of this statement is "of those who have stayed with the program," because several who had left the program of their own accord met an untimely and unnatural demise. For a detailed account of one such unfortunate individual, Brenda Paz, see Darren Brisco, "The New Face of Witness Protection," Newsweek, 2 May 2005, available at http://www.newsweek.com/id/51906. For an account of mobster Mario "Sonny" Riccobene, see Marcus Baram, "Start Snitching: Inside the Witness Protection Program," ABC News, 26 October 2007, available at http://abcnews.go.com/TheLaw/Story?id=3781361&page=1.

[224] Telephone interview with Thomas Wight, Deputy Assistant Director, Witness Security Division, United States Marshals Service, 5 December 2008.

[225] Although the DEA is one of the 16 members of the Intelligence Community, its de facto inclusion is on an infrequent, ad hoc, "as tasked" basis. That is, the DEA does not act as a member of the Community unless requested to do so for a specific purpose. DEA does not generally serve as, nor consider itself to be, an intelligence agency. Interview with DEA Director of International Operations Kevin Whaley, 7 June 2007.

[226] Gloria Freund, "Unmasking Networks: Drug Enforcement Administration Tradecraft for the Intelligence Community," in Improving the Law Enforcement-Intelligence Community Relationship: Can't We All Just Get Along? Timothy Christenson, ed. (Washington, DC: NDIC Press, 2007), 21-39, available at http://www.ndic.edu/press/5463.htm.

[227] Freund, "Unmasking Networks," 21.

and North Coast cocaine cartels.[228] As of this writing, the illicit drug trade is in the throes of another significant change because of DEA's successful tactics. Press reporting indicates that the cocaine drug trade is switching emphasis from marketing the cocaine product in the United States to Europe—largely because of DEA's successful interdiction efforts between South and Central America to the United States.[229] Has DEA won the War on Drugs? Certainly not, but it has had significant gains for being a relatively small agency and has done so by working closely with international partners—its foreign police counterparts. DEA has successfully harnessed the power of both formal and informal international police networks, which have become an exceptionally potent force multiplier for it. It has accomplished this feat largely by using its own informal, international trust-based networks.[230] And it has done so without resorting to over-classification.[231]

Yes, a Bit Worse

The biggest criticism about classifying and over-classifying information is that it renders information very difficult to work with. Information that is shared freely allows trends to be discussed, notes to be compared, and most of all cases and facts can be related to one another so that identification or recovery of dispersed data points is not stifled. Furthermore, as Gombert and Gordon suggest, "The first step toward defeating terrorism is for the U.S. government, especially the military and intelligence establishments, to stop treating information as the property of those who originate it and start treating information as a vital resource of those who need it."[232] Stacked requirements for appropriate security clearance and "need to know" designation inhibit the free flow of information to and from the large and diverse community of relevant federal, state, local, and private sector actors.[233]

---

[228] Mark Bowden, Killing Pablo: The Hunt for the World's Greatest Outlaw (New York: Atlantic Monthly Press, 2001). The author was stationed in Colombia within a few weeks after the death of Pablo Escobar and was present and participated in U.S. efforts that led to the downfall of the Cali Cartel. The author knows many of the principals portrayed in Bowden's book and can attest to many of the facts contained therein.

[229] Sebastian Rotella, of the Los Angeles Times, in a question and answer seminar held at the U.S. Embassy in Paris, 22 April 2008.

[230] Gloria Freund, "Unmasking Networks," in Improving the Law Enforcement-Intelligence Community Relationship, 21-39. The DEA makes a practice of carefully vetting the police they bring into their inner circle in the countries where they do business.

[231] Freund, "Unmasking Networks," in Improving the Law Enforcement-Intelligence Community Relationship, 21.

[232] Gompert and Gordon, War by Other Means, 130, 125.

[233] James B. Steinberg, Mary Graham, and Andrew Eggars, Building Intelligence to Fight Terrorism—Policy Brief 125 (Washington DC: The Brookings Institution, September, 2003), 2. http://www.brookings.edu/comm/policybriefs/pb125.htm.

such as the New York and Los Angeles Police Departments, would provide an opportunity for the worldwide, formal, and informal networks of law enforcement to connect the entire world with a vetted, relatively non-politicized, trustworthy network. Deflem explains, "While ideological sentiments, political responses, and formal laws on terrorism can be very diverse in the world, the target of terrorism at the level of police bureaucracy is defined in a language that can be shared among police institutions across the world.[242] With specific attention to international police cooperation in counterterrorism, Deflem adds, "The criminalization of terrorism by police has total aspirations. The net of social control is wide, it's mesh thin. Legal and moral considerations aside, a vague conception of terrorism becomes a powerful and highly consequential basis for police work."[243] Deflem sends the point home with these words, "From the worldwide police viewpoint, terrorism is a crime and is to be responded to accordingly. For police, 'the war on terror' is no war at all."[244] U.S. federal law enforcement agencies are in a unique position to engage the Blue Planet because U.S. law enforcement has been the dominant influence in international policing and has led to an "Americanization of police practices in foreign nations."[245] In short, according to Deflem, "Unlike the insularity that marked U.S. police work until the earlier half of the 20th century, police organizations from the United States, especially those at the *federal* level, have a very significant international presence.[246]

Because of the United States' great influence in international policing over the years, U.S. federal law enforcement is in a unique position to play a leadership role in international counterterrorism efforts.[247] While no one can deny that the FBI has taken a strong leadership role in international efforts after 9/11, there is much more to U.S. federal law enforcement than this one organization. One need only look at the numbers: In 2007, 164 FBI special agent/legal attaches lived and worked outside the U.S.[248] At the same time, according to the GAO's Combating Terrorism report, 696 DEA agents were assigned abroad, along with 298 Immigration and Customs Enforcement (ICE) attaches, 590 DSS Regional Security Attaches, 943 Customs and Bor-

---

[242] Deflem, Social Control and the Policing of Terrorism, 85.

[243] Deflem, Social Control and the Policing of Terrorism, 86.

[244] Deflem, Social Control and the Policing of Terrorism, 87. In this passage, Deflem was referring to international police work.

[245] Mathieu Deflem, "International Policing," The Encyclopedia of Police Science, Third Edition, Jack R. Greene, ed. (New York, NY: Routledge, 701-705, 2007), 704.

[246] Mathieu Deflem, "International Policing," 703. Italics inserted by the author for emphasis.

[247] Ideally in coordination with European and other world policing leadership.

[248] Michael A. Mason, Executive Assistant Director for Criminal, Cyber Response and Services Branch—FBI, 2007 Worldwide Personnel Recovery Conference, 10 January 2007, Power Point presentation. Available at http://proceedings.ndia.org/7040/12%20brief%by%20Mason.pdf.

der Patrol (CBP) officers, 54 Secret Service agents, five Alcohol, Tobacco, and Firearms agents, and 28 U.S. Marshals, for a total of 2,614 non-FBI, U.S. federal agents assigned overseas.[249] As the FBI declares in its 2004-2009 Strategic Plan, "Partnerships are essential if the FBI is to effectively address evolving threats that are too complex or multi-jurisdictional for one agency to handle alone."[250] According to the *New York Times* and former CIA officials, the number of that agency's officers assigned overseas amounted to fewer than 1,100 persons in 2004, which is about the same number of FBI agents staffing its New York field office alone.[251] Even if these numbers have now increased, any engagement with non-FBI, U.S. federal law enforcement agencies would have to be directed from above, because no individual agency would tread on the perceived turf of the behemoth agencies that have been afforded counterterrorism primacy. Nonetheless, the possibility exists for U.S. law enforcement (not exclusively the FBI) to pool its overseas resources and formulate a massive, police-based counterterrorism criminal intelligence network for intelligence and law enforcement ends alike. The U.S. is a law enforcement leader in mainstream crime and organized crime; it can also be a worldwide leader in combating the crime of terrorism, a crime that is often supported by criminal networks and criminal activities. Even today, if decision-makers in the U.S. government were to allow U.S. federal law enforcement agencies to unleash their potential, the foundation exists for a powerful, strategic, cohesive, global counterterrorism network.

Terrorist Networks Are Organized + Terrorism Is a Crime = Terrorism *Is* Organized Crime

U.S.-based international law enforcement has had significant success against international organized crime, against other network-oriented transnational criminal enterprises, and against criminal/terrorism networks. DEA has been largely behind the dismantling of the Medellin, Cali, and North Coast Colombian cocaine cartels and is having significant success against the Mexican drug gangs.[252] DEA interdiction efforts are currently being credited for a massive diversion in cocaine trafficking routes to West Africa on

---

[249] GAO "Combating Terrorism, Law Enforcement Agencies Lack Directives to Assist Foreign Nations to Identify, Disrupt, and Prosecute Terrorists," 7-10, and Michael A. Mason, Power Point presentation.

[250] Federal Bureau of Investigation, FBI Strategic Plan 2004-2009 (Washington, DC: FBI, 2004), 8. Available at http://www.fbi.gov/publications/strategicplan/strategicplantext.htm.

[251] Douglas Jehl, "Abundance of Caution and Years of Budget Cuts are Seen to Limit CIA," New York Times, 11 May 2004.

[252] Interview with Sam Houston, DEA Country Attaché, Paris, France, 12 September 2008. According to Houston, the current violence along the Mexican border is attributable in large part to DEA interdiction efforts which have placed enormous pressures on the gangs.

into Europe. The FBI, in partnership with vetted Italian police elements, the NYPD, and other local jurisdictions, has crippled Italian Mafia operations in the U.S.[253] U.S. Marshals, in tandem with the Diplomatic Security Service, have succeeded in locating and effecting the arrest and return of record numbers of fugitives from overseas. On the terrorism front, DEA again has been instrumental in inflicting serious damage on the Colombian rebel group, the FARC. The Bureau of Diplomatic Security has had remarkable successes with its Rewards for Justice program, which pays rewards for information that results in the capture of designated terrorists or averts terrorist attacks (Ramzi Yousef, Qusay and Uday Hussein, Mir Amal Kansi, Muhsin Khardr al-Khafaji, Khamis Sirhan al-Muhammed, Zacarias Mousawi, and Abu Sayiff group's leaders, Khadafy Janjalani, Hamisiraji Marusi Sali, Toting Craft Hanno, and Abu Solaiman).[254] DSS has also had significant successes against travel document fraud rings—which terrorists can use to enter the United States illegally, and a number of which had definable ties to terror groups and cells.[255] A recent RAND report concluded: "For terrorist groups that cannot or will not abandon terrorism, policing is likely to be the most effective strategy to destroy terrorist groups. The logic is straightforward: Police generally have better training and intelligence to penetrate and disrupt terrorist organizations. They are the primary arm of the government focused on internal security matters."[256]

A debate continues within the academic world as to whether terrorism constitutes organized crime.[257] What is certainly not in debate in those

---

[253] Larry McShane, "Italian Mobsters in Widespread Decline," USA Today, 10/25/2007. Available at http://www.usatoday.com/news/nation/2007-10-25-2782988282_x.html, and Reputed Mobsters Rounded Up in U.S. Italy, CNN.com, 02/07/2008, available at http://www.cnn.com/2008/CRIME/02/07/gambino.arrests.ap/index.html.
James B. Jacobs, Coleen Freil, Robert Raddick, Gotham Unbound: How New York City Was Liberated From the Grip of Organized Crime (New York: NYU Press, 2001); James B. Jacobs, Christopher Panarella, and Jay Worthington, Busting the Mob (New York, NY: NYU Press, 1996).

[254] Michael Bayer, "Operation Global Pursuit: In Pursuit of the World's Most Dangerous Fugitives and Terrorists," The Police Chief magazine 72, no. 8 (August 2008), 35-37. See also, Rewards for Justice, available at http://www.rewardsforjustice.net/index.cfm?page=success_stories&language=english.

[255] A case study documenting this success appears in Chapter 5 of the present work.

[256] Jones and Libicki, "How Terrorist Groups End: Lessons for Countering al Qa'ida," 27.

[257] Conversation with organized crime scholar Professor Phil Williams of the University of Pittsburgh, in Pittsburgh, PA, 22 March 2007.

A Who's Who Lineup of Global Terrorists and the Rewards for Justice Program.
Source: State Department, with permission.

circles is that terrorism is, in fact, a *crime*. It may be helpful from a prosecution standpoint that terrorism be considered *organized* (which it usually is) and a *crime* (which it certainly is) to make it definable as *organized crime* (regardless of whether the ultimate gain is financial or ideological). But it is the criminal aspect of terrorism that is crucial to the questions presented by this book. Transnational crime expert Louise Shelly argues that terrorism and transnational crime have converged to the point where terrorism has actually become "organized crime." Others hold the line by merely affirming the criminal aspect of terrorism, and terrorism's reliance on criminal enterprise and activity for funding and acquiring the tools of their trade. According to David Kaplan of *U.S. News*, "Both crime syndicates and terrorist groups thrive in the same subterranean world of black markets and laundered money, relying on shifting networks and secret cells to accomplish their objectives. Both groups have similar needs: weapons, false documentation and safe houses."[258] And to once again quote Sanderson and Nitikin: "Terrorist activity stretches across a bewildering variety of cultures, locations, languages, criminal linkages, support networks, and financing mechanisms."[259] A June 2005 report supported by a DOJ grant pooled together the work of some of the most well-respected scholars of transnational crime, international organized crime, and terrorism. The report addresses the convergence of organized crime and terrorism:

> There are striking similarities between terrorists and individuals engaged in organized crime. Both traffic in drugs and human beings. Both extort, intimidate and bribe. Both do business in the legitimate economy, too. Both use subterfuge to conceal their real purpose. Granted their motives appear different: organized crime focusing on making money and terrorism aiming to undermine political authority. But the perpetrators have similar profiles, and are often the same individuals.[260]

The report endorses the idea that police attention be directed at the most basic levels—at the local levels where terrorism originates and attacks and operations are planned:

> At a practical level, security planners are increasingly aware of the ways in which terrorists and organized crime cooperate, such as terrorists' involvement in money laundering and narcotics trafficking. But they fail to analyze that interaction in order to detect terrorist planning.[261]

A continuation of that logic would indicate that *international* law enforcement should be interacting at the levels where these types of activities take place—at the local police levels. This logic is supported by the following remarks:

---

[258] David Kaplan, "Paying For Terror," U.S. News and World Report, 5 December 2005, Available at: http://www.usnews.com/usnews/articles/051205/5terrror.htm. The present author would add money/funding to this list.

[259] Thomas Sanderson and Mary Beth Nikitin, "International Cooperation," in Five Years After 9/11: An Assessment of America's War on Terror, Julianne Smith and Thomas Sanderson, eds. (Washington, DC: The CSIS Press, 2006), 33.

[260] Louise Shelly, John Picarelli, et. al., Methods and Motives: Exploring Links between Transnational Organized Crime & International Terrorism (Washington, DC: National Institute of Justice, Office of Justice Programs, U.S. Department of Justice, 23 June 2007), 10.

[261] Shelly, et. al., Methods and Motives, 10.

In developing countries, criminals and terrorists tend to spawn more collaborative relationships that are closer knit, whereas in the developed world, organized crime is more likely to co-exist with terrorism through arms length business transactions. Terrorists in developed countries may, however, use crime to support their activities.

Terrorism investigators at U.S. federal, state, and local agencies are naturally inclined to focus on evidence of possible attacks in the United States, or the activities of groups operating overseas that are known to be hostile to the U.S. Yet the evidence given above suggests that a study of the structure and nature of this cooperation overseas is no less relevant. Indeed, it may be more fruitful than avenues of investigation focused too narrowly on the United States.[262]

The fact that law enforcement exists specifically to combat crime and has evolved to combat international crime makes it an ideal vehicle to combat transnational terrorism, specifically if it is a crime. Scholar Tamara Makarenko argues that "in many respects, the rise of transnational organized crime in the 1990s, and the changing nature of terrorism, have produced two traditionally separate phenomena that have begun to reveal many operational and organizational similarities. Security as a result, should now be viewed as a cauldron of traditional and emerging threats that interact with one another, and at times converge. It is in this context that the crime-terror continuum exists."[263] Other scholars maintain that the difference between crime and terrorism is so vague that there is no longer a point in making a distinction—and that law enforcement would be well served to acknowledge this point. Ludo Block of the Vrjie University in the Netherlands writes:

> The conclusion that the line between political and criminal violence is often blurred, is therefore nothing new. In that perspective, it is helpful to realise that the line between terrorism and organized crime is just a legal construct. It would be naïve to expect terrorists and criminals to stay within conceptual boundaries that were constructed independently of their reality.[264]

---

[262] Shelly, et. al., Methods and Motives, 12.

[263] Tamara Makarenko, "The Crime-Terror Continuum: Tracing the Interplay between Transnational Organised Crime and Terrorism," in Global Crime 6, no. 1 (February 2004), 130.

[264] Ludo Block, "Terrorism-OC Links: A Contemporary Issue?" ECPR Standing Group on Organised Crime Newsletter, vol. 5, no. 2 (May 2006), 14.

Rob McKusker of the Australian Institute of Criminology adds that "the key issue for law enforcement agencies is that the traditional separative method of policing organized crime and terrorism, respectively, is no longer applicable."[265]

These ideas further the concept of the basic "dragnet" strategy of law enforcement—that a "holistic" (whole Earth) approach to international law enforcement that provides avenues to combat all types of international crime will bear fruit in the identification of terror cells and operations in progress or at planning stages because terrorism is identifiable as a crime and often uses or requires criminal activities to support its operations. Shelly and Picarelli conclude that "the fight against terrorism is being undermined by a critical lack of awareness against terrorists' links with organized crime. Crime analysis must be central to understanding the patterns of terrorist behavior and cannot be viewed as a peripheral issue. Furthermore, resources taken away from the transnational crime arena in the post 9/11 era are giving criminals a greater chance to operate and even provide services to terrorists."[266]

It has been asserted that in the immediate aftermath of 9/11 a decision was made at the highest levels of the U.S. government that the threat of international terrorism was too much for our law enforcement assets to contend with. Therefore, the administration granted primacy to the military (and intelligence) communities in U.S. counterterrorism efforts.[267] A May 2007 GAO report affirmed that law enforcement agencies still lacked directives to engage their international resources toward counterterrorism. A June 2008 DOJ organized crime strategy paper implored U.S. law enforcement agencies to pool their resources to combat organized crime, yet no such call to action had ever been made to (non-FBI) U.S. law enforcement agencies to do the same toward counterterrorism. An inconvenient truth is that what should be an obvious, common sense, strategic approach to counterterrorism effort did not come to pass.

A Foregone Conclusion

This chapter argues that over-classification is commonplace and for agencies in the Intelligence Community over-classification is a reflexive, patterned behavior. Experts agree that the classification system can be abused and manipulated to advance bureaucratic interests and minimize perceived

---

[265] Rob McKusker, "Organised Crime and Terrorism: Convergence or Separation?" ECPR Standing Group on Organised Crime Newsletter 5, no. 2 (May 2006), 3.

[266] Shelly and Picarelli, Methods and Motives, 54.

[267] Philip B. Heymann, Terrorism, Freedom and Security: Winning without War (Cambridge, MA, The MIT Press, 2003), 10. Also, interview by author with Lt Gen (Ret) Brent Scowcroft in Washington, DC, 10 July 2007.

rivals. Classification under the current U.S. system is not particularly secure and, in fact, can be counter-productive in protecting sources and methods. Law enforcement employs operational and tactical security to protect information and the identities of informants who are at extreme risk, while at the same time allowing for information to be shared effectively and legally with trustworthy foreign counterparts. Scholars maintain that police entities, being more autonomous from the political centers of government than counterpart national intelligence services, are less likely to be compromised or manipulated by political forces.

Although not completely immune to the complicating and sometimes corrupting influences of politicization, law enforcement professionals generally steer away from such factors. On the other hand, intelligence agencies and the military, as powerful instruments of political power, are the court of first resort for (aggressive) political bodies (such as presidential administrations) and are ideally placed to garner positions of primacy in times of national crisis. Because intelligence agencies, and to a lesser extent the military, are mercenary, competitive, and insular, they are predisposed to wield any and all tools (classification procedures included) at their disposal to weaken the (perceived) competition. What we see as the phenomenon of over-classification is, in fact, a manifestation of these assertions of primacy and consequently a loss of the potential value of fully engaging the collaborative capabilities of international law enforcement through *all* of our law enforcement assets. "Can-do"-oriented instruments of political power, such as the (presidential) military/intelligence apparatus, have advantages in gaining positions of primacy. While some applications of these forceful instruments of political power are entirely appropriate in the fight against terrorism, this is not always the case. These "exceptions" will be the subject of the next chapter.

CHAPTER 4
Comparing Apples, Oranges, and Lemons on the Blue Planet

Military, intelligence, law enforcement, and diplomatic resources can be used to counter terrorism. Each discipline or instrument has its strengths, its advantages, its weaknesses, and its failings; and each applies its own measures of success and failure. Shortcomings of one instrument are often compensated for and complemented by the particular strengths of others, very much as the holistic concepts of *yin* and *yang* interact with each other. This principle justifies having in place the distinct instruments of national power and social control, and explains why it is strategically important that all instruments of national power be fully engaged in countering the multifaceted problem of terrorism.

As we have seen, a serious contest over turf and jurisdiction occurs between U.S. intelligence and law enforcement agencies in the international realm.[268] Fundamentally, this is a disagreement over sources. The author is not recommending that U.S. law enforcement agencies seek out their own "informants" overseas. This would be tantamount to espionage—if done without coordination with host-country authorities or accomplished in a manner inconsistent with national laws and sovereignty. However, it should be the duty and responsibility of U.S. federal law enforcement agents (country attaches) assigned outside the U.S. to liaise with host-country police counterparts to acquire terrorism-related, or terrorist-support, information. This can be accomplished by collaborating with the host-country police force, thereby gaining access to information provided by their informants or even direct access to the informants themselves.

Advantages of Applying Intelligence Practices and Resources toward Counterterrorism

The resources of the Intelligence Community can reach far beyond the scope of "legal" entities such as law enforcement and diplomacy. This is the strength of the Intelligence Community as an instrument of counterter-

---

[268] Mark Riebling's Wedge: The Secret War between the FBI and CIA presents a detailed accounting of U.S. misadventures in this regard.

rorism. Beyond its own collection and analysis capabilities,[269] one of the most potent tools the Intelligence Community has at its disposal is a wealth of liaison, coordination, cooperation, and joint operations activities with foreign intelligence services.[270]

A great advantage of intelligence services is the ability to operate outside of the confines of laws, international protocols, and diplomacy. As former CIA analyst Michael Scheuer writes, "CIA information … is best acquired clandestinely—by physical or electronic theft, or by persuading a foreigner to commit treason—and it is most useful when the originating country or group does not know it has been collected."[271] Military and civilian Intelligence Community successes since 9/11 underscore the usefulness of other intelligence services—notably in the success of Predator drones claiming kills of top al-Qaeda leaders in Pakistan,[272] and the near elimination of al-Qaeda in Iraq (AQI).

Bringing a Knife to a Shotgun Battle: Disadvantages of U.S. Intelligence Practices against the Networked World of Terrorism

Despite the foregoing acknowledgment that some inherent advantages exist for intelligence agencies as they engage in counterterrorism activities, the special aptitudes and capabilities of law enforcement personnel and their organizations also merit attention. Outside experts and government practitioners alike note the difficulty that intelligence services find in gaining access to terrorist cells, specifically those aligned with al-Qaeda. A *Washington Post* article symptomatic of this problem reads: "A decade after al-Qaeda issued a global declaration of war against America, U.S. spy agencies have had little luck recruiting well-placed informants and are finding the upper reaches of the network tougher to penetrate than the Kremlin during the Cold War."[273] Two former CIA employees explain why. Goodman maintains that the CIA rarely is able to recruit major foreign assets: "It is very difficult to

---

[269] Jeffrey T. Richelson, The U.S. Intelligence Community, 5th ed. (Boulder, CO: Westview Press, 2008).

[270] Pillar, Terrorism and U.S. Foreign Policy, 118. Also see Richelson, The U.S. Intelligence Community, 341-360. See also Michael V. Hayden, Statement for the Record, Senate Select Committee on Intelligence, 11 January 2007. Available at https://www.cia.gov/news-information/speeches-testimony/2007/statement_011107.htm.

[271] Anonymous (Michael Scheuer), Imperial Hubris, 187.

[272] David Ignatius, "A Quiet Deal with Pakistan," Washington Post, 4 November 2008, A17. See also Karen DeYoung and Joby Warrick, "Pakistan and U.S. Have Tacit Deal on Airstrikes," Washington Post, 16 November 2008, A01.

[273] Craig Whitlock, "After a Decade at War With West, Al-Qaeda Still Impervious to Spies," Washington Post, 20 March 2008, A01.

collect against the so-called "hard targets" with CIA operatives; the collection [results] by such assets are a very small part of the intelligence pie and are the most unreliable."[274] Turner claims that the system of assessment, pitch, and recruitment by the United States does not work particularly well with terrorists and that bureaucratically entrenched agencies like the CIA continue to resist making appropriate adjustments to the realities of our newest adversaries.[275] Al-Qaeda expert Peter Bergen follows a similar line of reasoning by asserting that the U.S.'s "traditional tools of intelligence gathering, which would have once been deployed against a rival like the Soviet Union, are not terribly effective against al-Qaeda."[276] In the face of these problems, a RAND study declares that "it is more important and more cost effective for the United States to create local capacity to develop and manage reliable HUMINT than it is for U.S. agencies to mind and manage agents directly.[277] The former National Coordinator for Security and Counterterrorism, Richard Clarke, also devotes several pages of his latest book to the intelligence agencies' limited ability to infiltrate terrorist elements and the inherent difficulties associated with individually selecting espionage targets in terror organizations.[278]

Law Enforcement vs. Intelligence, or Oranges and Lemons

Because of law enforcement's historical and professionally driven propensity for international cooperation, it offers an ideal vehicle for developing local capacity for overt, criminal intelligence or HUMINT, of which terrorism information is an inextricable part.[279] International law enforcement can overcome deficiencies of Cold War intelligence agencies' source acquisition practices, as well as some of the other natural limitations of intelligence. Because U.S. law enforcement has the ability to work closely with foreign police forces from headquarters to even the most local police units, avenues to fine-grained sources of information (informants, friends, family, neighbor-

---

274   Goodman, Failure of Intelligence, 341.

275   Turner, Why Secret Intelligence Fails, 94-95.

276   Peter L. Bergen, Holy War, Inc.: Inside the Secret World of Osama bin Laden (New York, NY: The Free Press, 2001), 228.

277   Gombert and Gordon, War by Other Means, 231.

278   Clarke, Your Government Failed You, 106-119.

279   Perhaps better terminology would be "CRIMINT," or "INFORMINT," to avoid confusion with the secret/covert employment of spies by the Intelligence Community.

hood sources, knowledge of criminal activity in areas of responsibility, active criminal cases) are often already established.[280]

The cultural affinity that police have for one another sets the stage for coordination between foreign police agencies and U.S. federal law enforcement organizations. In counterterrorism, the most valuable coordination occurs at the lowest levels, corresponding to the out-of-the-way places where terrorism breeds. Police in any country have a broad selection or range of available sources of information because criminal activity is ubiquitous, and also because police remain a recognized (if sometimes corrupt) component of society. Furthermore, police offer coverage that is both numerically and geographically better than that of the intelligence services, known in many societies as the secret police. Police also tend to network and talk to one another as they compare notes on trends and cases.[281]

Astute U.S. law enforcement officers assigned overseas who are trained to know what questions to ask of local police, and who understand what crimes are known to support terrorism (document fraud, credit card fraud, weapons dealing, drug trafficking, and thefts of explosives, among others), can become potent conduits for overt terrorism intelligence information.[282] In Muslim societies, "Even if they are not enamored with the state itself, Muslims who are concerned about family security, as most surely are, may accept and even cooperate with well-trained, well-led, well-behaved, and even-handed police.[283] Generally speaking, overseas U.S. law enforcement elements are welcomed as they coordinate criminal intelligence information with local police because it is professionally expedient for both sides. A foreign (U.S.) intelligence service ostensibly seeking similar information from

---

[280] In my 20+ years of experience, foreign police counterparts sometimes allow access to their informants. This observation extends to my federal colleagues in the international law enforcement arena, and is especially true for DEA, according to an interview with DEA-France Country Attaché, Robert "Sam" Houston, 18 September 2008, Paris, France.

[281] Unless they are cooperating on criminal cases, police agencies will speak only in generalities about particular cases. However, if circumstances warrant, more detailed data are shared.

[282] Unfortunately, we know from GAO reporting that (non-FBI) U.S. law enforcement elements assigned overseas are at present not well-trained in many of these areas. See GAO, *Law Enforcement Agencies Lack Directives*, May 2007.

[283] Gombert and Gordon, *War by Other Means*, 81.

host-nation sources may be less welcome.[284] It has been the experience of the author that coordination with Muslim foreign police officers is no different from coordinating with other categories of foreign police.

As noted earlier in the present work, former Assistant U.S. Attorney and now University of Illinois law professor Jacqueline Ross sees that law enforcement's ability to deal with locals extends far beyond that of purely intelligence organizations if one compares their ability to penetrate terrorist-related networks.[285] *Policing* involves the use of intelligence units to collect information on terrorist groups, penetrate cells, and arrest key members. The fact that law enforcement is *integral* to the everyday comings and goings of societies, especially the mundane aspects of daily life, makes penetration of local criminal or terrorism networks easier. They are participants, rather than only observers—which affords them advantages in gathering information and even infiltration: They know the local characters, the common schemes and scams and patterns of both community and criminal behavior. Furthermore, a law enforcement approach brings a public safety voice to legislative discussions of antiterrorism laws, often leading to criminalization of the activities that are necessary for terrorist groups to function, such as raising money or recruiting openly.[286]

Intelligence Agency Liaison as an Asset Multiplier

As is the case with law enforcement, host-nation intelligence agencies are of course far more adept at obtaining threat information within their own societies than are foreigners.[287] One of the noteworthy developments in the so-called war on terrorism is that the U.S. Intelligence Community has made effective use of liaison relationships with foreign intelligence services. Even inveterate CIA critic Melvin Goodman acknowledges the value of foreign intelligence services in this amorphous conflict.[288] In his overview of U.S. intelligence services, Jeffrey Richelson devotes an entire chapter to the sub-

---

[284] In Imperial Hubris, 186-187, former CIA analyst Michael Scheuer declares that "intelligence vital to national defense will not be given to us in a liaison relationship with foreign intelligence or police services. That information must be stolen or acquired from a traitor by the CIA." Author's note: This might be so if terrorism intelligence is targeting the host-nation. Third country terrorism information developed locally would likely be shared freely—as is common practice when State Department Regional Security Officers visit their host-nation police contacts. As a Regional Security Officer, I have often been given information on terrorist activities targeting the host-nation by counterterrorism police contacts. Furthermore, outside of the United States, terrorism information is rarely considered to be national defense or internal security information.

[285] Jacqueline Ross, e-mail interview, March 2008.

[286] Jones and Libicki, How Terrorism Ends, 11.

[287] Gombert and Gordon, War by Other Means, 81.

[288] Goodman, Failure of Intelligence, 341.

ject. The chapter begins with the observation that "Despite the huge investment in technical and human intelligence activities, the United States relies on liaison arrangements and cooperative agreements with foreign intelligence and security services for a significant portion of its intelligence."[289] Richelson in particular notes that the French are especially cooperative, and that former President Jacques Chirac ordered French intelligence services to place no limits on the terrorism information it would share with the United States. Richelson also identifies Jordan as a particularly important partner with the CIA.[290] Finally, former CIA Director Michael Hayden acknowledged the importance of foreign liaison in his early 2007 statement to Congress.[291]

Intelligence Agency Liaison and Asset Depreciation

Although the United States has enjoyed some success with international intelligence agency cooperation, all is not well in this domain. The requirements placed on national intelligence organizations dictate that, in the international arena, friends and allies are inconstant, and duplicity and subterfuge become virtues. The highly experienced (and now deceased) William Odom observed that cooperation does not come naturally in clandestine operations.[292] The use of "covers" and "covert operations" makes intelligence agencies inherently and necessarily dishonest. One may even suggest that it is the job of intelligence officers to be deceitful—lying is what they "do"— their "tradecraft."[293] One does not need a top secret security clearance to see duplicitous activities of intelligence services playing out around the world—a subscription to a good newspaper suffices.[294]

With their more direct ties to political power, intelligence services are not only susceptible to political influences, but they are also, as Ransom says, *object and instrument* of the political power structure of central governments.[295] The fact that they can operate outside the confines of the law,

---

[289] Richelson, The U.S. Intellgence Community, 341.

[290] Richelson, The U.S. Intellgence Community, 355.

[291] Michael V. Hayden, Statement for the Record, Senate Select Committee on Intelligence, 11 January 2007.

[292] Odom, Fixing Intelligence, 148.

[293] Former National Security Coordinator for Security and Counterterrorism Richard A. Clarke details this conundrum in his latest book, Your Government Failed You, 110-113.

[294] See, for example, Mark Mazzetti, "When Spies Don't Play Well With Their Allies," New York Times, 20 July 2008; "A Wild Frontier," The Economist, 20 September 2008, 55; Ron Moureu and Mark Hosenball, "Pakistan's Dangerous Double Game," Newsweek, 22 September 2008; Joby Warrick, "U.S. Officials: Pakistani Agents Helped Plan Kabul Bombing," Washington Post, 1 August 2008, A1; Rohan Gunaratna, Inside Al Qaeda, 52; and Steve Coll, The Taliban-Pakistan Alliance, at http://www.pbs.org/wgbh/pages/frontline/taliban/interviews/coll.html, posted 3 October 2006.

[295] Ransom, "The Politicization of Intelligence," 23.

and are steeped in the art of deception, means that intelligence services can manipulate counterpart intelligence services through misdirection and subterfuge.[296] For example, although the United States considers many of the present governments in the Middle East to be its allies in the war against terrorism, many of them *do* benefit when terrorist acts drive up the price of oil. In a very real sense, terrorism *does* benefit *them*.[297] It would be naïve to think that, even though they are ostensibly our friends, they will act in our best interests over their own. This becomes a problem around the world because this region tends to spawn and train international terrorists.

The U.S. Intelligence Community's prosecution of the war on terror has also purportedly caused friction with some erstwhile allies: "The unremitting hostility U.S. intelligence agencies face from broad sections of the European political spectrum affects both operational capabilities and the larger U.S. diplomatic effort, and the reputation of U.S. intelligence in many parts of the world where we must operate and find cooperation is worse than it has ever been."[298] The conventional wisdom that U.S. intelligence agencies continue to have problems sharing information and have the reputation of not playing well with others compounds the problem.[299] These are conditions not conducive to collecting detailed information on future, very real threats.

Fortunately, other counterterrorism instruments, especially law enforcement, are much more straightforward and less subject to intrigue. As a function of their autonomy, normally at some distance from the political centers of government, they will display at least the perception of trustworthiness in counterterrorism coordination. A savvy U.S. strategic national counterterrorism policy would take into consideration that, with intelligence services of allied countries likely having hidden agendas, law enforcement elements can provide other "safe" avenues for combating terrorism and gathering information. On the other hand, to the degree that counterpart intelligence services have the well-being of their own country's effective governance in mind, the opportunity exists for international intelligence service cooperation to identify and mitigate the effects of any law enforcement corruption or

---

[296] Bill Gertz alleges that a number of U.S. "friends" and allies are secretly working to advance their own interests. See Bill Gertz, Treachery: How America's Friends and Foes Are Secretly Arming Our Enemies (New York: Crown Forum, 2004).

[297] Although there may also be incentives to cooperate, it is all a matter of degree and, in this regard, it is the cooperating (helping) intelligence service that calls the shots. Ultimately, however, a United States with a destroyed infrastructure benefits no one but extremists—hence, a diminished United States, paying high oil prices, might be an ideal circumstance.

[298] Lewis and DeRosa, "Intelligence," in Five Years After, 30. See also Goodman, Failure of Intelligence, 195.

[299] Gombert and Gordon, War by Other Means, 75.

other potential drawbacks that might accompany international law enforcement cooperation.

Just as the United States experiences conflicts between intelligence and law enforcement, the author has observed that the syndrome occurs in most other countries as well. For example, the need for intelligence to protect its sources and methods can disrupt the normal judicial process for law enforcement and, conversely, the judicial process can impede intelligence operations, at least in the domestic arena. This can be a good thing because thorough integration of law enforcement and intelligence is a defining characteristic of a police state. In the author's experience, except for North Korea, Iran, and Myanmar, and former republics of the Soviet Union, some level of dissension between law enforcement and intelligence has been the rule. Because of their association with the political centers of government, intelligence services generally have a higher profile than police services. However, police personnel outnumber those in intelligence services and occasionally even in national militaries.

Endemic discord between police and intelligence functions extends to U.S. operations outside the U.S. For example, foreign law enforcement services will limit their cooperation if they are aware of intelligence involvement in a particular case. This causes intrinsic problems for the FBI, which, although traditionally a law enforcement agency, now advertises its intelligence focus as well.[300] The author has learned from foreign police representatives that they find it philosophically and even legally difficult to work with the FBI because of its intelligence role.[301] In this role, the FBI at times unavoidably interacts with host country intelligence services because of formalized agreements between them. Presently, the FBI maintains its network of law enforcement attaches in only 70 countries, whereas other U.S. federal law enforcement agencies, most often DEA and the Bureau of Diplomatic Security, are established in almost all of the world's 250 or so political entities.

Because law enforcement attaches do not cover the globe in a manner that focuses on terrorism, many criminal hot spots are covered by relatively few agencies—the broadest representation is by the State Department's Bureau of Diplomatic Security, operating in every U.S. Embassy and nearly every U.S. Consulate in the world in locations such as Mauritania, which is

---

[300] Federal Bureau Of Investigation, statement on Integrating Intelligence and Investigations, available at http://www.fbi.gov/hq/nsb/nsb_integrating.html.

[301] A well-known authority on criminal intelligence analysis, interviewed for this book, laments the "intelligencification" of the FBI (source requested confidentiality).

experiencing issues with radical Islamization;[302] Sierra Leone, which has a history of harboring Islamist militants;[303] South Africa, where a nascent Islamist radical movement is forming;[304] India and Bangladesh, where radical movements are fairly well established;[305] Azerbaijan, dealing with religious extremism;[306] Tajikistan, experiencing problems with Islamic radicalism;[307] as well as in those places experiencing Islamist insurgencies such as Thailand, Indonesia, and the Philippines; and in places where the threat of terrorist activities is high, as in the South Malaccan Straits;[308] the Caribbean region where al-Qaeda is making inroads;[309] and Guyana, with a growing problem with Islamic radicalism—Guyana, being the point of origin for the "Fort Dix Six" plot in the U.S.[310] In the period after the Dar es Salaam and Nairobi bombings in Africa, there were threats made against U.S. embassies the world over.[311] In South America, Bolivia appears to be a center of Islamist extremist activity.[312] Islamist terrorist activity or presence occurs in nearly every country on earth, and the only way to track or detect it may be through the auspices of international law enforcement. U.S. federal law enforcement is well represented the world over but, in contrast with the FBI, it has not yet been engaged in a routine, constructive way to combat international terrorism.

---

[302] Anour Boukars, "The Challenge of Radical Islam in Mauritania," in Unmasking Terror: A Global Review of Terrorist Activities, Vol. III (Washington, DC: The Jamestown Foundation, 2007), 243-247.

[303] Donald Temple, "Sierra Leone: An Obscure Battlefield in the War on Terrorism," in Unmasking Terror, 248-252.

[304] Anneli Botha, "PAGAD: A Case Study of Radical Islam in South Africa," in Unmasking Terror, 253-258.

[305] Aminesh Roul, "Student Islamic Movement of India: A Case Study," in Unmasking Terror, 320-323, and Andrew Holt, "Islamists Pose a Growing Threat to Stability in Bangladesh," in Unmasking Terror, 324-326. Also see David Montero, "Are Terror Groups Finding a Haven in Bangladesh?" Christian Science Monitor, 17 June 2009. Available at http://www.csmonitor.com/2009/0617/p99s01-duts.html.

[306] Anar Valiev, "Al-Qaeda in Azerbaijan: Myths and Realities," in Unmasking Terror, 343-347.

[307] Igor Rotar, Resurgence of Islamic Radicalism in Tajikistan's Ferghana Valley, in Unmasking Terror, 348-352.

[308] Zachary Abuza, "A Breakdown of Southern Thailand's Insurgent Groups," in Unmasking Terror, 354-360; Peter Chalk, "The Indigenous Nature of the Thai Insurgency," in Unmasking Terror, 361-365; Abu Dujana, "Jemaah Islamiyah's New Al-Qaeda Linked Leader," 397-399, and Noor Huda Ismail, "The Role of Kinship in Indonesia's Jemaah Islamiyah," in Unmasking Terror, 403-409; Zachary Abuza," MILF's Stalled Peace Process and its Impact on Terrorism in Southeast Asia, in Unmasking Terror, 410-143; and Catherine Zara Raymond, "The Threat of Maritime Terrorism in the Malacca Straits," in Unmasking Terror, 370-374.

[309] Chris Zambelis, "Al-Qaeda's Inroads into the Caribbean," Terrorism Monitor 3, no. 20 (21 October 2005), 475-480. Available at http://www.jamestown.org.

[310] Chris Zambelis, "The Threat of Religious Radicalism in Guyana," Terrorism Monitor 4, no. 15 (4 August 2006), 487-491. Available at http://www.jamestown.org.

[311] Recollections of the author.

[312] Nora Zimmett, "Bolivia Becoming a Hotbed of Islamic Extremists, Report Concludes," Fox News, 16 June 2009. Available at http://www.foxnews.com/story/0,2933.526753,00.html.

WANTED FOR MURDER

UP TO $5 MILLION REWARD
STRICT CONFIDENTIALITY

Fahid Mohammed Ally Msalam, Sheikh Ahmed Salim Swedan, and Haroun Fazul are believed to be responsible for the bombing of the U.S. embassy in Dar es Salaam, Tanzania on August 7, 1998. This attack indiscriminately killed 11 innocent civilians and wounded more than 80 others. These terrorists are believed to be part of an international criminal conspiracy headed by Usama bin Laden and Ayman al Zawahiri.

The U.S. Government is offering a reward for information leading to the arrest or conviction, in any country, of Msalam, Swedan or Fazul. Persons providing such information may be eligible for a reward of up to $5 million, protection of their identities, and relocation of themselves and their families. Persons wishing to report information on these men, or other terrorists, should contact the authorities or the Regional Security Officer at the nearest U.S. embassy or consulate. Information may also be provided by contacting:

REWARDS FOR JUSTICE
Washington, D.C. 20522-0303 USA
RFJ@state.gov
www.rewardsforjustice.net
1-800-877-3927

Suspects in the 1998 Bombing of the U.S. Embassy in Dar es Salaam, Tanzania.
Source: State Department, with permission.

Law enforcement international coordinating elements, generally designated as "country attaches," have the benefit of a common culture and mission and are also generally adept at assessing criminal activity which may be used to support terrorist activities. U.S. intelligence services are already multi-tasked and undermanned and are insufficiently prepared to deal with the nuances of criminal activity with local police elements.

The urgency and confusion that characterized the aftermath of 9/11 provided a climate for those in advisory roles to advance the cause and agendas of their own agencies. After 9/11, following the initial success of military and intelligence efforts in Afghanistan, those instruments achieved not merely *primacy* in foreign counterterrorism efforts but, with the addition of the FBI as an Intelligence Community agency, something approaching *exclusivity*.[313] It seems unlikely, given the importance both the *9/11 Report* and national security authorities attribute to the *foreign-domestic divide*,[314] that the exclusion of non-FBI U.S. federal law enforcement agencies from contributing to counterterrorism efforts overseas is an accident or an oversight. What is troubling from a law enforcement perspective is that our strategy appears to be a product, not of clever strategic planning, thoughtful insight, or careful consideration, but of organizational maneuvering.

Military vs. Law Enforcement—Apples and Oranges in Counterterrorism

"One of the great tragedies of the United States federal government is that it doesn't understand all the resources it has at its disposal."[315]

Authoritative studies show that military action is rarely successful against terrorists[316] and that police work, as a counterterrorism instrument, has had greater success, especially given today's greater focus on law enforcement intelligence to reinforce the application of this instrument.[317] Law enforcement organizations are better suited to counterterrorism because of their mission; that is, international law enforcement has specifically evolved

---

[313] Some recent initiatives by the U.S. military admittedly and forthrightly employ key advantages previously only afforded to international law enforcement. So too, military units engage the resources of law enforcement to track and investigate evidence obtained from the "pocket litter" of deceased insurgents as well as other material seized from the battlefield. Although these are positive steps in support of U.S. interests, these examples pale in comparison with the benefits that could be brought by open, overt coordination of worldwide law enforcement networks.

[314] As noted in Chapter One, the foreign-domestic divide has its roots in the National Security Act of 1947, in which the CIA was effectively prohibited from conducting domestic spy operations. The FBI held responsibility for domestic counterintelligence operations, which contributed to an already bitter rivalry between the FBI and the CIA. Later legislation, and legal directives from the Department of Justice, further contributed to the institutionalization of "the wall" between domestic and foreign operations and information gathering. According to national security expert James Steinberg, the "disconnect between foreign and domestic intelligence collection and analysis has been at the heart of post-9/11 analysis of 'what went wrong.'" See Steinberg, "Erasing the Seams"; Reibling's Wedge; and the 9/11 Report, 78-80, 353, 357, 400, 409.

[315] Interview with Frank Urbancic, then Deputy Coordinator for Counterterrorism (S/CT), U.S. Department of State, Washington, DC, 13 June 2007.

[316] Gombert and Gordon, War by Other Means, summary, xlviii.

[317] Jones and Libicki, How Terrorist Groups End, 27-29, and Osborne, Out of Bounds, 106, 139, 153, 155.

to avert and combat external transnational threats, especially the networked aspects of transnational criminality, through securing borders and tracking criminals and their networks—which strive to remain hidden. International law enforcement is especially attuned to dealing with networks—smuggling networks, organized crime networks, drug trafficking networks, human smuggling networks, and now terrorism networks—even if it were not regarded as a "crime." Law enforcement is designed to implement the "dragnet" strategy; that is, cast a "net" (typically at a border control point—or, more locally, over a busy street) which will intercept international or local movements of people and allow a system to sort out those who are up to no good or who are of interest to the police. Militaries do tend to be more effective against insurgent organizations that are large and well-armed, such as those in Afghanistan and Iraq. Police actions are more effective when the mission involves counterterrorism because "unlike the military, the police usually have a permanent presence in cities, towns, and villages; a better understanding of local groups and the threat environment in these areas; and better intelligence."[318]

In contrast with law enforcement groups, neither the intelligence nor the military communities are set up to take advantage of the globalized, networked structure and activities of al-Qaeda and other terrorist/insurgent groups.[319] Their insularity, elevation of secrecy, and outmoded means of protecting information, along with an overall obsession for security, places the Intelligence Community and particularly the CIA at a disadvantage when dealing with networks. Like a closed-circuit TV system, intelligence services are restricted to their own isolated means of communicating and sharing information. Obscured from their view are the myriad other networks that operate, comingle, and interact freely without interference or obstruction.

According to Slaughter and Raustiala, ideal "government networks are characterized by extensive sharing of information, coordinating enforcement efforts, and joint policy making activities. These activities plausibly exhibit network effects: the more regulatory agencies that participate in coordinating and reciprocating enforcement efforts for example, the better off are all the other agencies."[320] Sharing and coordinating are not traits typically shared by military and intelligence networks. Furthermore, again according to Slaughter, government networks, "can spring up overnight, address a host of issues and form 'mega-networks' that link existing networks."[321] Perhaps

---

318 Jones and Libicki, How Terrorist Groups End, 60.

319 Gombert and Gordon, War by Other Means, 42.

320 Slaughter, "Sovereignty and Power," 297, and Raustiala, "The Architecture of International Cooperation," 64.

321 Slaughter, "Governing the Global Economy through Government Networks," 179.

one of the best examples of these mega-networks is precisely what this work is presenting: the formal and informal networks of worldwide law enforcement with its common mission, common adversaries, common culture, and the vast number of individuals linked together. An example of the further linkages that can be formed might be Diplomatic Security's (DS) stewardship of the Overseas Security Advisory Council (OSAC)—a federal advisory panel through which DS, as a security and law enforcement agency, has formed an alliance with the American international corporate community. In this capacity, OSAC becomes a vehicle to communicate security concerns and advice to U.S. corporations with an overseas presence.[322] By establishing OSAC, Diplomatic Security created a network of American businesses with common international security concerns and linked them together with U.S. embassies through its Regional Security Offices. The significance of OSAC is that is has connected law enforcement networks with corporate networks and vice versa, although, thus far, OSAC has been used almost exclusively for communicating security information from the U.S. federal government to the U.S. international corporate community. Representing access to perhaps millions of foreign employees, the international business community has been opened up by OSAC as yet another possible unexploited source of transnational crime and terrorism information. Not only has OSAC opened up networks of communication with federal law enforcement, but also with the rest of the U.S. federal government system—to include U.S. intelligence, by proxy through the RSO in U.S. embassies and the U.S. Department of State. The OSAC model has proven so successful that it has spawned a domestic U.S. version run by the FBI: the Awareness of National Security Issues and Response (ANSIR) program,[323] and has generated a British government counterpart, Security Information for Business Overseas (SISBO).[324] OSAC has also attracted the interest of countries like France and Australia, which have expressed an interest in forming their own version. OSAC has a close alliance with the International Security Managers Association (ISMA), which connects the U.S. government and law enforcement with the remainder of the international corporate community—and all of their employees. Likewise, the FBI has a close relationship and partnership with the American Society for Industrial Security (ASIS), which connects it and the federal government with the U.S.-based American corporate community. In this manner networks can beget mega-networks precisely as Slaughter predicts. It is difficult to imagine

---

[322] OSAC is structured by a central U.S. council and is divided into individual country councils coordinated through embassy Regional Security Offices. The author is presently the program manager for the OSAC-France Country Council.

[323] FBI, http://www.fbi.gov/congress01/ansir040301.html.

[324] See http://www.sisbo.org.uk. SISBO is now officially partnered with OSAC.

85

that the military/intelligence apparatus of the United States would have access to such open networks.

Gombert and Gordon effectively tie together the phenomenon of terrorism and insurgency by characterizing Islamist-based terrorism as a tool and tactic embedded in a merger of "global-religious extremism with local-political conflicts" manifest in a worldwide, global Islamist insurgency. In their estimation, "terrorism cannot be defeated unless the insurgencies in which it is embedded are successfully countered."[325] They repeatedly note the efficacy of police as a tool against insurgency (and therefore terrorism) and decry over-reliance on the military as a counterterrorism instrument.[326]

Conversely, the military community is specialized to the point that its network interactions are with other military and military intelligence networks, with very limited corporate interaction. Militaries are accustomed to fighting militaries, not networks. Reed expects that future wars will move away from the principles of traditional warfare into the realm of "state and non-state entities organized as *networks* (author's emphasis) along social, economic, criminal, terrorist, gang, special interest, and ethnic lines, to name but a few.[327] It will take on the characteristics of war without national boundaries, where the distinctions between public and private, government and people, military and civilian—i.e., combatants and non-combatants—will again become blurred as they were prior to the Peace of Westphalia in 1648.

The "cultish" nature of law enforcement bears many parallels to international terrorism networks, first because international law enforcement has evolved alongside international terrorism and transnational crime, and also because both networks are based on the foundation of a common mission, a common profession, common enemies, common problems, common dangers, common causes, and ultimately upon trust.[328] Although there is a commonality among members of rival and allied intelligence services, and it too has famously been portrayed as a cult,[329] the relationships of intelligence personnel are not, should not, and cannot be based on trust because of the nature of the business; it rests instead on *mistrust*. Military personnel also can share cultural and organizational bonds based on common goals and common dangers (in the trenches), but such bonds are reserved for comrades in arms (esprit d'corps). Although military relationships can transcend some borders, really close international partnerships are reserved for countries

---

[325] Gombert and Gordon, War by Other Means, 3-7.

[326] Gombert and Gordon, War by Other Means, 186, 296, 289, and Jones and Libicki, How Terrorist Groups End, Preface, v.

[327] Reed, Why Strategy Matters, 15.

[328] Slaughter, "Sovereignty and Power in a Networked World Order," 288, 290.

[329] Victor Marchetti, CIA and the Cult of Intelligence (New York: Dell, 1989).

whose civilian leaders see political value in alliances. Law enforcement alliances cannot only transcend borders and other barriers, but they can also delve deeply into "human terrain" that other counterterrorism instruments would find hostile. James Sheptycki states that "the broad scope of human security is both theoretically comprehensible and practically realistic when encompassed by democratic policing means, whereas the broadening security agenda is simply incoherent and unrealistic to a mind-set beholden exclusively to military ones." [330]

Drawbacks of Law Enforcement in International Counterterrorism Efforts

Although this study advocates an expanded overseas law enforcement role in the fight against terrorism, this is by no means a panacea and has a number of potential drawbacks. Those drawbacks can be offset by other counterterrorism instruments in a fully-rounded, well-considered counterterrorism strategic policy. Nonetheless, because of imperfect strategy, drawbacks are persistent and include:

- The perception (with its kernel of truth) that law enforcement resources are fixated on legal process and investigative pretexts to collect information, or to initiate counterterrorism efforts and actions. This has especially been true for the FBI, whose by-the-book reputation is legendary. It is a less accurate description of hybrid security agencies like the Bureau of Diplomatic Security, and the civilianized military law enforcement services (Air Force Office of Special Investigations (AFOSI), the Naval Criminal Investigative Service (NCIS), and the Army's Criminal Investigation Division (CID), all of which use their security mandates to coordinate and liaise with foreign police services and do not require an investigative pretext to compare notes with foreign police counterparts).

- National police forces can be closely tied to the political centers of individual countries and may be difficult to work with (even if national police forces in general trend away from political centers of government). This is especially true if the police and the domestic intelligence services are one and the same.

- National police forces can be corrupt and/or incompetent. This can make them unreliable and difficult to work with. However, even though corrupt, some police agencies can be very effective and the corruption aspect can give them inroads and contacts that may not exist with legitimate police agencies. Working with corrupt police agencies requires extreme caution.

---

330 Sheptycki, "Policing, Intelligence Theory and the New Human Security Paradigm," 167.

- Law enforcement forces would not be effective on a military-style battlefield. This is especially so in the border areas of Afghanistan and Pakistan, and places where armed conflict is the norm—such as the Caucusus, Chechnya, Ossetia, Dagestan, etc. Gombert and Gordon nevertheless suggest that law enforcement can be effective even where insurgents are active.[331]

- Law enforcement operations would not be effective in situations where covert (not just clandestine) operations are necessary.[332] Law enforcement cannot overthrow governments, cannot illegally monitor communications, and cannot conduct black operations; this is the domain of intelligence services.

- Law enforcement operations are limited by international law and the rule of law.

- Police can be hated as much if not more than "secret police" by the local populace. This is as true in Los Angeles as in Moscow. However, police in many locations of counterterrorism interest to the United States do not just work among the poor and disaffected; they *are* part of the poor and disaffected—and not all of them are corrupt.

- Worldwide police networks, unencumbered by sovereignty constraints, can be dangerous to individual freedoms because they lack mechanisms for accountability—there is no way to regulate what police elements do or what they share. However, Slaughter asserts that such concerns are "overblown" and government networks have specific properties that are highly conducive to self-regulation.[333] The point can be made that if unleashing government law enforcement networks is so potentially powerful that it causes worry and consternation among the intelligentsia, then it could also be a formidable counter-balance to the advantages held by the global networks of extremist insurgency and terrorism.

Illustrative examples of these points will be presented in the following chapter.

---

[331] Gombert and Gordon, War by Other Means, 186, 289.

[332] According to the Interagency OPSEC Support Staff, a covert operation is an operation that is so planned and executed as to conceal the identity of, or permit plausible denial by, the sponsor. A covert operation differs from a clandestine operation in that emphasis is placed on concealment of the identity of the sponsor, rather than on concealment of the operation. A clandestine operation is synonymous with law enforcement's undercover operation. See: http://www.ioss.gov/docs/definitions.html.

[333] Anne-Marie Slaughter, "Governing the Global Economy through Government Networks," 180; Anne- Marie Slaughter, "Sovereignty and Power in a Networked World Order," Stanford Journal of International Law 40, (2004), 311.

Unintended Benefits

The strategic engagement of law enforcement networks, especially informal law enforcement networks, can deliver benefits beyond what may be immediately discernible. Slaughter maintains that because of advances in communications and technology, and the forces of globalization in general, the traditional dynamics of diplomacy and international relationships are migrating to the middle, operational (sub-state) levels of governments, of which the author and his international law enforcement colleagues are a part. From these increasingly efficient and potent relationships, new power structures are emerging.[334]

From the perspective of the author, it is easy to see how these power structures can come about. As Branch Chief of Diplomatic Security's International Criminal Investigative Liaison program (CIL), I was in charge of a section that would take (and usually accommodate) requests for international investigative assistance from other federal law enforcement agencies and U.S. police departments. Being in a position to assist others in the business seemed to make me a somewhat valuable commodity in law enforcement circles. After a time it became apparent that I was being specifically sought out by not only my peers but by those far senior to me in rank. In other words, I was *valuable*, and therefore *powerful*—far beyond my pay grade—by virtue of the international relationships at my disposal.[335] My superiors also recognized this disproportionate allotment/odd displacement of "juice." When the Deputy Director of DSS tried and failed to secure a liaison position with the newly formed Homeland Security Department's (DHS) Bureau of Immigration and Customs Enforcement (ICE), he asked me to see what I could do, knowing that I had ties at relatively high levels throughout U.S. federal law enforcement. With a phone call and a few personal visits to hammer out the details, the position was secured—to the mutual benefit of Diplomatic Security and ICE.

Slaughter argues that such sub-state interactions are redefining not just traditional notions of sovereignty but sovereignty itself. In the world of international criminal investigative liaison, this interaction manifests itself as "informal" law enforcement. Because CIL is not a "formal" pathway for conducting international criminal investigations, nearly every lead run, nearly every contact made, nearly every action taken would necessarily be interpreted as *informal*. The reader should not, however, confuse *informal* with

---

334 Slaughter, "Sovereignty and Power in a Networked World Order," 283-327.

335 I must confess that, having moved on from that branch chief position, I deeply miss being in the thick of the international liaison and investigative community.

illegal. As viewed by Deflem and den Boer, informal pathways are the conduit for the lion's share of international police, "cop-to-cop" business. Formal pathways are those conducted under the prescribed and negotiated treaties and procedures of the state; they are under the auspices of sovereignty. As Slaughter indicates, "Government networks bypass a great deal of cumbersome and formal, international negotiating procedures."[336] In other words, they bypass the conventions of sovereignty. This was, and is, CIL's stock in trade.

CIL has acquired a reputation within the international law enforcement community that allows it to accomplish in a few hours, or a few days—by working the informal police networks—what it would take Interpol or more traditional agencies weeks or even months to fulfill. There is no legal agreement more representative of the assertion of sovereignty than an extradition treaty, usually contained within a Mutual Legal Assistance Treaty (MLAT) between countries. CIL, in coordination with the U.S. Marshals Service, pioneered the use of a legal procedure which enables the return of American fugitives from overseas if extradition treaties prove unworkable or if there is none in place. While the details are operationally sensitive, U.S. fugitives hiding overseas can be subject to expulsion or deportation from other countries if properly coordinated. Because Diplomatic Security is present in nearly every country and has investigative resources and close ties with host-nation police services the world over (because of their security mandate to protect U.S. embassies and facilities overseas), DS's Regional Security Officers (who are fully authorized federal special agents for investigations and arrests) are perfectly oriented to engage their police contacts to locate, arrest, and deport American citizen fugitives. While this tactic does not work everywhere (particularly where MLAT treaties are followed to the letter—and particularly in Western Europe), it works in a large part of the world and has revolutionized the fugitive return procedure for the U.S. federal government. CIL is able to accomplish similar feats and "circumvent cumbersome international protocols" for almost any type of investigation. Instruments of governmental networks like CIL can serve to "pierce the shell of sovereignty," as Slaughter observes.[337] CIL has become so proficient and efficient that it has become the "discovery" of other results-oriented and progressive federal investigative agencies. Over time, partnerships and alliances have been formed with agencies like the U.S. Marshals, which partnered with DSS for its international fugitives program;[338] DHS-ICE, which successfully

---

[336] Slaughter, "Governing the Global Economy through Government Networks," 180. It should be noted that Slaughter is referring to government networks generally and is not singling out law enforcement. It is not solely law enforcement that is bypassing sovereignty.

[337] Slaughter, "Government Networks," 227-229.

[338] Secured by a Memorandum of Understanding, at the Marshals' request, DSS has a permanent Special Agent position in the International Investigations Office of the Marshals.

teamed up with DSS to bring international muscle to "Operation Predator;"[339] the U.S. Postal Inspector;[340] the Secret Service, to address the explosive increase in transnational financial fraud; and even the FBI, to assist with its nearly overwhelming overseas caseload.[341]

Some scholars of international policing have expressed concern about potential encroachment by police on national sovereignty and the imposition of Western ideas on the rest of the world through policing practices. Slaughter portrays this as a disadvantage of governmental networks, that they can be seen as an "effort to insulate the decisions of the powerful from the input of the weak," and in an international context that "many countries, both developed and developing, may see government networks as a device whereby the most powerful countries penetrate the defenses of national sovereignty to impose their policy templates on everyone else."[342] This is precisely the point Andreas and Nadelmann make in *Policing the Globe*. They assert that the "moral entrepreneurs" of the Western powers have contrived externalized policing as a means of imposing their moral and emotional convictions on the rest of the world—particularly in the realm of drug and narcotics policies and narcotics regimes.[343] According to Andreas and Nadelmann,

The underlying impetus of all international criminal law enforcement activities is the initial fact of criminalization by the state. New laws turn once-legal cross-border activities into criminal activities, resulting in a sudden and sometimes dramatic overall increase in transnational crime. And new criminalizations often inspire and justify the creation of new international law enforcement capabilities, which in turn can invite additional laws and other initiatives. Thus criminalization has been a powerful motor for state expansion—and based on current trends, we can expect it to be an even more important source of growth in the years ahead. The policing face of the state is becoming more and more prominently displayed, with its gaze increasingly extending beyond national borders.[344]

---

[339] "Operation Predator is a comprehensive initiative designed to protect young people from child pornographers, alien smugglers, human traffickers, and other predatory criminals (under the provisions of the 2003 Protect Act)." Sources: http://www.ice.gov/pi/predator/news-releases.htm and http://www.ice.gov.pi/news/factsheets/operationpredator.htm

[340] The Postal Inspectors fund a position in the CIL office at DSS headquarters in Rosslyn, Virginia.

[341] DS's second biggest client in the fugitive return business, after the Marshals, is the FBI.

[342] Slaughter, "Governing the Global Economy through Government Networks," 180.

[343] Andreas and Nadelmann, Policing the Globe, 223-226.

[344] Andreas and Nadelmann, Policing the Globe, 225.

Slaughter maintains that these concerns are overblown. However, the present author considers that the forces of globalization (rather than the imperatives of "moral entrepreneurs") are tectonic in nature and that the tendencies for international governmental cooperation, of which international policing remains but a small part, are too monumental to be contained. Slaughter maintains that governments increasingly must "intervene" in one another's affairs because "fundamental threats to their own security, whether from refugees, terrorists, the potential destabilization of an entire region, or a miasma of disease and crime may well have their origins in conditions once thought to be within a state's exclusive jurisdiction." Slaughter sums up her position by declaring that "States can only govern effectively by actively cooperating with other states and by collectively reserving the power to intervene in other states' affairs."[345]

Dragnetworking: Strategic Advantages of Federal Law Enforcement Networks

Based on his experience, the author agrees with Slaughter that governmental and, in particular, international law enforcement networks, can be fast, flexible, and very economical. As Chief of Diplomatic Security's Criminal Investigative Liaison Branch in Washington from 2003 to 2006, it amazed me that I could authorize and coordinate criminal investigative operations on the other side of the world which could be happening in real time. Cell phones and e-mail made communication easy and effective. Investigative requests from U.S. domestic police departments and federal law enforcement agencies, long hampered by formal procedures and other sorts of international red tape, could be carried out in a matter of hours or a few days. As strong and weak nations alike find and acknowledge "non-military" ways to wage war, the strategic canvas will be redone. Further, this development will not be limited to nation-states; it will be employed by networks, including super-empowered individuals and groups.[346] Under these conditions, the United States would be well-served to fully leverage the best counterterrorism instruments, starting with U.S.-led, international law enforcement networks.

Because military and intelligence networks are hindered by their insularity and their propensity to control information, they are unlikely to enjoy the potential benefits of government networks.[347] On the other hand, international law enforcement—a "trust-based," efficiency-driven govern-

---

[345] Slaughter, "Sovereignty and Power in a Networked World Order," 285.

[346] Reed, Why Strategy Matters, 17.

[347] Gombert and Gordon, War by Other Means, 79.

mental network—can do just that. Just as police are driven by the quest for professionalism, so can diverse national governments enjoy the functional benefits of an enhanced capability to confront common, fluid international threats.[348] It is not military and intelligence networks but law enforcement networks that are cited as paragons of international networking.[349] Slaughter marvels at the flexibility and the efficiency with which government networks can now accomplish their goals through informal means.[350] Her sentiments are echoed by another observer:

> Law enforcement agencies view information and intelligence as a precious commodity. Trust and reciprocity are thus essential for success in cross-border investigations. Studies in the field of international police cooperation show that informality is a prerequisite for trust: without the consolidation of an informal network, police cooperation will not succeed.[351]

As Andreas and Nadelmann say, "The sentiment that a cop is a cop, no matter whose badge is worn, and a criminal a criminal regardless of citizenship or where the crime was committed, signals the emergence of a transnational value system that can override both political differences and formal procedures. It provides the oil and glue of international law enforcement."[352]

Among policing scholars, a metaphorical transnational state appears to exist where policing fits into "interstitial spaces" between governed territories. These spaces are "grey areas" where national laws and procedures do not necessarily exist and where normal international protocols and other matters of sovereignty do not necessarily apply.[353] The author believes it is possible, even likely, that this is where the sub-state transactions that Slaughter refers to are taking place, and it is here that mid- to high-level governmental managers are finding functionality and success.[354] If these processes are indeed redefining sovereignty, then this is an area for national leaders and strategists (and international law enforcement) to exploit these "economies of circumstance" toward combating terrorism. In other words, the new circumstances that are

---

348 Deflem, "Bureaucratization and Social Control," 760; Slaughter, "Government Networks," 224.

349 Gombert and Gordon, War by Other Means, summary, iv.

350 Slaughter, "Governing the Global Economy through Government Networks," 192.

351 Monica den Boer, "Law Enforcement Cooperation and Transnational Organized Crime in Europe," in Transnational Organized Crime & International Security, Mats Berdal and Monica Serrano, eds. (Boulder, CO: Lynne Rienner, 2002), 111.

352 Andreas and Nadelmann, Policing the Globe, 232.

353 Author's interpretation of Sheptycki's construct. James Sheptycki, "Transnational Policing and the Makings of a Postmodern State," British Journal of Criminology, vol. 35, no. 4 (Autumn 1995), 629-630.

354 Slaughter, "Sovereignty and Power in a Networked World Order," 288.

now appearing as a consequence or by-product of globalization—the fact that inexpensive international phone service and even cheaper e-mails enable direct international communications for the functional levels of governments to coordinate mutual interests with one another and form these "interstitial spaces"—present an opportunity for motivated decision-makers to counter the network advantages long since held by criminal and terrorist elements. These network and cyberspace advantages which have been the hallmark and masterstroke of transnational Islamist terrorist groups like al-Qaeda have also been the subject of much consternation and criticism in terms of our own failure to capitalize on systems that we pioneered. By overcoming outmoded assertions of turf and conferring the substate and interstitial advantages of government networks to the particular talents of U.S.-led international law enforcement, we can finally confront the threat of transnational terrorism in the arena of its strength.

Andreas and Nadelmann refer to the emergence of terrorism as an international global prohibition regime—that is, terrorism is on its way to being nearly universally recognized as a "common" crime—in the same way as the United States has managed to identify international narcotics trafficking. Through "regularization" of international policing "police have sought to cut through red tape, to avoid diplomatic imbroglios, and to obtain more and better assistance from foreign colleagues. Their cumulative progress has been substantial. No longer do police plead in vain, as they did just a few decades ago, to be allowed to communicate directly across borders instead of via foreign ministries and consulates."[355]

The author believes that the adoption of a global regime against terrorism is as attributable to the steady progress toward a globalized civilization as to the imposition of a global hegemony by the "great Satan." After all, the United States was attacked on 9/11 much to the horror of the "civilized" world. It was not the hegemony of any nation that drove the civilized world to abhor genocide after the holocaust—it was, and is, the force of civilized society—the unstoppable force of civilization; the force that drives us to do better, to be better, to improve the collective lot of the human inhabitants of this planet. Policing is a civilizational construct—true, it can be, and is, abused and corrupted, but it remains an irreplaceable force to advance the greater good.

Andreas and Nadelmann are correct in observing that "what distinguishes the contemporary era is the relatively greater transnational nature and reach of some terrorist networks and the growing fear of catastrophic criminality involving the use of weapons of mass destruction by non-state actors.

---

[355] Andreas and Nadelmann, Policing the Globe, 232.

As the technologies to create such weapons become more diffused, responsible governments have little choice but to coordinate their control and enforcement efforts ever more effectively. As with other types of transnational criminality, deviant or "outlaw states" and government agents represent a major part of the law enforcement challenge.[356] For better or worse, it is a fact that the United States holds a leadership role in international policing—just as in the arena of international diplomacy and international policy. But this role of the United States can be a force for *civilizational hegemony* in the fight against terrorism.

Parallel Universes

In the same way that globalization has created opportunity for terrorism networks to grow toward a worldwide insurgency, globalization has and is providing opportunities for long-established, well-organized sectors of national governments to evolve into ultra-efficient and eminently responsive entities in their own right—with potential benefits that have yet to be imagined and realized. No matter what the concerns are, the application of the power of international law enforcement has to be preferable to torture and other dubious practices to which the forces of intelligence and the military have resorted. In this sense, the negative aspects of efficient international policing are the lesser evil.

Thus, the networks of law enforcement are ideally suited to combat the networks of worldwide terrorism and insurgency, and are the best available instrument to fight networks with networks. Unfortunately, the closed networks of intelligence and military forces are not conducive to taking advantage of rapidly evolving and mutating networks of international terrorism. Up to the present, the talents of informal law enforcement networkers in the U.S. have lain mostly dormant. Acknowledging and acting on the advantages conferred by U.S. international law enforcement can bring an entirely new and much-needed dimension to U.S. counterterrorism strategy, a strategy that is in danger of stagnating. Informal law enforcement networks can bring the added benefit of providing neutral pathways for cooperation from U.S. allies and non-allies alike that may find our military and intelligence practices and even our policies objectionable. In the end, by following this path, we will have what amounts to a shrewd and genuine counterterrorism strategy.

---

356 Andreas and Nadelmann, Policing the Globe, 233.

CHAPTER 5
Tales of the Blue Planet

The Practitioner's World—Beyond Academic Discourse

My time as Branch Chief of the Department of State's International Criminal Investigations Section (CIL) prepared me to appreciate the relationship between the concepts set forth in the previous chapters and the realities of everyday diplomatic service. In this chapter I will highlight, through examples drawn from personal experience, best practices that resonate with the concerns and exhortations of academic discourse.

The cases and scenarios to follow are representative of those that took place during my time as Chief of CIL and of cases I became aware of as Chief of the U.S. Embassy's Regional Security Office in Paris, as well as from interaction with colleagues. In all likelihood, they are not dissimilar to cases encountered at other posts. These cases are selected for demonstrating the particular arguments and academic points raised in this book, but they are not otherwise extraordinary in terms of what Diplomatic Security and other federal law enforcement agencies encounter on a daily and weekly basis. During my time in CIL we processed, as a yearly average, over 3,000 requests for overseas assistance originating from U.S. domestic police departments and other federal law enforcement agencies. Additionally, we coordinated two or three overseas fugitive locates, arrests, and returns (to the U.S.) per week. The reader should not presume that because Diplomatic Security is a relatively small and not so well-known agency that we do not receive "the cream" of the criminal investigative international work. The reader will see that DSS agents very often deal with "the worst of the worst" of the world's criminals and terrorists, and it is because of DS's broad representation the world over that we are sought out by our fellow agencies. One might suggest that smaller agencies such as DS, in part because of their relative obscurity, possess an ability to adapt and adjust quickly to confront new problems.

In previous chapters we have identified the following benefits of international law enforcement networks and, more specifically, the informal networks.

1. Law enforcement entities are flexible, accustomed to ever-changing, mutating aspects of crime, including international crime.

2. Informal law enforcement networks can adapt, adjust, and act quickly to address issues that require immediate action.

3. The culture of law enforcement can, and does, transcend borders, politics, religion, nationalism, and other impediments to cooperation.

4. A global capability to "connect the dots" is possible if the devices of law enforcement are strategically enabled.

5. Law enforcement agencies, particularly in their interactions with each other, trend toward autonomy and away from the effects of political influence.

6. Law enforcement is ubiquitous, worldwide, and agencies are legion.

7. Law enforcement's sphere of influence and ability to obtain information extends from the most basic levels of civilization (the villages and back alleys) to the highest levels of industrialized society.

8. Law enforcement can take advantage of emerging, sub-state international governmental networks, which are presently revolutionizing relationships and rendering obsolete the traditional pathways of sovereignty.

9. Informal networks of law enforcement can be spectacularly powerful and successful.

10. U.S. law enforcement is in a unique position to lead and coordinate international law enforcement counterterrorism efforts.

11. International law enforcement networks can empower agencies in weaker states—especially through exercising "soft power."

12. The crime of terrorism, insofar as it is internationally recognized, provides a powerful incentive for law enforcement to cooperate internationally.

13. Law enforcement agencies commonly work with one another, including with foreign counterparts, and share information in a manner consistent with privacy considerations, national laws, and operational security.

14. Law enforcement, particularly U.S. law enforcement, is accustomed to working with sensitive information and is successful at protecting what the Intelligence Community refers to as "sources and methods," without the need to resort to unreliable and overly restrictive classification practices.

15. Law enforcement networks have a great deal of experience with, and significant successes against, international networks, which makes them ideally suited to combating the network aspects of al-Qaeda-style transnational terrorism.

16. The technological aspects of law enforcement and border control are already a big factor in worldwide counterterrorism efforts, which can be exponentially more effective if other aspects of globalized law enforcement can be further engaged and coordinated.

Law Enforcement Entities Are Flexible, Accustomed to the Ever-Changing, Mutating Aspects of Crime, Including International Criminal Networks and Enterprises, and Are Not Subject to Cold War-Era Procedures and Tactics

A telling example of the benefits conferred by law enforcement networks over those of the Intelligence Community and other counterterrorism instruments was the recent apprehension of Victor Bout, the so-called "Merchant of Death"—a weapons dealer renowned for his lack of discretion in choice of clients. Bout's exploits were fictionalized in the 2005 movie *The Lord of War*, starring Nicolas Cage. He specialized in providing arms for various Third World conflicts and was widely rumored to have supplied clients as varied as the Taliban and warlord-turned-dictator Samuel Taylor in Liberia. On one occasion, Bout was alleged to have air-dropped 10,000 AK-47s into Peru that passed to Colombia's narcoterrorist insurgent group the Revolutionary Armed Forces of Colombia, better known as the FARC.[357] Bout was captured in a sting operation in Thailand engineered by the U.S. Drug Enforcement Administration. For this operation, DEA employed informants and well-established connections with foreign law enforcement to lure Bout into a bogus arms sales agreement with what he thought were representatives of the FARC.[358] Thai police arrested Victor Bout on 6 March 2008. He had been a thorn in the side of the United States for quite some time, and had embarrassed the U.S. by allegedly working as a subcontractor for such well-known firms as Kellogg, Brown, and Root (KBR) and Federal Express, ferrying supplies into Iraq for the Iraqi war effort.[359] According to Bruce Falconer, writing in the non-profit investigative journal *Mother Jones*, the DEA sting operation was to take place in Romania, but Bout became concerned about being arrested there and wanted to change the location.[360] DEA, taking advantage of the flexibility of its international networks, successfully switched the venue to Thailand, a country where it has especially powerful ties.[361] According to a senior DEA official, "We were asked to go after Bout. We DEA accomplished in six months what the Intelligence Community could not do in over eight years."[362]

Informal Law Enforcement Networks Can Adapt, Adjust, and Act Quickly to Address Issues that Require Immediate Action

In July 2004, as I arrived in the office, one of the CIL special agents grabbed my arm to relate a story she had heard on the local news segment of the *Today* show, reporting that a local Maryland man, Thomas Koucky, an admitted molester of over 300 underaged boys, had fled the country after being released on $3,000 bond from a Virginia courthouse. I told the agent to start making some phone calls to see where the fugitive investigation stood. Upon consultation with the U.S. Marshals and the Northern Virginia Fugi-

---

[357] Bruce Falconer, "Victor Bout's Last Deal: How an Elite DEA Unit Brought Down the World's Most Notorious Arms Dealer," Mother Jones, 18 March 2008. Available at: http://www.motherjones.com/news/feature/2008/03/viktor-bout.html.

[358] Falconer, "Victor Bout's Last Deal."

[359] Falconer, "Victor Bout's Last Deal."

[360] Falconer, "Victor Bout's Last Deal."

[361] Interview with a senior DEA Official, 25 August 2008.

[362] Interview with a senior DEA Agent, 25 August 2008. Although the DEA is a formal member of the Intelligence Community, it is solely a "taskable" relationship. DEA cannot take unilateral action in intelligence operations—it must be tasked by the Intelligence Community. From an interview with DEA Director of International Operations, Kevin Whaley, 7 June 2007.

tive Task Force, it had been determined that Koucky had fled to Guatemala with a friend who was a Guatemalan native. Investigation determined that the friend, a waiter in a Virginia restaurant, was from a particular neighborhood outside of Guatemala City. The fugitive task force asked CIL if we could help. We replied that we would try and requested a photo of the subject. Within a few hours, a local Foreign Service National Investigator (FSNI) for the Regional Security Office in Guatemala City spotted the fugitive in a poor neighborhood on the outskirts of the city—the same neighborhood that the investigation had determined Koucky's friend to be from. By early evening, the Regional Security Officer had developed an operations plan with the Guatemalan National Police, and the RSO requested authorization to proceed with the operation—which I gave. At 6:00 a.m. the next morning, police surrounded the building in which Mr. Koucky was staying, and by 7:00 a.m. he was in custody. At the airport in Guatemala City, Guatemalan authorities gave custody of Koucky to the RSO, who escorted him back to the United States. By 6:00 p.m. that day, Diplomatic Security special agents, U.S. Marshals, and Arlington County Police officers marched Koucky into the Arlington County Jail. Less than 36 hours after learning of the case, DSS agents had located the fugitive, coordinated the arrest, and returned a notorious criminal to face justice. Koucky had been in Guatemala less than ten days, and by Guatemalan law this fact allowed the immigration authorities to deport him as an undesirable person without further procedure. Koucky received a sentence of 10 years in a Virginia prison. International police resources in this case involved the Arlington County, Virginia, Police Department, the U.S. Marshals, Immigration and Customs Enforcement of the Department of Homeland Security (DHS-ICE), the Diplomatic Security Service, the Guatemalan National Police, and Guatemalan immigration authorities. The Koucky case illustrates how spectacularly fast and flexible governmental/law enforcement networks can be. Furthermore, the speed of the case precluded lengthy court proceedings on extradition—in support of Slaughter's claim that intergovernmental networks can also be "economical."

The Culture of Law Enforcement Can Transcend Borders, Politics, Religion, Nationalism and Other Impediments to Cooperation

Cuba

Few relationships in the annals of international affairs have been as acrimonious as that between the United States and Cuba in recent decades. The United States has not had diplomatic relations with Cuba since January

1961.[363] This acrimony extends well beyond severed diplomatic ties into the economic realm, involving a trade embargo and travel restrictions. Cuba's disdain for the United States is apparent in speeches made at the United Nations and in aggressive, hostile intelligence activity against the United States both domestically and abroad.[364]

On 13 September 2002, U.S. Postal Inspectors and Miami Police arrested Angel Rafael Mariscal for producing child pornography. Mariscal was accused of producing, starring in, and distributing pornographic videos featuring him and others engaging in sex acts with children. The Postal Inspector's investigation determined that more than 100 minors had been sexually abused on camera, the youngest a 7-year-old girl. Mariscal had amassed over 500 hours of pornographic footage involving sex acts with children. After painstaking investigation, officials ascertained that the videos had been filmed in Cuba. Although the prospects for conducting any sort of investigation in Cuba seemed remote, postal inspectors and police contacted Diplomatic Security to see if any assistance was possible. Diplomatic Security worked within the State Department to obtain special dispensation to work with the Cuban police to locate the child victims in this case. With approval in hand, DSS Regional Security Officer Pat Durkin, assigned to the U.S. Interest Section in Havana,[365] contacted the local Cuban police hierarchy regarding the case. After expressing initial astonishment at the request, the horrified Cuban authorities agreed to help, and soon began a monumental effort to locate the victims.[366] The DSS Regional Security Officer, who as a U.S. Federal Special Agent had investigative and arrest authorities, was granted permission to interview the abused children, whereupon he provided written reports and photographs of the locations where the abuses took place—and authorized the documentation as evidence. In addition, investigators learned that Mariscal was HIV-positive and had infected at least seven of his child victims in Cuba.

---

[363] See Department of State Fact Sheet, "U.S.-Cuba Relations," at www.state.gov/p/wha/rls/fs/2001/2558.htm.

[364] Stephane Lefebvre, "Cuban Intelligence Activities Directed at the United States, 1959-2007," International Journal of Intelligence and CounterIntelligence 22, no. 3 (Fall 2009), 452-469.

[365] The United States has a rudimentary presence in Cuba under the diplomatic umbrella of the Swiss Embassy in Havana, an office known as the U.S. Interest Section. Although without an official diplomatic role, that entity does work with U.S. citizens who have familial and legal issues in Cuba.

[366] According to then-Regional Security Officer Pat Durkin, Cuban authorities cooperated out of self-interest. Kevin Whitelaw, "DS Gets Its Man," Foreign Service Journal (September 2005), 40, also available at http://www.afsa.org/fsj/sept05/whitelaw.pdf. See also Bayer, "Operation Global Pursuit," 34-35.

At his trial, the government presented evidence that Mariscal had traveled to Cuba and Ecuador frequently over a 7-year period to produce child pornography. He distributed his CD-ROMs and VHS tapes throughout the United States by mail and Federal Express. In November 2004, Mariscal received a sentence of 100 years in prison for his crimes.[367]

Many themes of this book are represented by this case—the idea of a trust-based common culture that transcends politics and ideology; the concept of a "common enemy"—in this case pedophiles; and the idea that even in a highly regulated society like Cuba's, the police can have a significant measure of autonomy, even if cooperation is self-serving—as it usually is.[368] Subsequent instances of collaboration between U.S. law enforcement, through the Bureau of Diplomatic Security, and Cuba have occurred, all with the consent and supervision of the U.S. Department of State.

On 30 September 2006, David Ray Franklin stole a Cessna 172 Hawk XP airplane at the Marathon, Florida, Airport and flew to Cuba with his minor son—of whom he did not have legal custody—in a case of parental abduction.[369] On 27 October, through the intervention and cooperation of DSS, the Government of Cuba returned David Franklin to U.S. custody. On 10 November, the Cuban government also allowed Diplomatic Security special agents to enter Cuba to seize the plane as evidence and fly it back to Florida.[370]

In another recent case, Friday the 13th of June 2008 was a bad day for Leonard Auerbach—it was the day he was returned to the United States from Cuba, where he had fled to avoid prosecution on child pornography charges.[371] On 14 November 2008, Auerbach was sentenced to 15 years for producing child pornography. The DHS-ICE press release cites field and coordination work by the Bureau of Diplomatic Security as instrumental in the case.[372] Auerbach had been on DHS-ICE's list of top-ten most wanted fugitives.

In these cases, because they are often the only U.S. law enforcement representation in country, Diplomatic Security officers engage their close law enforcement contacts for assistance. Even in countries like Cuba and China,

---

[367] Whitelaw, "DS Gets Its Man," 2005, 40. See also Bayer, "Operation Global Pursuit," 34-35.

[368] Although it is likely that the Cuban police had high-level approval to cooperate—as did Diplomatic Security, the Cuban police did manage to convince the Cuban governmental hierarchy that cooperation was in their best interests.

[369] As the FBI has jurisdiction over all abduction cases, this case was coordinated with the Bureau.

[370] See "Diplomatic Security Special Agents Return Stolen Cessna From Cuba," at http://www.state.gov/m/ds/rls/75855.htm. Also see "Suspect in Parental Kidnapping Returned from Cuba," at http://www.state.gov/m/ds/rls/75281.htm.

[371] See http://www.ice.gov/pi/nr/0811/081114oakland.htm.

[372] See http://www.ice.gov/pi/news/newsreleases/articles/080616miami.htm.

Diplomatic Security RSOs will necessarily have police contacts to carry out their security directives—because it is almost always the national police who provide the first layer of defense for embassy security.[373] RSOs universally try to establish friendly relationships with national police elements, fundamentally because embassy security is a matter of life and death.

China

In a particularly heinous case, international fugitive and accused child rapist and pornographer Kenneth John Freeman was returned to the United States from China on 18 October 2007. Freeman, a former competitive bodybuilder, was charged with one count of producing child pornography, one count of transporting child pornography, three counts involving transporting a minor across state lines and producing child pornography, three counts of first degree rape of a child, and one count of bail jumping. Freeman had fled the United States in March 2006, and had been placed on the U.S. Marshals' 15 "Most Wanted Fugitives" list, as well as DHS-ICE's top-ten fugitives listing.[374] A break in the case came when the U.S. television show *America's Most Wanted* aired a segment in which Freeman's abused daughter told her story. Soon after, the National Center for Missing and Exploited Children (NCMEC) received telephone calls which linked the girl to Internet videos posted some years earlier. A team of investigators from the federal Marshals Office, ICE, the Benton County Sheriff's Office, and the Diplomatic Security Service tracked Freeman as he moved through China—where he allegedly had been traveling on business. Julie Meyers, then-Assistant Secretary for Homeland Security, Immigration, and Customs Enforcement said of the case, "The arrest of this accused child molester proves the global reach of our law enforcement partnership."[375]

Not only does the Freeman case demonstrate extraordinary cooperation between U.S. law enforcement elements and a country not traditionally known for law enforcement cooperation, it also demonstrates how networks can build upon themselves to form mega-networks, as Slaughter asserted: In this case a television network (FOX) and the networks associated with an

---

[373] In a related case, Diplomatic Security assisted the U.S. Marshals Service in effecting the return of a fugitive who had been hiding out in Cuba—for more than 40 years—after a conviction on fraud charges. See Alfonso Chardy, "Cuba Sends Fugitive to Face U.S. Justice After 4 Decades," Miami Herald, 26 April 2007. Available at http://newsgroups.derkeiler.com/pdf/Archive/Soc/soc.culture.cuba/2007-04/msg01127.pdf.

[374] U.S. Marshals Service, Former Lawman and Accused Child Rapist Returned to Washington State to Face Charges. Available at www.state.gov/m/ds/rls/93721.htm.

[375] National Center for Missing and Exploited Children (NCMEC), "NCMEC Applauds U.S. Marshals and ICE for Capture of Nation's Most Wanted Accused Child Pornographer." Available at http: // www.missingkids.com/missingkids/servlet/PageServlet?LanguageCountry=en_US&PageId=3155

NGO (non-governmental organization)—NCMEC—all contributed to the successful conclusion of an exceptionally disturbing fugitive case.

A Global Capability to "Connect the Dots"

In the movie *The Lord of War*, a character portrays the sadistic son of the ruthless president—armed with a gold-plated AK-47—and terrorizes both his enemies and the people of his country. This is the fictionalized representation of "Chuckie Taylor," the U.S.-born son of the brutal Liberian warlord-turned-dictator Charles Taylor. There was no need to embellish Chuckie's exploits for the cinema; his real-life series of atrocities is legendary. He was allegedly involved in killings, rapes, beatings, and torture. According to an *Associated Press* report, torture victims were held in water-filled holes in the ground, beaten and sexually abused, and forced to drink urine and eat cigarette butts:[376]

It was July 2002 and civil war had been rampaging through Liberia for 13 years, transforming one of Africa's oldest democracies into a ghoulish landscape. Drugged-out militias manned checkpoints decorated with human intestines and severed heads. Small children were forced into battle by the thousands. Women were raped and turned into sex slaves known as "bush wives." Enemies were disemboweled, cooked and cannibalized. All told, human rights groups estimate, more than 600,000 Liberians were murdered, raped, maimed or mutilated in the conflict.

In the midst of this reign of terror, Chuckie was among the most-feared men in the country. Only 25, he created and commanded the Anti-Terrorist Unit (ATU), the president's personal security force—a source of such pride that Chuckie had the group's emblem, a crest of a hissing cobra and a scorpion, tattooed on his chest. In the capital, he cut a terrifying figure, scattering crowds as he raced through traffic in a Land Cruiser with a license plate that read "demon." When he appeared in public, he was almost always fitted out in black or camouflage fatigues, a well-built figure strapped with a 9mm, a cigar in hand. His face—the dark eyes, the round cheeks, the neatly trimmed beard—was immediately familiar to Liberians who had endured the long civil war. Not only because of menacing reputation but because of the man he so closely resembled, his father, Charles Taylor, the president of Liberia, who had set the region ablaze with four devastating wars over the span of two decades.[377]

---

[376] Curt Anderson, "Activists Want Charles Taylor's Son Tried for War Crimes, Torture," Associated Press, 5 August 2006.

[377] Johnny Dwyer, "The All-American Warlord," The Observer, 23 November 2008, 32. Available at http://www.guardian.co.uk/world/2008/nov23/liberia-war-crimes-chucky-taylor.

On 29 March 2006, the Regional Security Officer in Port of Spain, Trinidad, received an urgent phone call from an agent with DHS-ICE requesting immediate assistance in determining the existence of a passport in the name of Charles McArthur Emmanuel. Emmanuel was known to have gone by another name—Charles "Chuckie" Taylor. Whenever RSOs receive requests from other agencies, the proper procedure is to vet the request through DS/CIL and then the Branch Chief (at that time, the author) determines whether to render assistance.[378] In this case, passport information is considered privileged, "privacy act" information. Caution must be exercised in releasing that information to another agency. Examination of the passport records indicated possible passport fraud; the passport application appeared to have been falsified to conceal the fact that Charles Taylor was his father.[379] To share the passport application with ICE, DSS opened a passport case on Chuckie, then passed the lead for further action on to ICE.[380] On 30 March 2008 Charles "Chuckie" Taylor was charged with passport fraud upon his entry into the United States from Trinidad. On 30 October 2008 he was found guilty of torture and related crimes. This brought the first conviction under the U.S. Torture Prevention Act of 1994.[381]

In law enforcement, investigative leads can open a window on provocative interrelationships. Chuckie had ties to Israeli arms trader Leonid Minin. Chuckie's father was one of the primary customers of Victor Bout. Charles Taylor has been accused of harboring members of al-Qaeda. Victor Bout allegedly supplied arms to the Taliban. He is also alleged to have smuggled drugs in empty planes returning after dropping off arms shipments, like Minin. This illustrates the many tendrils of international crime and criminal enterprises. It is in this manner that the resources of law enforcement can provide information about the larger picture of terrorist and other illicit networks. While it is the responsibility of intelligence agencies to track such information, any fixation on "secret" information as the only "valuable" data precludes a full and thorough accounting of the overall intelligence picture.[382]

---

[378] Sometimes requests are outlandish, illegal, or otherwise beyond the capacity of often over-tasked Regional Security Offices. As a headquarters element, CIL can recommend proper and legal measures to accomplish investigative goals.

[379] An Associated Press article stated, "Prosecutors say he lied on his passport application about the identity of his father, who was arrested the day before..." See Curt Anderson, "Activists Want Charles Taylor's Son Tried for War Crimes, Torture," Associated Press, 6 August 2006. Available at http://www.prosecutions.org/news/archives/002607.html.

[380] Source: Professional files and recollections of the author.

[381] DHS-ICE–Bayer e-mails dated 7 December 2006 and 30 October 2008. See also Amnesty International, "Chuckie Taylor Convicted of Torture," 31 October 2008. Available at http://www.amnestyusa.org/doctument.php?id=ENGNAU200810317933&lang=e.

[382] Interview with an intelligence agency supervisory analyst who requested confidentiality. Ironically, this source desired confidentiality because he feared professional retribution.

Law Enforcement Agencies Trend Toward Autonomy and Away from the Effects of Political Influence

The U.S. relationship with Pakistan is complicated—particularly between our respective intelligence services. In many other countries, as well as in the United States, intense rivalries exist between intelligence services and the national police. Such is the case in Pakistan.[383] During the heated search for Daniel Pearl in the days and weeks following his kidnapping, this rivalry may have played to the advantage of RSO Randall Bennett in Karachi. According to Pearl's journalist wife Mariane, Bennett led the Karachi-based U.S. investigation in the hunt for Pearl and his kidnappers.[384] By securing the cooperation of the Pakistani National Police through a longtime trusted contact, Tariq Jamal, the Deputy Chief of the Karachi police, Bennett was able to establish a trusting relationship with the man who would lead the investigation to locate Pearl and bring his kidnappers (and in the end, murderers) to justice. Although ultimately unsuccessful in rescuing Daniel Pearl before he was killed, the investigation exposed a sophisticated terror cell whose careful precautions were overcome, resulting in their arrest shortly after Pearl's body was found. Significantly, the Pakistani Intelligence Service (ISI) was allegedly complicit in protecting the kidnappers.[385] Daniel Pearl had written articles that likely irritated and embarrassed the ISI, giving it an incentive, at least, not to cooperate with the police search.[386]

The duplicity and political motives of the Pakistani Intelligence Service are a recurring theme in Mariane Pearl's book. Of the ISI's role in the investigation, she writes "Where is the ISI's national pride? Why has it shown such minimal interest in the kidnapping? The agency leaves its mark on every aspect of Pakistani politics; you would think that even for appearance's sake, it would want its presence known."[387] When she is speaking of the central suspect's ability to remain free, even though some Pakistani authorities knew where he was, she writes, "Someone has been protecting him. Somewhere between corrupt politics and false preachers, Omar found a shelter."[388] The ISI's adversarial role with respect to U.S. interests may be limited to certain

---

[383] E-mail correspondence with the Regional Security Officer in Pakistan, Steve Smith, 4 December 2008.

[384] Mariane Pearl, A Mighty Heart (New York: Scribner, 2003).

[385] Pearl, 182.

[386] Pearl, 149-150.

[387] Pearl, 141.

[388] Pearl, 160.

extremist elements within the ISI, but it is difficult to tell who is who, and our own intelligence agencies suffer from not knowing.[389]

On the other hand, Pearl speaks very favorably of the police, although recognizing some corruption. She writes that Bennett considered his police contacts in Karachi to be "trusted brothers."[390] Later in the book she notes, "I recall Randall's reference to Tariq Jamil as his brother, and the respect he showed Captain. It reassures me to see that all these men seem to consider him Bennett a real friend."[391] The one military intelligence officer who worked for the police on the Pearl case had his career destroyed and he ultimately became a police officer.[392] The lead police investigator she knew as "Captain" came out unscathed and was even honored for his role in the case—despite the powerful influence of the ISI. These developments offer good evidence of the political autonomy of police.

Even in such politically volatile environments as Pakistan, the police (and other intergovernmental networks) can assume positions of autonomy and even mild opposition to political forces. These dynamics occur continuously in our counterparts' countries, although Pakistan may seem a pronounced example. It appears wise to take advantage of the opportunities brought by the professional autonomy of police agencies.

The Forces of Law Enforcement are Ubiquitous, Worldwide, and Agencies Are Legion

In the province of law enforcement, little things can mean a lot. Police are accustomed to focusing on minute details—they know that they can lead to big breaks. Recall that Timothy McVeigh was originally arrested on a weapons possession charge after a traffic stop 90 minutes after the Oklahoma City Murrah Federal Building bombing.[393] Would-be millennium bomber Ahmed Ressam was arrested after a routine customs inquiry.[394] D.C. Beltway snipers John Allen Muhammad and Lee Boyd Malvo were arrested by Maryland State Troopers after a citizen noticed their car parked at a rest stop and called the

---

[389] Mark J. Roberts, Pakistan's Inter-Services Intelligence Directorate: A State within a State? Joint Force Quarterly 48 (2008), 104-110; see also Richard A. Clarke, "Plans of Attack," Washington Post, 7 December 2008, B01.

[390] Pearl, 35.

[391] Pearl, 98.

[392] Pearl, 226.

[393] Nolan Clay, "Lawman who caught Timothy McVeigh speaks of arrest," The Oklahoman, 29 August 2008. Available at http://newsok.com/article/3290630/.

[394] Lisa Meyers, Foiling Millennium Attack was Mostly Luck, MSNBC, 29 April 2004. Available at http://www.msnbc.msn.com/id/4864792.

emergency number 911.[395] Intelligence elements, often relatively few in number, need to "target" their efforts. Implicit in that goal is the presumption of a certain amount of foreknowledge—the need to know just what information they require and from whom they can obtain it. Little room exists for error, nor can the agent expect felicitous happenstance or chance. Law enforcement, on the other hand, has the ability to cast a wide net (dragnet) to identify persons of interest and important information before or after an event. As we have seen in the vignettes here, such information often turns out to be preventive; that is to say, it is "actionable intelligence." Both instruments can be effective, but each has different approaches and particular talents. A balanced and intelligent counterterrorism strategy would wholly incorporate the talents of both and benefit from the contributions of each.

Law Enforcement's Sphere of Influence and Ability to Obtain Information Extends from the Most Basic Levels of Civilization (the Villages and Back Alleys) to the Highest Levels of Industrialized Society

In the fall of 2007, DHS-ICE and the Regional Security Office in Togo collaborated on a sexual predator case that originated in Bangladesh—involving a retired AID (Agency for International Development) officer who had allegedly been sexually abusing young boys in that country. One of the harsh realities of the Third World is that in places like Bangladesh an opportunistic pedophile with a little cash can buy nearly anything, including the company of children. This former AID officer had a detailed knowledge of the country and was able to accommodate his proclivities. Pedophiles, however, are customarily reviled even in a poor country like Bangladesh. While the investigation was underway, the subject left the country and disappeared for a time. Almost a year later, the U.S. Embassy in Lomé, Togo, had some interaction with a former AID officer who had established a residence on a mountaintop above a village in a remote region of Togo. As time went on, some at the Embassy in Lomé expressed bewilderment as to why this person was living on a mountaintop in the middle of Togo. At an embassy social event, several persons were discussing the odd man who lived on the mountain and the Regional Security Officer happened to overhear the conversation. When the RSO asked the name of the man on the mountain, it sounded familiar. After some checking, and some very high-quality dot-connecting, the RSO determined that the man on the mountain was the same man as the one wanted in Bangladesh. Upon this discovery, the RSO immediately notified DHS-ICE, and the hunt

---

[395] CBS News, "Trucker: I'm no Hero," 25 October 2002. Available at http://www.cbsnews.com/stories/2002/10/25/earlyshow/main526939.shtml.

was on. Within a week, the Regional Security Office and ICE had formulated a plan. RSO would gather a force of local Gendarmerie and they would venture into the remote mountains, where the Gendarmerie would arrest the subject. ICE would simultaneously make accommodation for some special agents to fly to Togo to escort the subject back to the United States to face prosecution. The RSO and his deputy, the Assistant Regional Security Officer, assembled their force and went into the mountains.

Upon arriving at the village, the Gendarmerie asked a man walking along the street where they might find the white man who lived among the villagers. The man was hesitant to answer but, after some time and a payment of a few loaves of bread, he pointed to a road that led to a modern-style house that sat above the village. Perched on top of the house were enormous solar panels and large water tanks. It occurred to the officials that the subject was providing clean water and electricity to the villagers. This could get sticky—so they would need to act quickly. The original plan to take the time to recon-noiter the subject's residence had to be abandoned because the RSOs realized he could be tipped off by the villagers and he could disappear. They decided that the Assistant RSO would speak to the subject and inform him of the U.S. warrant for his arrest and that the Gendarmerie was there to take him into custody. While this was going on, word spread quickly throughout the village that the Americans were there to kidnap their white chief. While the police and the RSOs were taking the subject into custody, an angry mob of approxi-mately 100 people surrounded the front of the house, blocking the official vehicles. As the RSOs assessed the situation and tried to calm the local chiefs, the crowd grew to approximately 250 angry persons, now armed with bows and arrows, spiked clubs, guns, and machetes. As the crowd grew even more agitated, they began aggressive movements. The situation was explosive. The RSOs succeeded in calming the crowd enough so their ace card could enter the fray. They called in their Foreign Service National Investigator (FSNI), nicknamed Big John—a chief well-known in his own right and whose size and voice carried an air of authority and gained respect among the crowd. Initially, the RSOs had decided that Big John would wait and monitor the situation from off site, in deference to the Gendarmerie—in effect, letting them handle the situation. When the situation escalated to the point where the Gendarmerie and the RSOs were being shoved and pushed about, Big John stepped in. Within a short period of time, the crowd had calmed and the tribal chiefs directed the crowd that the Gendarmerie and the RSOs should be able to leave with the subject in custody. The rapid turn of events meant that the subject would be expelled from Togo earlier than anticipated and that ICE agents would miss the deportation if they travelled all the way to Togo. Once again, in timely response to changing events, one tired Assistant RSO and a fresh FSNI escorted the subject to France, from where he was returned to the United States by appreciative ICE agents.

This case demonstrates just how small the world can be when law enforcement agencies collaborate. From a casual conversation at an embassy cocktail party to a mountaintop rural village in Togo where a neighborhood chieftain calms an angry mob, law enforcement is everywhere, whereas other counterterrorism instruments are not. It is this distinction that can make a difference in a world where causing mass loss of life and destruction has become a political strategy. As a branch chief in CIL, I encouraged RSOs to assist other agencies and their host-nation counterparts with criminal cases whenever they could. The first reason is because it engenders goodwill and trust among counterpart agencies—and we might need them for a favor at some point. Second, it helps keep the RSO apprised of what criminal and terrorism activity is taking place in his assigned country. Third, it keeps the RSO apprised of the activities of other law enforcement agencies, which is necessary for coordination purposes. Fourth, and most important, it places RSOs in closer contact with their host-country police counterparts, in the realm where the host-nation police are most comfortable—dealing with criminal matters. When RSOs deal with host-nation police on a multitude of levels, they are better able to relate to police at any particular level. This close working relationship can result in critical information being passed at the right time. For a security officer at a high-value target like a U.S. embassy, this can mean the difference between life and death for members of the embassy community.

Law Enforcement Can Take Advantage of Emerging, Sub-State, International Governmental Networks

Slaughter maintains that intergovernmental networks can circumvent cumbersome bureaucratic procedures and red tape. As chief of CIL, I always tried to exploit the informal networks of law enforcement, understanding their efficiency. Ironically, I found that the most difficult countries to work with were those which were ostensibly our allies—countries with which the United States had formal Mutual Legal Assistance Treaties. These treaties tend to turn law enforcement cooperation into a bureaucratic exercise with requests and responses going through diplomatic channels. Very often these interactions would be processed with very little human interaction and when one country refused to honor a request for whatever reason, be it a technicality or opposition to the death penalty, the answer was often final. This was particularly true with countries in Western Europe, which sometimes seemed almost spiteful in their reluctance to cooperate.[396]

In France, the notorious Ira Einhorn case exemplifies the situation. In this case, a well-known counter-culture radical of the 1960s and early 1970s was accused of murdering his girlfriend, then hiding out in Europe and ultimately in France. It required a monumental effort, and a promise not to impose the death penalty in Pennsylvania, to ultimately gain Einhorn's extradition.[397] Even now, it is a painstaking and time-consuming exercise to obtain extraditions and other types of official cooperation. But law enforcement officers are resourceful—particularly in the same Western European countries where policing, and informal policing in particular, were pioneered, according to Deflem, den Boer, Andreas, and Nadelmann. The United States has an MLAT with France, for example, and it does indeed restrict what we have come to know as informal policing. But there is very often some wriggle room, and one need only look for it.

In November 2006 the San Francisco District Attorney's Office requested Diplomatic Security's assistance with the difficult prosecution of a violent, multiple-charge rape case. The accused rapist in that case had been charged with sexually assaulting two women. The prosecution alleged that the defendant had gone to a home shared by the two female roommates, along with some of their friends. After the friends had left for the evening, the defendant regained entry to the apartment under the pretext of having left his keys and cell phone behind. Upon reentering the apartment the defendant violently physically assaulted and raped the terrified women using a corkscrew as a weapon. The case presented difficulties for the prosecution because the charges were predicated almost solely on uncorroborated verbal testimony of the women and some minimal circumstantial evidence. During the initial trial, police investigators discovered that the defendant had a previous conviction for rape in France. Prosecutors moved to introduce that conviction as evidence, but the presiding judge refused based on the defendant's right to face his accuser. The judge allowed the prosecution to attempt to locate the victim and convince her to testify. Because of the need for quick action on this case, the French Foreign Ministry agreed to allow U.S. authorities to attempt to locate and convince the French rape victim to testify. Desperate, the District Attorney's office and the San Francisco Police Department appealed to the Regional Security Office in Paris for help. Immediately, the RSO engaged

---

[396] Craig Whitlock, "Extradition of Terror Suspects Founders," Washington Post, 21 December 2008, A01. http://www.washingtonpost.com/wp-dyn/content/article/2008/12/20/AR2008122002096.html?hpid%3Dtopnews&sub=AR.

[397] CNN, "France Postpones Extradition of U.S. Fugitive," CNN.com, 12 July 2001. http://archives.cnn.com/2001/WORLD/europe/07/12/einhorn.france/index.html.

his FSNIs[398] to locate the French victim. Unfortunately, the victim declined to testify, fearing that the defendant would not be vigorously prosecuted and would be able to harm her for her role in testifying against him. The trial ended in a hung jury. After the trial, the prosecutor told the investigators that he would be willing to re-try the case if the French victim could be convinced to testify. Once the witness was relocated, the RSO, over a period of several weeks, gently persuaded the frightened witness to testify.[399] The San Francisco District Attorney's office paid for the victim to be flown to San Francisco. In February 2007, based on the testimony of the French victim, the defendant was convicted of assault with a deadly weapon, first-degree burglary with the intent to commit a sex offense, and using a deadly weapon in the commission of sex offenses. On 9 November 2007 the defendant was sentenced to two consecutive life terms of 35 years each, with a *minimum* of 70 years to be served, and $30,000 in fines and restitution of $5,000 per victim.

Without such intervention and assistance, a brutal rapist would be walking free. The French victim was ecstatic about the conviction—her assailant had been given a minimal sentence for her rape and assault in France—thus prompting her fear of a similar outcome in the California trial. To this day, the French witness remains in contact with the RSO and recently conveyed her intention to travel to San Francisco to meet with the other women victims for empathy and support from their common harrowing experiences. She recently delivered her first child.

This case demonstrates that, even in highly restrictive and regulated environments, intergovernmental networks of informal policing can prevail over established and rigid formal systems.

Informal Networks of Law Enforcement Can Be Spectacularly Powerful and Effective

In October 2004 the Pennsylvania State Police called the author at CIL headquarters in Washington to request assistance to solve an 11-year-old cold case murder investigation. In December 1993 deer hunters discovered the nude body of an unidentified woman in a wooded area near South Middleton, Pennsylvania. The woman had been raped and then brutally murdered, her corpse abused. In June 2004 DNA evidence from her attacker was matched to Theodore John Solano—a convicted sex offender who had served prison time for dis-

---

[398] Foreign Service National Investigators are hired by Regional Security Offices to conduct security investigations on behalf of U.S. embassies abroad. Generally, FSNI positions are highly coveted positions among retired, high-level police officials of the host country. These positions often give RSOs an extraordinary amount of clout and access in the host nation.

[399] With the permission of the French National Police.

tribution of child pornography. Police tracked Solano to Canon City, Colorado, where they interviewed him. Under questioning, Solano provided police with the name of a woman with whom he had a "marriage of convenience." Investigation led police to believe that the woman was Natalia Andreevna Miller, a young Russian who had immigrated to the United States in hopes of marrying an American man and gaining U.S. citizenship. But since the police could not positively establish the identity of the body, they were unable to charge the prime suspect—Solano. Even though they had a considerable amount of circumstantial evidence against him, without a positive ID on the body they could not adequately tie Solano to the murder. The state trooper's investigation led to a family that had hosted Natalia, and some possible names of the girl's parents, plus the information that they were likely from the area of St. Petersburg, Russia. The DSS lead agent assigned to the case informed the Pennsylvania Police that there was an excellent chance that DSS could locate them. Within a day of the initial phone call to CIL, and based on the names provided, the Assistant Regional Security Officer Investigator[400] in St. Petersburg engaged his Russian police contacts—who quickly located the parents. The parents eagerly came to the U.S. Consulate to provide blood samples, which were sent to DSS headquarters and, through an evidentiary chain, on to the Pennsylvania State Police. DNA analysis confirmed the identity of Jane Doe as Ms. Miller and, on 3 December 2004, police arrested Solano. "It was a real-life episode of Cold Case Files," Cumberland County District Attorney Skip Ebert observed. "What DSS can bring to the table is fantastic—I never knew these folks existed before."[401]

What was once an 11-year-old cold murder case was resolved by the tenacity of the Pennsylvania State Police, the County Coroner, the development of DNA technology and, importantly, the ongoing, real-time evolution of intergovernmental networks—the informal networks of international policing. No mutual legal assistance treaty, letters rogatory, or diplomatic demarches were required for this case—only cops talking to cops. On 4 January 2008 Solano pleaded no contest to third-degree murder for the strangulation death of Miller and will serve 17 to 40 years in state prison.[402]

---

[400] Diplomatic Security has Assistant Regional Security Officer Investigators in particular posts overseas whose sole function is criminal investigation. They serve there in addition to the Regional Security Officer. DSS has added 50 ARSO-I positions for 2009.

[401] Bayer, "Operation Global Pursuit," 34. See also Tiffany Pakkala, "'Jane Doe' Suspect Nabbed," The Sentinel, 4 December 2004, available at http://www.cumberlink.com/articles/2004/12/04/news/news01.prt, and Erik Harkreader, "Murder Suspect in Court," The Sentinel, 1 December 2005, available at http://www.cumberlink.com/articles/2005/12/01/news/news01.txt.

[402] Matt Miller, "Husband Sentenced in 'Jane Doe' Murder," The Patriot-News, 4 January 2008. Available at http://www.pennlive.com/midstate/index.ssf/2008/01/_if_olga_shugar_has.html.

U.S. Law Enforcement Is in a Unique Position to Lead and Coordinate International Law Enforcement Counterterrorism Efforts

Presently, in matters of transnational crime, the United States holds an almost universally accepted leadership role in international law enforcement.[403] The Americanization of international law enforcement is a matter of fact, of record, and is recognized by scholars. As the most widely represented national law enforcement assemblage on earth, the United States is positioned to be a leader in counterterrorism initiatives as well. In counterterrorism, leading the charge for the United States in law enforcement is the FBI; it is, without question, a force to be reckoned with and it is indeed a positive force. Few law enforcement organizations can muster a fraction of the FBI's resources, investigative skill, and technical know-how. But by this agency's own admission, it cannot succeed alone.[404] We know from the May 2007 GAO Combating Terrorism Report that, with the exception of the FBI, U.S. federal law enforcement capabilities have not been adequately engaged. We also know from that report that, as a practical matter, the number and worldwide geographic distribution of the non-FBI, U.S. federal law enforcement presence overseas are greater than the overseas representation of the FBI.[405] The United States is in a position to be a more effective leader if U.S. law enforcement is more completely engaged in counterterrorism activity. The following case indicates just how effective this leadership can be.

Operation Triple X—Diplomatic Security Service

Operation Triple X was an international, criminal undercover operation, led by the U.S. Department of State's Bureau of Diplomatic Security in partnership with the Indonesian National Police. The investigation revealed that organized criminal syndicates in Indonesia were conspiring to perpetrate a massive manipulation of the U.S. government's visa issuance process to facilitate trafficking in women and children to work in the sex industry, drug trafficking, weapons trafficking, pedophile networks, and money laundering. Some of these criminal syndicates were affiliated with Jamaah-al Islamiya (JI), a ruthless and deadly terrorist group. The leadership of JI had sworn allegiance to Osama bin Laden and al-Qaeda and was responsible for the bombings in Bali in 2003 which killed 202 people, and the 2004 bombing

---

[403] European policing looms large in this equation as well. See Mathieu Deflem, "International Policing," 703; also Andreas and Nadelmann, Policing the Globe, 241-245, who see the Americanization of international law enforcement as a means of imposing American hegemony. Kal Raustiala, "Architecture of International Cooperation," 24-25, also accepts as a given that networks tend to "strengthen the power of the already powerful, and favor strong economic actors such as the U.S."

[404] FBI Strategic Plan 2004-2009, 8.

[405] GAO, Combating Terrorism Report.

of the J.W. Marriott Hotel in Jakarta that killed at least 12. In 2003, JI was behind a potentially devastating plot to bomb U.S. diplomatic facilities in Singapore and U.S. military bases in the South Pacific. Additionally, the U.S. Embassy in Jakarta and the U.S. Consulate General in Surabaya were closed several times in 2005 and 2006 because of similar terrorist activities. The investigation yielded 84 arrests and over 4,800 fraudulent documents, including Indonesian passports, U.S. passports and visas, Indonesian national identification cards, marriage, birth, and family records, vehicle registrations, and drivers' licenses. More than 8,000 individuals were identified as having engaged the services of these criminal syndicates for the purpose of getting into the United States. The potential for serious violence became clear when one of the syndicate's clients was arrested for attempting to smuggle automatic weapons from Indonesia into Los Angeles.

Operation Triple X—An Indonesian Passport, an Identification Card, and the Marketing of Fraudulent Documents.

Source: State Department, with permission.

BJBS, one of the main Indonesian front companies for the massive fraud network, was raided by police. The raid uncovered a direct link between criminal syndicates producing fraudulent documents and JI. According to an article in *Police Chief* magazine, "One JI operative brought $30,000 to BJBS to pick up three complete sets of counterfeit identification documents. An undercover officer working inside overheard the would-be terrorist declare, 'I am a member of JI—now I'm going overseas.'" An important link between Surabaya's fraudulent document brokers and terrorists arose on 9 June 2007, when Indonesian police arrested JI's Arif Syarifuddin. Arif Syarifuddin is an alleged JI member who specialized in providing false documentation, safehouses, and safe passage for JI operatives, and was considered a rising star among the JI leadership. Syarifuddin was arrested by an elite Indonesian antiterrorism task force called "Detachment 88," for which DS has provided antiterrorism training for many years.[406] These cases have succeeded not on the basis of national strategic policy—but because of the professionalism of the law enforcement entities involved—both on the U.S. side and that of our international partners. These cases have succeeded not *because* of our national policy (of the previous U.S. administration); they succeeded *in spite of* it—because overseas information coordination for terrorism has been viewed as the domain of the Intelligence Community.

The massive scope of the investigation, as troubling as it is, is all the more troubling because DS's Surabaya office is relatively new. If it had not established operations in Surabaya, this chain of fraud would likely be continuing unabated, and a lethal terrorist group would have a reliable pipeline for travel directly to the United States. Although DS is the most broadly represented U.S. law enforcement agency worldwide, it very likely still does not operate everywhere it is needed—as the 9/11 Commission reported, "for terrorists, travel documents are as important as weapons"[407]—who knows how many more Surabaya(s) remain in the world?

The effective application of several layers of the "soft power" of policing, as illustrated here, places federal U.S. law enforcement agencies in a logical position to become a much more effective leader in the international struggle against terror. Peter Chalk, an analyst with the RAND Corporation, suggests

---

[406] Richard J. Griffin, "Operation Triple X: Hitting Hard at Illegal Document Trade," The Police Chief 74, no. 10 (October 2007). Available at http://www.policechiefmagazine.org/magazine/index.cfm?fuseaction=display_arch&article_id=1295&issue_id=102007.

[407] The 9/11 Commission Report, 385. Available at http://www.9-11commission.gov/report/911Report.pdf.

that "Jakarta's decision early on to assign police, rather than the military, to take the lead gave crucial legitimacy to the terrorism crackdown."[408]

Operation Triple X was also successful because of the development of informal, personal relationships among the law enforcement participants. According to the former Assistant Secretary for Diplomatic Security, Richard A. Griffin:

> One good tip, some old-fashioned police work, and a solid partnership with a host of law enforcement authorities around the world was all it took to shut down more than two dozen document counterfeiting operations in Indonesia, enhancing U.S. national security. It is worth noting here that DSS achieved such success with Operation Triple X even though its personnel have no law enforcement authority in other countries, outside of the actual U.S. diplomatic facilities. How, then, did DSS special agents achieve such tangible results against criminal operations? Besides good and thorough investigative work, perhaps the most significant element for success in any international investigation—or, indeed, any investigation involving more than one agency—is to establish trust and confidence through good working relationships with all partners at the managerial, investigative, and operational levels. It is a lesson that DSS learned long ago, applied in Operation Triple X, and successfully puts into practice every day throughout the world.[409]

In this case, the tip came from a group of counterfeiters that the Indonesian police had rounded up. The Indonesian police permitted Regional Security Officer Kevin Whitson to interview them (through the powerful, informal, trust-based networking capability of law enforcement). The counterfeiters never thought they would face prosecution, so they arrogantly spoke freely to Whitson.[410]

This case exemplifies the importance of having an ability to connect the dots in an unrestricted manner. In this instance, an important vulnerability in U.S. national security was discovered and rectified—a vulnerability which could have enabled al-Qaeda-affiliated Jamaah al-Islamiyah access and entry to the United States—a vulnerability which, in this instance, was cor-

---

[408] Alex Kingsbury, "Lessons from the Near-defeat," U.S. News & World Report, 28 October 2008. Available at http://www.usnews.com/articles/news/world/2008/10/28/lessons-from-the-near-defeat-of-a-once-feared-al-qaeda-affiliate-in-indonesia.html.

[409] Griffin, "Operation Triple X."

[410] Griffin, "Operation Triple X."

rected through *criminal investigation.*[411] DSS followed national security and State Department policy by not classifying information—case information is available to all who have a legitimate interest—including foreign law enforcement.[412] If DSS had classified this information, important leads would have been suppressed and unavailable to those who would find it useful.

Operation Triple X— Indonesian Officers with Masses of Confiscated Fraudulent Documents.

Source: State Department, with permission.

Law Enforcement Networks Can Empower Weaker States— Especially through "Soft Power"

According to some of the premier experts in the field, intergovernmental networks can empower weaker states.[413] As Deflem argues, police elements, as participants in intergovernmental networks themselves, will aspire toward efficiency, professionalism, and expertise—through which they can achieve a significant measure of autonomy from the political center of the state. States tolerate a measure of autonomy by the police because competency

---

411 As noted earlier in this book, law enforcement and security officers do not need to restrict their interactions with host-country security elements only to criminal cases. They can, and should, discuss trends, ongoing cases, if appropriate, or simply matters of speculation and suspicion.

412 The unfortunate flip-side of this point may be that, because the information is unclassified, it may not be considered as important as classified information by some in the Intelligence Community.

413 Raustiala, "Architecture of International Cooperation," 24-25; Slaughter, "Governing the Global Economy," 203.

in a police force reinforces public confidence and serves to combat crime—a parasitic influence on any country. Because international police networks, especially informal police networks, empower police by improving efficiency, international police networks can empower weaker states. Because it is often in the interest of weaker states to tolerate intergovernmental networks, it is also in their best interests to tolerate autonomy from their police—because it ultimately benefits the state. This is why police entities are often formidable adversaries of intelligence services;[414] it is also why police networks are ideally suited to deal with another formidable network, the networks of Islamist terrorism and insurgency.

Colombian Official
Pointing to GAULA
Operating Areas.
Source: State Department,
with permission.

Just as international police networks have limited some activities of Jamaah al-Islamiyah and other groups in Southeast Asia, international policing efforts are finding success in another part of the world, the narcoterrorist stronghold of Colombia.[415] The following observations from a *Washington Post* article by Kevin Whitelaw are telling:

> Once the most visible symbols of Colombia's troubles and a key revenue source for the nation's guerrillas, kidnappings, have plummeted from a high of 3,572 victims in 2000 to 521 in 2007, according to the Ministry of Defense. The sharp drop has been driven by several factors, including much larger security forces that have put the guerrillas on the run.

---

[414] Police are formidable because they possess power in their own right—separate from the political state. Police are literally a "force" of numbers, authority, and autonomy and can represent competition or even a threat to intelligence services vying for influence within governments and states.

[415] While Indonesia and Colombia are examples of U.S.-led law enforcement international network successes, they are successes in spite of current U.S. counterterrorism policy. This point will be addressed further in Chapter Six.

"In the past, there were some areas with no police presence, so FARC, the prime kidnappers, had areas where they could keep 20 people at a time, like a hotel," says Col. Umberto Guatibonza, the commander of the police wing of the elite anti-kidnapping forces known as GAULA GAULA is the Spanish acronym for Unified Action Groups for Personal Liberty. "We occupied those areas."

Colombian officials also credit an important but little-known program, run by the U.S. State Department's Bureau of Diplomatic Security, that has trained more than 600 GAULA members. The DSS training, offered under its Anti-Terrorism Assistance program, has focused in particular on rescuing hostages. "Before, there was the will and the people, but you want to turn it into something professional, especially for how you do a careful rescue," says Colombian Vice-Defense Minister Sergio Jaramillo. "When it gets to the nitty-gritty, you need expertise."

The $3.4 million ATA Anti-Terrorism Assistance effort is only a tiny part of the broader *Plan Colombia*, the U.S. aid program that has funneled some $5 billion in aid to Colombia since 2000 under the aegis of the U.S. war on drugs. [Funding for] *Plan Colombia*, the bulk of which goes toward the Colombian military, has a decidedly mixed record when it comes to fighting drugs (overall production has remained relatively steady). "For the United States, it was always about narcotics," says Arlene Tickner, who teaches at the National University of Colombia. "For the Colombian government, the interest was born out of a need to combat an insurgency."

And indeed, the aid effort has helped the Colombians turn the tide against the FARC guerrillas. U.S. officials estimate that FARC, which numbered some 40,000 fighters at its peak, has dwindled to about 9,000. What only recently looked more like an intractable civil war now seems, perhaps, manageable. "The Colombia of 2008 might as well be a different country on a different planet in a different galaxy," says William Brownfield, the U.S. ambassador to Colombia.[416]

---

[416] Kevin Whitelaw, "Inside Colombia's War on Kidnapping," U.S. News & World Report, 27 February 2008. Available at http://www.usnews.com/articles/news/world/2008/02/27/inside-colombias-war-on-kidnapping.html.

Colombian GAULA Troops and Their Special Equipment.
Source: State Department, with permission.

ATA is not the only means at Diplomatic Security's disposal for exercising soft power. Its Rewards for Justice (RFJ) program has contributed to the cause as well.[417] In October 2003 a "concerned" individual saw a *60 Minutes II* story on three Americans who had been kidnapped by members of the FARC after their plane had crashed in the Colombian jungle earlier that year. This individual, along with two associates, contacted the Government of Colombia and the U.S. Embassy in Bogota concerning the location of the camp run by Edgar Navarro, a FARC commander believed to have been involved in the kidnapping. The three sources hiked through the jungle to lead the Colombian security forces to Navarro's camp site. On 19 October 2003, the Colombian forces entered the campsite to arrest Navarro and his unit. A gun battle ensued, killing Navarro and 11 of his bodyguards. The sources received a reward of $300,000 each—a reasonable price to deliver a serious setback to a deadly terrorist/insurgent group.

Of course, the biggest successes of U.S.-led law enforcement in Colombia do not belong to the Diplomatic Security Service; that distinction goes to DEA. DEA has been at the forefront of assisting the government of Colombia first rid itself of the Medellin Cartel, the Cali Cartel, and the North Coast Cartel, and most recently, the narcoterrorist group the FARC.[418] DEA is also seeing success with interdiction efforts that are diverting drug ship-

---

[417] For more on ATA's successes see Jeffrey W. Culver, "Stronger Partners: Program Celebrates 25 Years of Fighting Terrorism, State Magazine, December 2008, 14.

[418] To be fair, other counterterrorism instruments have been very active in many of these actions in Colombia, but it is the efforts of law enforcement and the "umbrella" of law enforcement that has provided the impetus for the modest successes thus far achieved in Colombia.

ments away from the United States and toward Europe—to ports that are not quite so risky for traffickers.[419]

A principal factor contributing to the nearly unprecedented popularity of Colombian President Alvaro Uribe has been his government's successes against the FARC.[420] 2008 saw the demise of two of the FARC's founding members (one by natural causes, the other by an unnatural cause), and the rescue of 11 hostages, to include Ingrid Betancourt, a former candidate for the Colombian presidency along with three U.S. defense contractors. It is under these circumstances that international police efforts are paying off by empowering weaker states. Andreas and Nadelmann maintain that U.S.-led international drug enforcement efforts are one of the many ways that the United States imposes its own policies and morality on other states—thereby sustaining its own hegemony.[421] At the same time, other states are benefitting by defeating terrorist groups or violent insurgencies, and are professionalizing their police forces to boot.[422]

Colombian Counterterrorism Analyst at Her Work Station.
Source: State Department, with permission.

---

[419] Interview with senior DEA official, 3 November 2008. See also, Joseph Kirschke, "The Coke Coast: Cocaine and Failed States in West Africa," World Politics Review, 9 September 2008. Available at http://www.worldpoliticsreview.com/article.aspx?id=2629.

[420] Anastasia Moloney, "Colombia's Uribe at Six Years: A Positive but Fragile Legacy," World Politics Review, 21 August 2008. Available at http://www.worldpoliticsreview.com/article.aspx?id=2589.

[421] Andreas and Nadelmann, Policing the Globe, 242.

[422] Of course, corrupt national police forces are a hindrance, but over time, as evidenced in examples presented here, police forces are capable of professionalizing themselves through international cooperative policing efforts.

The Crime of Terrorism Provides a Powerful Incentive for Law Enforcement to Cooperate Internationally

In the wake of 9/11 the United States experienced worldwide sympathy and support. In that context, the U.S. attack on Afghanistan was largely seen as justified by the rest of the world. It has since become conventional wisdom that the U.S. lost a significant share of that support by choosing to invade Iraq. Also disturbing to the rest of the world was the perception that the United States had abandoned its principles as a champion of justice and human rights in favor of militarism and political intolerance. The United States can regain some of the goodwill that has been lost by re-adopting an emphasis on the "rule of law" in its counterterrorism policies and endeavors.

If terrorism is a "unifying" force for police, then an appropriate means of exploiting that force is through the already potent networks of law enforcement. Policing scholar Anthony Balzer asserts that one of the unifying aspects of police culture is a common cause, the notion of "fighting a common enemy."[423] Althhough Operation Triple X is a fine example of how police have cooperated in counterterrorism efforts, perhaps the best way to express the idea of the "common enemy" is to step out of the context of terrorism. The reader may have noticed that, in the case studies examined above, cases often involve pedophiles. It has been the author's experience that no other category of criminal activity engenders so much international cooperation as crimes against children. In 2004, DSS located and participated in the apprehension and return of 108 American fugitives from overseas. Of those, 25 were fugitives wanted for sex crimes committed against children—the next highest category of fugitives were those wanted for narcotics trafficking with 16, followed by those wanted for murder with 11.[424]

In 2004, shortly after my assignment as head of CIL, I was briefed on a case where an astute parent in the American expatriate community in Tunisia felt uncomfortable about an American child psychologist who had a practice there. The parent knew the psychologist was from the Chicago area and asked that his name be checked against a sex offender registry. The man's name popped up as a pedophile who had adopted an 8-year-old boy and had

---

[423] Anthony J. Balzer, "International Police Cooperation: Opportunities and Obstacles," in Policing in Central Asia and Eastern Europe: Comparing Firsthand Knowledge with Experience from the West (Slovenia: College of Police and Security Studies, 1996). Available at http://www.ncjrs.gov/policing/int63.htm.

[424] In 2005, out of 114 DSS fugitive locates and assisted apprehensions and returns, 27 were pedophilic in nature; in 2006, there were 23 pedophile cases out of 123 total DSS fugitive returns; in 2007, out of 105 total fugitive returns, 31 were pedophile cases—with pedophile cases far outnumbering other categories of fugitive crimes. Source: Author's professional files and DS/CIL.

allegedly sexually assaulted him until he was 14 years old. The parent reported the man to the RSO who referred the case to CIL. After meticulous investigation, CIL located a Chicago-area warrant for the man.[425] Further inquiry revealed that the subject had absconded before his trial on child molestation charges and that he had been convicted in absentia in 1993. CIL then went to work. According to RSO Tunis, the Tunisian police were eager to remove the subject from their country, but lack of an extradition treaty with the United States posed an impediment to cooperation. The police volunteered, however, that they could consider an Interpol Red Notice a warrant under their laws, and if we somehow obtained one then they could conceivably eject the subject. Because CIL has agents working at Interpol headquarters in Lyon and at the National Central Bureau in Washington, DC, we were able to press for and receive an expedited Interpol Red Notice. Upon its issuance, the RSO asked the Tunisian police to deport the subject to the United States. They agreed to do so, but they went further than that: They considered the crime to have been so reprehensible that they arranged for the deportation order to be signed by President Zine El Abidine Ben Ali. The Tunisians considered the return of the subject to be an extradition, while the United States considered his return to be a deportation. Regardless, according to a DOJ Office of International Affairs (DOJ-OIA) attorney at the time, the exchange was unprecedented—no fugitive had ever been returned from Tunisia to the United States up until that point.[426] Upon his return to the United States, after more than a decade, the subject, John Pierre Bourgignon, was sentenced to 24 years in prison.

This case demonstrates that particular crimes (and types of criminals) can and do serve as a motivation for police to cooperate—and in some cases exceedingly so. Deflem argues that recognizing terrorism as a criminal action can produce many similar examples.

Law Enforcement Agencies Are Accustomed to Working Together and with Foreign Counterparts—and Share Information in a Manner Consistent with Privacy Considerations, National Laws, and Operational Security

The discipline involved in preparing cases for trial tends to keep police finely attuned to the demands of proper procedure and legal process. However, even the most meticulously conducted and carefully laid out inves-

---

[425] The warrant had not been placed in the national criminal indexes and had to be manually tracked.

[426] As recollected by the author. See also Frank Main, "Tunisia Returns Longtime Fugitive in Sex Abuse Case," Chicago Sun-Times, 25 January 2004, 3A, and Matt O'Connor, "Fugitive in Sex Case Brought Back to City," Chicago Tribune, 25 January 2004, Section 4, 3.

tigations can fall victim to unanticipated technicalities or nuances of law and result in what the press might cavalierly refer to as a "botched investigation." Potentially worse is the notion that cases that have involved countless hours and sometimes years of effort can be squandered when a case is "blown"— especially when it is for reasons deemed avoidable. Generally speaking, we in law enforcement are used to playing by the rules and operating under certain constraints. Some of us would never admit it, but constraints such as Miranda warnings in the U.S. can strengthen the credibility of cases. Information that passes investigative muster is said to be "vetted." Fluid communications between law enforcement agencies and police departments both domestically and internationally permit sharing and cross-checking in a way that the tight controls on dissemination of intelligence and classified information prevent.[427] So too, law enforcement entities work well on a reciprocity basis, as in "one good turn deserves another."[428] In fact, the principle of mutual recognition is the basis of police and judicial cooperation in the European Union.[429] Such are benefits and constraints of the "rule of law."

But even operating under the rule of law there is "wriggle room" to accomplish goals. DSS uses CIL as an instrument of goodwill among our own law enforcement agencies to encourage communication and cooperation in support of our primary security mission to protect U.S. personnel and facilities overseas. We also try to assist foreign police whenever possible with their requests to the degree that such requests are legal and reasonable. DSS understands that law enforcement is reciprocal in nature,[430] and we may need to call in a favor to protect our interests overseas.

A few years ago, a police liaison officer with the German Embassy in Washington, DC, called me to assist him with a security issue at his consulate in Los Angeles.[431] The liaison officer, who later became my good friend Klaus, explained that a German national living in Los Angeles had made threats to bomb the German consulate there. The man making the threats was wanted in Germany for having sent a live bomb to the German Parliament building. Although the man was in DHS custody, he (Klaus) was having difficulty convincing the U.S. Attorney's Office in Los Angeles to extradite or deport the fugitive back to Germany. I told Klaus that I would do what I could to help. After calling the DSS section responsible for protecting foreign missions, I

---

[427] E-mail discussion between Jacqueline Ross, Professor of Law, University of Illinois, and Mike Bayer, 25 November 2008.

[428] Ross – Bayer e-mail, 25 November 2008.

[429] Monica den Boer – Bayer e-mail attachment, 20 February 2009.

[430] Ross – Bayer e-mail, 25 November 2008.

[431] Diplomatic Security oversees security for all foreign embassy missions in the United States.

called the Assistant U.S. Attorney handling the case and persuaded him by explaining that we relied on our foreign counterparts to protect our interests overseas and that it was important that we cooperate with them if we hope for them to cooperate with us. After some complaints about being squeezed by the State Department, the Assistant U.S. Attorney complied. After lengthy court filings and appeals, the subject was ultimately deported back to Germany.

Klaus and I worked this case, with its delicate international judicial and diplomatic implications, because we both knew and understood the implications. Klaus had to be careful about his own country's legal procedures and privacy laws, and I had to be aware of them as well, yet be able to artfully convince an overworked U.S. Attorney's Office that it was in the best interests of the U.S. government to accommodate the German's request.

This case highlights the reciprocal nature of police work. Klaus and I established a relationship based on trust. I helped him because he is a fellow law enforcement officer and because he asked me. That is all he needed to do. Now, if I ever need a favor from the German police, I know he will spare no effort to try to help me. Likewise, he knows he can ask me a favor again, even though he "owes me one," and I too would spare no effort to help. Such are the unwritten rules of law enforcement—and their power is proved daily.

Law Enforcement, Particularly U.S. Law Enforcement, Is Accustomed to Working with Sensitive Information

Hand in hand with understanding how "the system" works is knowing how to protect information. As mentioned earlier, law enforcement officers have a strong, vested interest in sharing information for cross-checking and verifying information and establishing connections to other cases and crimes, but at the same time protecting the information so a case is not blown or an informant hurt or killed—or worse, from our standpoint, the investigator harmed. The previous example showed not only how the system can be worked, but the importance of trust and how it is established between law enforcement officers. Trust is a small but important part of the vetting and protection process and it is essential if informal law enforcement networks are to be effective. One of the arguments against engaging law enforcement in any international problem is the wild card of police corruption. Law enforcement officers experienced in international law enforcement know that corruption is a fact of life with some police entities, particularly in the Third World, but we also know that there are ways to overcome problems associated with corruption. Sound operational security practices are one way of overcoming such obstacles.

In May 2004 the Department of Justice's Office of International Affairs (OIA) sought the assistance of the Regional Security Officer in Kampala, Uganda, in a fugitive fraud case in which over 4,000 U.S. persons were alleged to have been defrauded of more than $200 million. Two subjects, Van A. Brink (aka Gilbert Zeigler) and Douglas Ferguson, were alleged to have used their ill-gotten gains to purchase an organic vegetable farm in Oregon and luxury homes in Oregon, Nevada, Grenada, and a "palace" in Uganda.[432] In the United States, Van Brink and Ferguson faced charges of money laundering, mail fraud, and wire fraud, among others. The two men had allegedly fled the island nation of Grenada just ahead of law enforcement authorities after the failure of two banks they had started and controlled. The RSO in Kampala, responding to a DOJ request, began to ask questions about the pair, and was told that the two men had friends at the highest level of the Ugandan government—it was asserted that they lived in Idi Amin's old palace. The RSO worried that the men, or their friends in high places, would be tipped off if he investigated through normal channels. Through his trusted police contacts, the RSO knew that there was an especially vetted anti-corruption unit within the Ugandan police department. His contacts arranged for him to go to them for assistance. They agreed to help and DOJ-OIA notified the FBI that an apprehension operation was underway.[433] Within a few weeks, the Ugandan Police and the RSO had developed a plan of action for the apprehension. Meanwhile, the FBI sent a team of special agents to escort Van Brink and Ferguson to the United States for trial. No one else knew of the operation—not the RSO's trusted contacts nor anyone in the hierarchy of the government. The RSO warned CIL that the apprehension might be a little tricky, given that Brink and Ferguson's compound was protected by armed guards. The RSO informed CIL that the vetted unit was genuine and that he trusted it unconditionally. Based on the RSO's assertions, CIL advised him to proceed with the operation but to stay out of any gunfights. Indeed, as the raid got underway, a gun battle erupted and one of Brink and Ferguson's guards was killed. The next day, FBI agents escorted a stunned Brink and Ferguson back to the United States. While awaiting trial, Van A. Brink, aka Gilbert Zeigler, died of natural causes. On 27 August 2007 Ferguson, age 74, was sentenced

---

[432] Caribbean Net News, "FBI Arrests Former Grenada Bank President," 2 June 2004. Available at http://www.caribbeannetnews.com/2004/06/02brink.htm.

[433] The Van Brink and Ferguson case "belonged to" the FBI. DSS does not presume or assume jurisdiction when honoring assistance requests from other agencies.

to four years in prison and was ordered to pay $26 million in restitution.[434] Every aspect of the apprehension and return of the fugitives was done through informal police channels and methods.

This case demonstrates the efficacy of information security within police circles, even in the international arena. DEA's proficiency at protecting its own sources (informants) and measures (methods) has been noted earlier. The sensitive U.S. Marshals' Witness Security Program, which relies on unclassified operational security methods to protect identities and information, remains a prized program. The case discussed in this section demonstrates how operational security at the international level can remain flexible, effective, and relatively easy to implement. A potentially deadly situation for all involved was avoided because of situationally-oriented operational security. Information was not classified, but remained uncompromised. Also, the idea that a police unit could fearlessly pull off an operation that might upset powerful members of a central government lends credence to Deflem's assertions that police elements may drift away from the political centers of government—and perhaps with the informal approval of that very government.

Law Enforcement Networks Have a Great Deal of Experience and Significant Success against International Criminal Networks, Which Makes Them Ideally Suited to Combat Highly Networked, Transnational Terrorism

Dealing with criminal networks, including terror networks, is a large part of what law enforcement units do, especially as they operate together informally. As this chapter was being written, Italian police were carrying out mass arrests of Sicilian Mafia in Palermo. Italian police maintain that this operation "decapitated" the Mafia in Sicily.[435] In Chapter Three the author observed that the FBI and the New York Police Department (NYPD) had managed to cripple the Mafia in New York and that law enforcement efforts have contributed to the downfall of the Medellin, Cali, and North Coast drug cartels in Colombia. In the present chapter, the author has discussed how law enforcement efforts appear to have been instrumental in weakening the Colombian FARC and the Southeast Asian al-Qaeda-affiliated Jamaah al-Islamiyah and Abu Sayif Groups. Operation Triple X was still another exam-

---

[434] Van Brink and Ferguson's accomplices were also ordered to pay restitution in excess of $80 million. See Joseph B. Frazier, "2 Plead Guilty in Grenada Bank Scam," FOXNews.com, 28 March 2007; CBC News, "Canadian Gets 6 Years in Scam that Netted Millions and a Yacht," 28 August 2007. Available at http://www.cbc.ca/world/story/2007/08/28/offshore.scam.html.

[435] "Sicilian Mafia 'Decapitated' by Mass Arrests, Say Police," CNN.com/Europe, 16 December 2008. Available at http://www.cnn.com/2008/WORLD/europe/12/16/mafia.raid.italy/index.html.

ple of the takedown of an organized criminal enterprise through informal police collaboration.

In my own experience, the case of trafficking in women involving the Czech Republic had strong elements of organized crime throughout—so much so that the case was prosecuted out of the Eastern District of New York's organized crime section—the same section that prosecuted John Gotti and countless other mob figures. This case began in 1996 when I was a criminal investigator for Diplomatic Security's Visa Fraud Branch. The case started as a simple employee malfeasance, visa fraud case. In August 1996 I received a referral from the State Department's Fraud Prevention Program Office (FPP). It was alleged that a female Czech national employee of the Consular Section at the American Embassy in Prague had been screening visa applicants for processing and had cleared an inordinate number of visa applications for 18- to 24-year-old female applicants. The number of clearances was flagged as a definitive fraud indicator, because this category of applicant, young adult females, typically had a difficult time qualifying for visas—usually because they lacked sufficient ties to their homeland to guarantee their return home. I set the case aside for attention later in the busy day. Within an hour or two, I received a call from the Regional Security Officer in Prague. The RSO explained that he had been visited by a Czech police inspector who wanted to inform him that a U.S. Embassy employee may be collaborating with an organized crime group that they were investigating. The scenario the RSO laid out matched the case I had on my desk. The RSO explained that the Czech police investigation revealed that a female Czech national visa screener at the embassy was in league with a criminal enterprise in the Czech town of Pardubice that had been obtaining visas for young Eastern European women and had been sending them to the United States to work in the sex industry— mostly in the New York City area but also in Miami, Florida, and Houston, Texas. The RSO explained that the criminal enterprise had ties with Russian organized crime and had a strong presence in New York City. The RSO also related that the Czech police believed that a NYPD detective might be involved with the gang. The RSO sent by overnight delivery the translated transcripts of gang conversations mentioning the name of a NYPD detective. For a criminal case, the possibility of a bad cop can be a deal-breaker because, with police departments, that case becomes a priority. Regardless, I was duty-bound to bring the bad news to the NYPD, so I set up a trip to New York and made an appointment with its Internal Affairs Division. I had anticipated meeting with one or two detectives, but found myself sitting among several high-level NYPD officials. It was clear they were taking this matter very seriously. I explained the scenario to them, passed them copies of the Czech police transcripts, and articulated that I had no intention of getting involved in an internal affairs case. I informed them that I would wait until they finished with their investigation before I continued on with mine. They seemed relieved to hear that I would leave them alone to conduct their own internal investigation. The NYPD officials then told me that there had been an arrest in the Queens section of New York City that bore remarkable similarities to some of the elements in my case. They gave me the number of a NYPD vice detective who had made the arrest and advised me to call him. Later that day, I received an urgent message to call the RSO in Prague. Upon calling, the RSO related to me that the Czech police had monitored more conversations and it became clear that the NYPD detective discussed in the first transcript had been attempting to help some young women escape from the gang in New York. He had not been in league with them at all. I immediately relayed that information to the NYPD. In relief and gratitude, they offered me full support with my investigation. Soon after, I met with the vice detective who explained that he had arrested a young Czech woman for prostitution. He said that the young woman had run away from the Czech gang that brought her to the U.S., and was in fear for her life because the gang was known to be violent. He gave me the address and phone number of the young woman. She became my informant and provided me with names and information on other young women from the Czech Republic and other countries in Eastern Europe that the gang had brought to the United States. My informant told me that many of the young women had been duped into coming into the U.S. thinking they would become lingerie models or waitresses. With that information I scheduled a trip to the Czech Republic.

There, I met with my counterpart investigator. We compared notes and determined that the gang had all the hallmarks of a traditional Mafia or organized crime gang. They specialized in dealing stolen cars, drugs, and weapons, and they were deeply involved in trafficking women and prostitution. They had also been known to take contracts for murders. I suggested that if the Czech police could help me with the investigation of the embassy employee, perhaps she would inform or testify against the gang in the Czech Republic. Together, we concocted a plan to use a young, attractive Czech police officer to come to the embassy to pose as a last-minute visa applicant sponsored by the gang. After the operational plan was approved in Washington, we proceeded with the undercover sting operation. It worked. The young woman admitted to the scheme, named her accomplices, and agreed to cooperate in the investigation—to the elation of my Czech police counterparts. Based on her information, the Czech police arrested all the members of the Czech gang in Pardubice. These were dangerous and bad men and the police were glad to be rid of them. I asked the police if they would help me take down the other half of the gang in New York. They agreed.

First, they took me to meet a young woman who had managed to escape the gang in New York. She shared the harrowing tale of how she responded to a newspaper ad and had been recruited to work as a lingerie model in New York. She said she found herself in a peepshow the first day there. She also said she and her family had been threatened with harm if she did not do as she was told. She said she cried the entire first day at the peep-show, and refused to participate at all after that. As the gang became more frustrated with her the threats became more heated. She planned an escape with another young woman who had been duped. They arranged to purchase airline tickets and get replacement passports from the Czech Consulate in New York, as the gang had confiscated theirs. When the gang discovered the women missing, they sent out a search party to find them. They located the young women as they were getting into a taxi with their suitcases. The women spotted the gang members at Kennedy Airport after they had checked their bags and sprinted through the gate before the gangsters could react. Unfortunately for them it was not over. They spotted more men waiting for them at the baggage claim area at the Czech airport so they left their bags and departed in a taxi while the gang waited for them. She became my second informant.

With names, information, and patterns of travel, I was able to find hundreds of visa applications related to the gang's prostitution and peep show enterprise. With the help of my informant in New York, I was able to find several more disgruntled witnesses and informants. NYPD helped me find several more. On the day of the raids in New York, I had the assistance of NYPD and the Immigration and Naturalization Service (INS, now DHS-ICE). Over 150 police officers and special agents took part in the raids. We eventually arrested all principal gang members and received convictions. All told, the raids netted 45 arrests in the United States and six in the Czech Republic. The peep shows in New York City are well known to have been controlled by the Colombo and Gambino Italian crime syndicates—which by the 1990s were in league with Russian organized crime groups.[436] One of the key cooperating witnesses from the peep show business was alleged to have been involved with Russian organized crime and had served as a go-between for the Czech, Russian, and Italian organized criminal groups. The two ringleaders were sentenced to five years each for Mann Act violations and two others were sentenced to six months and time served for witness tampering.

436 Bill Berkely, "Code of Betrayal, Not Silence, Shines Light on Russian Mob," New York Times, 19 August 2002. Available at http://query.nytimes.com/gst/fullpage.html?res=9E00EFDA 103DF93AA2575BC0A9649C8B63.

This case exemplifies how even routine criminal cases can grow into complex cases involving international criminal networks. It also demonstrates how well law enforcement agencies can deal with such networks and how rapidly they can adjust to changing situations and scenarios—even internationally. One of the reasons that I pursued this case so aggressively was to show just how vulnerable our visa issuance process was and how, if criminal networks could exploit the system, so too could terrorists. Prior to 9/11, my exhortations in this regard had fallen on deaf ears.

According to former Assistant Secretary of State for Diplomatic Security Richard Griffin:

- The 19 9/11 attackers applied for 23 visas and obtained 22. Two more conspirators obtained visas but did not participate in the attack.

- The 19 hijackers managed to conceal their identities by using 364 aliases, fraudulent entry/exit stamps, and altered passports.

- Over the course of 21 months, the conspirators attempted to enter the United States 34 times through nine airports. They succeeded all but once.

- Through these fraudulent means, the 9/11 terrorists obtained legitimate passports and tourist visas, entered the United States, and carried out the worst terrorist attack in U.S. history.[437]

U.S. international law enforcement efforts were not well coordinated before 9/11. According to the GAO they still are not. Perhaps this is a good time to start.

The Technological Aspects of Law Enforcement and Border Control Are Firmly in Place in Worldwide Counterterrorism Efforts, but Can Be Exponentially More Effective if Other Elements of Globalized Law Enforcement Can Be Further Engaged and Coordinated

On 22 May 2007, as a result of "the most far flung and exotic fugitive investigation ever conducted by the U.S. Marshals Service," fugitive child molester Rabbi Alan Horowitz was arrested at the Newark, New Jersey, Airport, having been escorted from India by a Diplomatic Security Service special agent. Horowitz had been spotted loitering near a school in Mahabalipuram, India, by a local man who was suspicious of his intentions. The local man found out that Horowitz was a rabbi, so he spent some time researching sex-

---

[437] Griffin, "Operation Triple X."

offender rabbis on the Internet until he came across Horowitz's photograph on an *America's Most Wanted* website. The man immediately notified the nearest U.S. Consulate, whereupon Diplomatic Security became involved. DSS notified local police and coordinated Horowitz's apprehension and deportation through the U.S. Marshals Service. When Horowitz fled the United States, the U.S. Marshals petitioned Interpol to issue a Red Notice on Horowitz. The Indian government agreed to deport Horowitz based on the Red Notice, which they recognize as an international arrest warrant.

Interpol Red Notices are tied into a number of databases—usually border-crossing databases will flag fugitives unwise enough to use their true identities. The Interpol notice system can be linked with criminal history indexes which can also flag wanted persons when they are arrested. Interpol member countries can now subscribe to a worldwide lost and stolen database in which all reported lost and stolen passports are listed. Persons attempting to use those passports as false identification can be detained until identified.

Just as with the Horowitz case, different methods, factored together, can result in policing successes. If international informal policing is permitted to flourish, it can add yet another dimension to what is rapidly becoming a technology-driven worldwide dragnet. Whether ensnaring a terrorist or a criminal, or finding a missing person, the technological dragnet enhances law enforcement's ability to find who it is looking for—and sometimes find persons of interest who have not before raised suspicions. Informal networks of policing deliver the person-to-person, intangible benefits that technology will never replicate. Together they make up a potent counterterrorism tool.

The Beginning of the End

Through the real-world applications presented here, a clearer picture emerges of the versatility of U.S. law enforcement and its worldwide, collaborative networks. It is abundantly clear that U.S. federal law enforcement can deliver benefits that other counterterrorism instruments cannot. Yet, the powerful advantages of informal international policing have not been engaged to their fullest potential. The next chapter will advance the argument that a greater range of governmental counterterrorism instruments can be engaged without harming or diminishing any agency or element that has contributed to the war on terrorism thus far. If we are finally able to combine the particular talents of all our instruments, we might finally adopt the best course to contain and even defeat this worldwide scourge.

CHAPTER 6
Emergence of the Blue Planet

The U.S. government has access to a vast amount of information. When databases not usually thought of as "intelligence," such as customs or immigration information are included, the storehouse is immense.[438]

In earlier chapters, the author drew on professional experiences as a frame of reference for the observations of scholars and other practitioners. In that light, he can confirm the validity of the recent GAO report, *Combating Terrorism: Federal Law Enforcement Agencies Lack Directives to Assist Foreign Nations* (May 2007). As noted in the report, law enforcement and security officers in the field really do lack the implementing directives that would guide the exertion of counterterrorism leadership. What we do contribute, we achieve on our own, sometimes isolated, initiatives as law enforcement and security officers.[439] Leaders seeking to implement these directives should be cognizant that there is an inherent danger in over-managing law enforcement. As discussed at length in this work, law enforcement seeks to professionalize through autonomy. Government directives impose restrictions and constraints which may affect efficacy. Leaders, in an effort to secure their own positions (and agency turf), may not be able to resist the temptation to impose those restrictions upon law enforcement relationships in an effort to control information and power—much like what happens now with traditional-power agencies. In effect, attempting to control informal relationships serves to politicize the entire process, rendering it inoperable. Efforts to implement directives should encompass the autonomy that law enforcement needs to remain effective.

The *9/11 Report* pointedly asks the question: Who is the quarterback? The answer has always been, of course, the traditionally entrenched parochial interests of the most powerful counterterrorism agencies—those that saw us through the Cold War.

Earlier in the report we detailed many missed opportunities to thwart the 9/11 plot. Information was not shared, sometimes inadvertently or

---

[438] 9/11 Commission Report, 416-417.

[439] The U.S. State Department Coordinator for Counterterrorism, General Dell Daily, agrees with this point. Most of us in law enforcement do our best, but there is no uniformity of approach or training. If there is no personal willingness for an RSO or other special agent assigned overseas to coordinate with foreign police counterparts, there is nothing to compel that person to do so. Interview, 31 July 2008.

because of legal misunderstandings. Analysis was not pooled. Effective operations were not launched. Often handoffs of information were lost across the divide separating the foreign and domestic agencies of the government.

However the specific problems are labeled, we believe they are symptoms of the government's broader inability to adapt to how it manages the problems of the 21st century. The agencies are like a set of specialists in a hospital, each ordering tests, looking for symptoms and prescribing medications. What is missing is the attending physician who ensures they work as a team.

One missing element was effective management of transnational operations. Action officers should have drawn on *all available knowledge in the government*.[440] This management should have ensured that information was shared and duties were clearly assigned across agencies, and across the foreign-domestic divide.[441]

Critics as diverse as Amy Zegart, Michael Turner, and the 9/11 Commission point out that these heralded Cold War agencies, namely the FBI and the CIA, were slow to adapt to the post-Cold War universe—which led to a variety of intelligence failures and ultimately to 9/11. These critics maintain that those same conditions still exist today—primarily because entrenched agencies resist change and wish to retain their positions of power and prominence. The way in which we deal with terrorism information is a case in point. A clearly ineffective classification system for protecting terrorism information is routinely used—and inappropriately—to deal with a problem that, according to our own established guidelines, should not normally require such measures. It appears to be more than coincidental that this same classification system is acknowledged, again by our own guidelines, to be a source of abuse for agencies to retain control and maintain power. It is also not accidental that newly introduced reforms for the information-sharing environment present the appearance of facilitating the sharing of information but, in fact, may preserve the status quo.[442] It is not only information classification systems that reflect a misappropriation of counterterrorism resources; rather it is entire structures and infrastructures of agencies that were created for one purpose—to oppose the nation-state adversaries of the Cold War—which now face an enemy they are not structured to confront. The irony is that federal resources are in place and ideally suited to confront that very enemy.

---

[440] Italics inserted by the author.

[441] 9/11 Report, 353.

[442] And, by adding additional levels of sensitivity to unclassified designations, may actually enhance these agencys' ability to control information.

The 21st century has brought a new and fluid enemy in Islamist, net-worked terrorism. This enemy was driven to near oblivion in 2002, yet has regrouped and morphed into a new and more insidious entity in the Feder-ally Administered Tribal Areas in Pakistan. According to the *New York Times*, al-Qaeda's resurgence has been facilitated by "years of missteps in Washing-ton and Islamabad, as well as by sharp policy disagreements and turf battles among American counterterrorism agencies.[443]

How Can We Solve a Problem Like al-Qaeda? How Can We Catch a Cloud and Pin It Down?

The 2007 *National Intelligence Estimate: The Terrorist Threat to the U.S. Homeland*, expected the U.S. homeland to face a persistent and evolving ter-rorist threat and asserted that al-Qaeda will remain the most serious threat.[444] For good measure, and adding yet another threat to the mix, then-Homeland Security chief Michael Chertoff noted that "Hezbollah makes al-Qaeda look like a minor-league team."[445] Even as our current national security leaders talk up the ongoing threat of Islamist extremism, the academic world debates the "real" threat posed by Islamist, extremist-based terrorism. On one side of the academic debate are those who argue, like Bruce Hoffman, that al-Qaeda is "alive, well, resurgent, and more dangerous than it has been in several years."[446] On the other side is Mark Sageman, a scholar-in-residence with the NYPD, who maintains that the main threat no longer comes from a central-ized al-Qaeda, but from radicalized individuals who meet and plot in their neighborhoods and on the Internet. Sageman refers to them as "bunches of guys"—who have carried out locally-based terrorist attacks such as the train and subway attacks in Madrid in 2004 and in London in 2005. Hoffman sees al-Qaeda as still a very dangerous organization that is resilient and far from being defeated.[447]

For the forces of international policing, disagreement over al-Qaeda's capabilities is moot. If permitted to "take the gloves off," empowered transna-

---

[443] Mark Mazzetti and David Rohde, "Amid U.S. Policy Disputes, Qaeda Grows in Pakistan," New York Times, 30 June 2008. Available at http://www.nytimes.com/2008/06/30/washington/30tribal.html?pagewanted=1&_r=1&ref=todayspaper.

[444] Office of the Director of National Intelligence, National Intelligence Estimate: The Terror-ist Threat to the U.S. Homeland, Washington, DC, 17 July 2007. http://dni.gov/press_releases/20070717_release.pdf.

[445] Fox News, "Chertoff: Hezbollah Makes al-Qaeda Look Like a Minor-League Team," 29 May 2008. http://www.foxnews.com/story/0,2933,359594,00.html.

[446] Elaine Scolino and Eric Schmitt, "A Not Very Private Feud Over Terrorism," New York Times, 8 June 2008. http://www.nytimes.com/2008/06/08/weekinreview/08sciolino.html.

[447] Bruce Hoffman, Commentary: Al Qaeda Isn't Dead Yet," CNN.com, 9 September 2008. http://www.cnn.com/2008/POLITICS/09/09/hoffman.alqaeda/index.html#cnnSTCText.

tional law enforcement networks and dragnets will catch what they catch. If al-Qaeda is resurgent and morphing, the strengthened networks will catch a portion of that upsurge. If the organization is weakened and fading, the newly harnessed international policing networks could cripple them even further. If terrorism is structured from the top down, international policing networks will be targeting cell activity. If they are structured from the bottom up, police networks will again be targeting cell and operational activity. Whatever the state of al-Qaeda and/or Islamist terrorism, if the (informal) forces of international law enforcement are enabled and relatively unfettered, there will be more plots uncovered, more terrorists located and arrested, and more criminal support activity disrupted than now.

From the perspective of the author, those who maintain that groups such as al-Qaeda are on the wane, or have been nearly defeated, are not being constructive—especially when there is so little known about these adversaries.[448] The author has experienced the damage caused by prematurely asserting a diminished security threat in his time with the Bureau of Diplomatic Security. In 1987, as a result of the Inman Commission study, DSS was created to focus on State Department security. Car bomb attacks on the U.S. Embassy in Beirut in 1983 and 1984, and the attack on the Marine barracks in Beirut in 1983, exposed the Department's inattention to security.[449] My first seven years with the Department were salad days for the newly created DS. However, in the mid-1990s, as the State Department underwent serious funding cutbacks, DSS was one of the components of the Department that took the most serious hits. Wilson would likely attribute this, at least in part, to an organizational culture that does not see security as its main mission, therefore making it an expendable program. Because there had not been an attack on an embassy in nearly 10 years, cutbacks in security were seen as justifiable and necessary.[450] However, on 7 August 1998 two massive truck bombs exploded in Nairobi and Dar-es-Salaam killing over 200 and injuring thousands.[451] In April 1999, the then-president of the American Foreign Service Association,

---

[448] For another example see Peter Bergen, "Commentary: WMD Fears are Overblown," CNN.com. http://www.cnn.com/2008/POLITICS/12/05/bergen.wmd/index.html#cnnSTCText.

[449] Wilson, Bureaucracy, 91.

[450] Interview with Admiral Bobby Ray Inman, NewsHour with Jim Lehrer transcript: "Searching for Answers," PBS Online NewsHour, 10 August 1998. Please see http://www.pbs.org/newshour/bb/africa/july-dec98/bomb_8-10.html. See also Fred Burton, "The Boom and Bust Cycle in Counterterrorism Spending," Stratfor.com, 28 March 2007, available at http://www.stratfor.com/boom_and_bust_cycle_counterterrorism_spending.

[451] In Nairobi, 200 Kenyan citizens and 12 U.S. diplomats were killed, and over 4,000 Kenyans were injured. In Dar-es-Salaam, 11 Tanzanians were killed and 85 persons were injured, to include two Americans. See the Special Report, "African Embassy Bombings," PBS Online NewsHour, at http://www.pbs.org/newshour/bb/africa/embassy_bombing/map/html.

in a statement to the House Appropriations Subcommittee on Commerce, Justice, State, and the Judiciary, declared:

> Over the years, our leaders have focused on embassy security only after a tragedy. We saw it in the 1970s after Khartoum. We saw it in the 1980s after Beirut. We see it again today in the wake of Nairobi and Dar-es-Salaam. However, as the memory of each loss fades, attention wanes. Commitment declines. Funding is diverted until a new tragedy ensues. For some embassy security is an academic issue. For us, literally it is a matter of life and death.[452]

Extrapolate what happened at the State Department to what is happening now—equivocation about the threat of terrorism in the press and academia—and we have the first steps toward letting our guard down. This is not to say that overspending for homeland security and counterterrorism does not occur, or that a wise reallocation of resources is not called for.

The Criminal Commons

Because most terrorist acts involve supportive criminal activity, how can we change the current U.S. political and security landscape toward a more effective vision that gives fuller play to the security contribution of international law enforcement? We can now outline a low-cost, low-impact path to correct this anomaly.

According to a respected source, the attacks of late 2008 in Mumbai were supported by the notorious organized criminal syndicate of Dawood Ibrahim—which had joined forces with Lashkar-e-Taiba in pulling off the assault. This source asserts that the Ibrahim group sold blueprints for the city's hotels to the Lashkar terrorists.[453] According to other reporting, India is seeking the extradition of Ibrahim from Pakistan for his role in the attack.[454] Chapter Three documented extensively the convergence of terrorism, international crime and, ultimately, organized crime. If the Ibrahim group were involved, this adds further credence to such convergence and to the argument for full inclusion of international law enforcement resources in the fight.

---

[452] Daniel F. Geisler, "Statement of Mr. Daniel F. Geisler, President, American Foreign Service Association, to the House Appropriations Subcommittee on Commerce, Justice, State, and the Judiciary, 15 April 1999," available at http://www.afsa.org/congress/041599testimony.cfm. After 1998, spending for security remained relatively constant until 11 September 2001, when additional funding was made available.

[453] Mansoor Ijaz, "Zardari and Mumbai," Forbes.com, 6 December 2008. Available at http://www.forbes.com/2008/12/05/zardari-mumbai-laskar-oped-cx_mi_1206ijaz.html.

[454] Ayaz Gul, "Pakistan Offers to Help Investigate Mumbai Terror Attack," VOANews.com, 2 December 2008. Available at http://www.voanews.com/english.2008-12-02-voa31.cfm.

Another news report on Ibrahim claims he played a crucial role in the 1993 Bombay (Mumbai) serial bombings by engineering "the smuggling into India of tons of explosives provided by Pakistan's spy agency, the Directorate for Inter-Services Intelligence."[455] The 1993 Mumbai bombings featured a series of 15 bomb explosions which targeted the Bombay Stock Exchange, hotels, offices, and banks, killed 257, and injured 1,400.[456] Ibrahim has also been linked to the 2005 New Delhi bombings in which 60 were killed.[457] Ibrahim has also been associated with the Mumbai rail blasts of 2006 in which 209 persons were killed and over 300 were injured.[458] According to the BBC, Ibrahim is linked to both al-Qaeda and Lashkar-e-Taiba, and is involved in "large scale shipment of narcotics in the UK and western Europe."[459] Kaplan asserts that "crime syndicates and terrorist groups thrive in the same subterranean world as black markets and laundered money, relying on shifting networks and secret cells to accomplish their objectives. Both groups have similar needs: weapons, false documentation and safe houses."[460]

Meanwhile, on 25 September 2007, then-Director of National Intelligence Mike McConnell told the Senate Judiciary Committee that the greatest threat [to the U.S.] is from al-Qaeda; that it could be training operatives to move explosives into the U.S. by exploiting the United State's visa program.[461] In so doing, McConnell tacitly acknowledged the need to engage the worldwide resources of international law enforcement for our counterterrorism efforts. The terrorism advisor for President-elect Obama also weighed in with an assessment that U.S. policymakers have been inattentive: our counterterrorism setup "lacks a sheriff to lead the posse."[462]

---

[455] "A Godfather's Lethal Mix of Business and Politics," U.S. News and World Report, 11 November 2005. Available at http://www.usnews.com/usnews/news/articles/051205/5terror.b.htm.

[456] NationMaster, "1993 Mumbai Bombings," NationMaster.com, available at http://www.nationmaster.com/encyclopedia/1993-Mumbai-bombings.

[457] "A Godfather's Lethal Mix."

[458] Dow Jones, "Al-Qaeda Link to Mumbai Blasts," 11 July 2006. Available at http://www.news24.com/News/0,,2-10-1462_1966228,00.html. The Indian police were also said to have blamed the Pakistani Inter-Services Intelligence, operating in collaboration with Lashkar-e-Taiba. The 209 deaths statistic came from a CNN article—which is the source of the Indian police attribution: CNN, "India Police: Pakistan Spy Agency Behind Mumbai Bombings," CNN.com, 1 October 2006. Available at http://www.cnn.com/2006/WORLD/asiapcf/09/30/india.bombs/idex.html?section=cnn_world#.

[459] BBC, "Profile: India's Fugitive Gangster," BBC News, 12 September 2006. Available at http://www.bbc.co.uk/2/hi/south_asia/4775531.stm.

[460] David Kaplan, "Paying For Terror," U.S. News and World Report, 5 December 2005.

[461] CNN, "Terrorists Could Exploit Visa Program, Intelligence Chief Warns," CNN.com, 25 September 2007. Available at http://www.cnn.com/2007/US/09/25/dni.alqaeda.threat/index.html.

[462] Mark Mazzetti, "Behind Analyst's Cool Demeanor, Deep Anxiety Over American Policy," New York Times, 26 December 2008. Available at http://www.nytimes.com/2008/12/27/washington/27reidel.html?_r=1&ref=todayspaper.

Who's Driving This Bus?

According to the *9/11 Report*, "national intelligence is still organized around the collection disciplines of the home agencies, not the joint mission. The importance of all-source analysis cannot be overstated. Without it, it is not possible to 'connect the dots.' No one component holds all the relevant information."[463] Also, according to the *9/11 Report*, by engaging the world-wide resources of international law enforcement, we not only improve our "whole earth" intelligence capability, but we vastly improve and increase our chances of "getting lucky" or, more accurately, of finding the key lead that prevents a terrorist attack on U.S. soil, or the soil of our allies in the war on terror. Unfortunately, according to the Government Accountability Office:

> almost 6 years after the 9/11 attacks, the United States lacks clear implementing guidance for integrating the variety of overseas LEA activities to help foreign nations to identify, disrupt, and prosecute terrorists. We found that, because most LEAs have not been provided clear directives, they generally lacked (1) clearly articulated roles and responsibilities to assist foreign nations; (2) guidance on setting funding priorities and providing resources; (3) performance monitoring systems to assess LEA progress; (4) formal structures to coordinate LEA operational and technical assistance to foreign nation LEAs; and (5) comprehensive country needs assessments to tailor LEA technical and operational assistance to specific foreign nation needs.[464]

According to the latest all-star panel on national security reform, "When knowledge is compartmentalized—as in the infamous 'unconnected dots' preceding the 9/11 terrorist attacks—it is difficult for the national security system to adjust its behaviors appropriately in order to meet system goals."[465]

Time for a change?

How can we get more out of the system?[466]

The new U.S. President, elected to effect change, has at his disposal a "sleeping giant" counterterrorism instrument in the underutilized networks of U.S. federal law enforcement. This instrument can:

---

[463] 9/11 Report, 425.

[464] GAO, "Combatting Terrorism: Law Enforcement Lacks Directives," 3.

[465] James A. Locher III, et. al., Project on National Security Reform: Forging a New Shield (Arlington, VA: Project on National Security Reform), November 2008, 200.

[466] Frances Fragos Townsend, former National Security Advisor to the President for Counterterrorism and Homeland Security, interview in Washington, DC, 7 June 2007.

1. Open an untapped reserve of overt terrorism intelligence and information—a "whole earth" intelligence resource based on the reach and scope of international law enforcement.

2. Create new international pathways of exchanging and sharing not only overt terrorism intelligence but also intelligence on other types of transnational criminal activity that can also affect our national security.

3. Create an innovative means of engaging super-efficient international, inter-governmental networks.

4. Create a pathway for a national security entity that can step beyond politicization and can "naturally" professionalize itself and increase stability in weaker states.

5. Create *another* constructive pathway for exerting "soft power" through law enforcement's international, intergovernmental networks.

6. Create a means to work around the crushing parochialism and bureaucratic constraints that hinder our counterterrorism efforts and our standing as a leader in promoting the "rule of law."

Harnessing law enforcement networks can open up an untapped reserve of overt terrorism intelligence and information—a "whole earth" intelligence resource based on the reach and scope of international law enforcement.

As discussed in Chapter Five, law enforcement's domain stretches from the richest levels of a society or country to the poorest levels; in fact, law enforcement is an ever-present participant in the comings and goings of life. Further, international law enforcement channels can be tapped informally, whether for normal investigative activity, collecting information on terrorist trends, or for patterns of behavior that indicate the presence of terrorist cells. This power is available to savvy leadership, which can harness its potential without destroying it through formalization, regulation, or over-bureaucratization. A "whole earth," overt intelligence resource is waiting to be finally engaged.

Harnessing law enforcement networks can create new international pathways of exchanging and sharing not only through overt terrorism intelligence but also intelligence on other types of transnational criminal activity that can also affect our national security.

As part of a "whole earth," overt intelligence capability, law enforcement networks can create pathways to enhance cooperation on organized crime, identity theft, credit card fraud, 419 fraud scams, and counterfeiting at U.S. and world levels—activities that affect the well-being and ultimately the survival of U.S. citizens. With this capability in play, U.S. intelligence agencies themselves, whether for criminal investigative or national security purposes, can monitor patterns of international criminal activities for potential threats to the United States, including the trafficking of nuclear materials or large shipments of illegal weaponry.

While present U.S.-based investigative methods might provide some insight as to the type of crimes that support terrorism overseas and possibly cells within the United States—terrorism information generated under the auspices of criminal investigations is a matter of "getting lucky"—that is, if an activity is noticed by law enforcement to the degree that it generates a criminal investigation, then it can lead to the "uncovering" of terrorist-related activity. However, much suspicious behavior does not meet courtroom standards of generating a criminal case. Local police, and sometimes federal agencies, have a public safety and national security mission/mandate that is not necessarily reliant on courtroom standards of criminal investigation. Just as a beat cop might take note of a new face in the neighborhood as a potential source of trouble, there are activities that can, and should, generate inquiries that are not necessarily criminally investigative in nature, but may engender suspicion of U.S. law enforcement—particularly overseas. Many types of activities are not necessarily criminal in other countries that are crimes in the United States—document fraud, weapons trading, and money laundering, to name but a few (and all can be used to support terrorism)—and a hard sell to present to U.S. attorneys to prosecute in U.S. federal courts. Furthermore, if U.S. law enforcement lacks leadership directives to pursue acquiring information on this type of activity that probably does not meet investigative or prosecutorial standard, then critical information (*overt* intelligence) can be lost. If U.S. law enforcement has been cut out of the counterterrorism equation overseas—as had been asserted by former Vice President Cheney, then U.S. strategic policy has disregarded an important source of terrorism information/intelligence.

Poster Urging the American Public to Help Stop the Financing of Terrorist Actions.
Source: State Department, with permission.

Without better international police cooperation, overseas criminal activity that supports terrorism—that can directly impact the United States (or our allies)—often remains hidden from us. If not for the wherewithal of the Regional

Security Officer in Surabaya, Indonesia, Operation Triple X would not have transpired—he had no directive to concentrate on document fraud; his pursuit of the case was based solely on his own determination to do so—another person assigned to Surabaya would likely not have pursued such an endeavor, particularly if he/she had limited criminal investigative experience. DS, like other U.S. federal agencies, receives no direction, and therefore no funding, from strategic policymakers to concentrate on *overseas* activities that could lead to the generation of terrorism information (or criminal cases) from overseas police contacts that could be of value in the big picture of intelligence analysis.[467] Law enforcement does gather information for public safety or for generation of criminal cases—an activity possibly misnamed by the relatively new term of "intelligence-led policing."[468] This is true overseas, and information is legally accessible through our numerous law enforcement attaches posted overseas. U.S. law enforcement personnel assigned overseas routinely report to their headquarters on information relevant to their investigative authorities and mandates, and there does not need to be a prohibition on acquiring and reporting potentially valuable information to law enforcement (or ultimately intelligence consumers) on overt, legally acquired, basic criminal information. Hybrid law enforcement/intelligence elements, like the National Counterterrorism Center (NCTC), can be the ultimate analysis element for information acquired in this way (as it was established to do). Underemployed coordinating elements like the State Department's Office of Counterterrorism (S/CT), in conjunction with the National Security Council, can be the ultimate arbiter of just how this information is handled.

Law enforcement networks, particularly informal ones, can create an innovative means of engaging super-efficient international, intergovernmental networks.

Princeton's Anne-Marie Slaughter[469] describes intergovernmental networks as being fast, flexible, and economical. Informal law enforcement

---

[467] Diplomatic Security does, however, manage a successful program to gather information pertaining to U.S. travel documents to attempt and identify terrorist activity—but this does not generally entail the continuing or immediate engagement of the extensive informal police networks available to Regional Security Officers overseas. The establishment of a Visa and Passport Security Program within the Department of State's Bureau of Diplomatic Security is designed to safeguard the integrity of U.S. travel documents. The program is required to target and disrupt terrorist travel and includes the following four components: Analysis of Methods, Identification of Individuals and Documents, Identification of Foreign Countries Needing Assistance, and Inspection of Applications. For more information on this program, please see http://www.state.gov/m/ds/rls/rpt/c.s0978.htm.

[468] Law enforcement has practiced this art since long before it was named intelligence-led policing.

[469] Anne-Marie Slaughter is now Director of Policy and Planning for the U.S. Department of State.

networks might be the ultimate example of that argument. The cases explored in Chapter Five demonstrated just how fast, effective, and economical informal law enforcement networks can be. The difference between law enforcement networks and other types of intergovernmental networks is that law enforcement authorities enjoy the operational flexibility that other intergovernmental entities lack. So too, law enforcement authorities can apply best practices without engaging bureaucratic processes that require endless levels of approvals and justifications.[470]

Law enforcement networks create a pathway for a national security entity in any country that can step beyond politicization and can "naturally" professionalize itself and increase stability in weaker states.

According to Mathieu Deflem, whose work contributed to the present study, law enforcement gravitates toward professionalism and efficiency. Promoting efficient law enforcement networks (informal ones being the most efficient) creates a cycle of autonomy that further promotes the quest for professionalism and efficiency. As explained in Chapters Three and Five, because they empower police by improving efficiency and encouraging autonomy from political centers, international police networks can also bureaucratically empower weaker states by engaging them in productive, efficient relationships. Because it is often in the best interests of weak(er) states to tolerate intergovernmental networks, it is also in their best interests to tolerate autonomy among their police force—in the present study, we have found that an autonomous police force is the midwife to meaningful intergovernmental security arrangements.

By preferentially employing military and intelligence agencies in counterterrorism efforts, the United States has inadvertently limited its capacity to make itself more flexible and efficient—because these agencies do not seek autonomy from the central government; rather, they *are* an integral *part of* the central government. Their resistance to change will be challenged by reintroducing law enforcement into national security information gathering and exploitation.

---

[470] Apparently, even the formalistic FBI has recognized the need for its agents to have more autonomy. See Carrie Johnson, "Rule Changes Would Give FBI Agents Extensive New Powers," Washington Post, 12 September 2008, A02. http://www.washingtonpost.com/wp/content/article/2008/09/11/AR200891103306_pf.html; also see Eric Lichtblau, "Terror Plan Would Give F.B.I. More Power," New York Times, 13 September 2008. http://www.nytimes.com/2008/09/13/justice.html?ref=us.

Engaging law enforcement networks can create a constructive pathway for exerting "soft power" through law enforcement's international, intergovernmental networks.

Commenting on his national security team, President-elect Obama declared that "They share my pragmatism about the use of power, and my sense of purpose about America's role as a leader in the world… Now more than ever, we have a stake in what happens across the globe."[471] This approach suggests his intention to apply the principles of soft power that had been important throughout the Cold War.

International legal scholar Kal Raustiala, in a much-referenced work, asserts that in international, intergovernmental networks "common interests predominate" and it is soft power rather than hard power that is at play—that in these network relationships it is persuasion and attraction rather than coercion and compulsion that prevail.[472] The author finds that, in his experience, this has been the case with the informal networks of international law enforcement.

Engaging international law enforcement networks can create a means to work around the crushing parochialism and bureaucratic constraints that hinder our counterterrorism efforts and our standing as a leader in promoting the "rule of law."

Reengaging U.S. law enforcement assets in relation to national security sends a message to allies who have taken issue with a policy dominated by the military/intelligence apparatus: that the United States has resumed a path which respects the "rule of law." An expert advisory panel has concluded that, "The basic deficiency of the current national security system is that parochial departmental and agency interests, reinforced by Congress, paralyze inter-agency cooperation even as the variety, speed and complexity of emerging security issues prevents the White House from effectively controlling the system … after more than seven years, the U.S. government has proved unable to integrate adequately the military and nonmilitary dimensions of the complex war on terror."[473]

---

[471] David E. Sanger, "Obama's Advisers to Back Soft Power," International Herald Tribune, 1 December 2008. http://www.iht.com/articles/2008/12/01/america/obama.php#top.

[472] Raustalia, "The Architecture of International Cooperation," 24.

[473] Walter Pincus, "Experts' Report Urges Changes in National Security System," Washington Post, 4 December 2008, A06. Available at http://www.washingtonpost.com/wp-dyn/content/article/2008/12/03/AR2008120303382.html.

Engaging the devices of international law enforcement as a source of overt criminal and terrorism intelligence will be a prudent means of integrating an element that had been conspicuously absent. A means will be needed to deconflict overlapping efforts as they are identified, but creating what amounts to a new, overt intelligence source presents an obligation for intelligence agencies to analyze the data. As they do so, a further measure of integration will take place. So too, national security policymakers will have another asset at their disposal, even as that asset naturally seeks distance from political processes, manipulation, and bias.

The Final Frontier: A New and Blue World

This work has addressed the question: **How can the United States engage international partners more effectively to address the worldwide manifestations of destabilizing violence, which is often indiscriminately labeled "terrorism"?**

Answer: By bringing to bear the full potential of U.S. federal law enforcement's international policing networks—particularly its demonstrably effective, informal international law enforcement networks. Through invoking a *war on terrorism*, U.S. leadership precluded the international (foreign) participation of non-FBI, U.S. federal law enforcement capabilities. Because U.S. law enforcement agencies are recognized as leaders in international policing efforts and are represented the world over, coordination can be widespread. International law enforcement enjoys a professionally cooperative culture, an identifiable target in the criminal commons of terrorism, strength in numbers, and access to all levels of societies the world over.

In view of this principal question, can we overcome the entrenched parochial interests of the most powerful agencies (law enforcement, intelligence, and military) to bring greater coordination to the task of combating this violence and thus to bring to bear the benefits and advantages of individual agencies and local police departments?

Answer: Yes, through the will of political leadership of the United States, and by creating a "dual track" approach that will accommodate the particular talents of all counterterrorism instruments—without disrupting processes, relationships, and methods that are already in place and that have been successful in keeping us free from an attack on U.S. soil since 2001.

An effective national security strategy will recognize that in a free society there will always be a dichotomy between law enforcement and intelligence that manifests as the difference between legal and extralegal. For this reason, there will always be a perceived "wall" between law enforcement and intelligence. Full integration of intelligence and law enforcement not only implies a police state; it is the very manifestation of a police state. But this does not mean "the wall" cannot be porous.

We can assert that the vast majority of terrorism information has nothing to do with national security and should not be classified. A new and distinct "law enforcement track" would provide a means for overt, international criminal and terrorism information developed through the vast networks of formal and informal law enforcement to be collected, transmitted, analyzed, and ultimately shared through unclassified, but controlled, channels. Reporting procedures would follow procedures for the transmission of unclassified, law enforcement sensitive information that are already in place. Information that contains personal data can be sanitized or approved so that it can be shared. As a result of the USA PATRIOT Act, there now exist elements and procedures through which this information can be evaluated and shared. Ultimately, however, if this track is implemented, as we have seen, the parochial interests of the most powerful, "premier" agencies will be served because they have lead investigative or lead response authorities on any information generated by this track.

An "intelligence track" would continue to employ classified procedures for processing information. No current methods or operations would be disrupted, and all "secret" information will stay secret.

As it stands, then, the only way to activate an effective dual-track mechanism is through the will of the present administration—with directives, funding streams, missions, and mandates for the law enforcement track clearly articulated and supported. Only then can a pristine law enforcement track develop and flourish to support the overall intelligence and law enforcement missions.

Another Question: What Will This Cost Us?

Answer: Potentially very little. The means and tools already exist to engage U.S.-based international law enforcement networks at almost no further cost. U.S. federal law enforcement is already represented at embassies around the world. Most of these agencies maintain host-country law enforcement contacts for the investigative mission, and can expand that mission to include a counterterrorism component. That expansion might require overtime pay for a 50-hour work week. Various means of transmitting information securely from overseas already exist and can easily accommodate whatever information might be forthcoming—if they are properly funded and provided with the power and authority to do what they were set up to do. The National Counterterrorism Center (NCTC) was created to evaluate and interpret such information.[474] Furthermore, other agencies with counterterrorism authorities and mandates have analysis assets in place. It is possible that, if this initiative generates a great deal of terrorism information, the national security interests of the United States will be the beneficiary and more analysts will be hired. It is also conceivable that additional Special Agents would need to be hired to provide coverage in areas that are notably deficient in representation, most notably the Caribbean region. It is a certainty that additional funding for training U.S. law enforcement attaches overseas must be in place to provide a uniformity of effort and a comprehensive means of coordinating and sharing information with foreign counterparts. Most agencies already have annual training conferences for their overseas attaches, and most necessary training could be integrated at reasonable cost into that curriculum.

According to the Government Accountability Office, "Below the Executive Office of the President, the State Department is the lead federal agency for U.S. government activities to combat terrorism overseas." The Coordinator for Counterterrorism—an ambassador-rank position—heads the State Department's efforts to combat terrorism.[475] This is one asset that would certainly require additional funding, as it holds the authority for information coordination and deconfliction efforts, but cannot adequately do so because it is grossly underfunded.[476]

In particular, how can U.S. law enforcement effectively harness the power of international, informal police networks without destroying them by adopting formalized procedures?

Answer: By leaving law enforcement elements alone to do what they do best, just as they are doing now under their own mandates and investigative authorities. Trust them to evaluate what they find out and to report what is relevant. Provide training and instruction to law enforcement attaches, before they travel overseas, on how to acquire terrorism information in an

---

[474] Unfortunately, the National Counterterrorism Center is widely regarded as not having fulfilled its potential and mandate—as a result of the parochialism of Intelligence Community agencies. According to the Project on National Security Reform report, published in December 2008, "Existing national structures like interagency committees or even recent specialized and high-priority institutions like the NCTC cannot overcome the basic rigid structure of the national security system, which favors the independence of the functional departments and agencies at the expense of integrating mechanisms." Guiding Coalition of the Project on National Security Reform, Project on National Security Reform: Forging a New Shield (Center for the Study of the Presidency, November 2008), 239.

[475] GAO, "Interagency Framework for Combating Terrorism."

[476] GAO, Combating Terrorism, "Law Enforcement Lacks," 35, declares: "A 2006 report from State's Office of Inspector General found that State lacked adequate resources to meet its mandate to coordinate all U.S. counterterrorism assistance abroad, and was too underfunded to provide advice, coordination, and action on counterterrorism issues to its embassies."

open and forthright manner—just as they would acquire information under their present authorities and agency mandates. Then turn them loose.

The Blue Planet: Value-Added or Zero-Sum

While these measures might sound deceptively simple to implement and make unequivocal common sense, making these practices a reality will require careful and dedicated marshalling by deft and knowledgeable hands at the National Security Council level. Appeals that proclaim "don't fix what isn't broken" (a claim cashiered by the argument in the present work) and promote obfuscation will create tremendous pressures to "stay the course" on the path of current military/intelligence exclusivity. Likewise, rationalizations that current counterterrorism efforts work well, even though hidden to the public by secrecy, or that law enforcement efforts will disrupt active, international intelligence relationships and operations, fail to take into consideration that deconfliction is to be carried out by the NCTC and the State Department's Office of the Coordinator for Counterterrorism. These counter-arguments also fail to take into consideration the vast scope and scale of international law enforcement networks and the unique value that full inclusion of these assets will bring.

National Security Council oversight, direction, and leadership of this initiative will send a positive message to law enforcement agencies that their contributions are valued—and will encourage enthusiastic participation. National Security strategists—or individuals at the State Department's Office of the Coordinator for Counterterrorism—could provide guidance to the field to target specific groups or specific areas of interest, all the way down to the neighborhood level. These efforts could deconflict initiatives with the "clandestine" side of the effort. Nonetheless, it will take time to reorient our international police networks toward counterterrorism—building reliable pathways and new relationships does not happen overnight.

By carefully incorporating the contributions of U.S. law enforcement (and consequently worldwide law enforcement) into a comprehensive national security counterterrorism strategy, the National Security Council can build a formidable "new" counterterrorism instrument. As this approach is adopted, we will no longer need to confront the manifest threat to U.S. citizens here and abroad with only a part of our information arsenal.

BIBLIOGRAPHY

"African Embassy Bombings." PBS *Online NewsHour*. Last accessed 27 June 2009, *http://www.pbs.org/newshour/bb/africa/embassy_bombing/map/html*.

"A Godfather's Lethal Mix of Business and Politics." *U.S. News and World Report*, 11 November 2005. *http://www.usnews.com/usnews/news/articles/051205/5terror.b.htm*.

Albright, David, and Corey Hinderson. "Unraveling the A.Q. Khan and Future Proliferation Networks." *The Washington Quarterly* 28, no. 2 (Spring 2005), 112.

Alexander, Yonah, ed. *Combating Terrorism: Strategies of Ten Countries*. Ann Arbor: University of Michigan Press, 2002.

Al-Zawahiri, Ayman. "*Realities of the Conflict Between Islam and Unbelief*." Last accessed 27 June 2009, *http://www.lauramansfield.com/j/_12206.asp*.

Amnesty International. "Chuckie Taylor Convicted of Torture." 31 October 2008. *http://www.amnestyusa.org/doctument.php?id=ENGNAU200810317933&lang=e*.

Anderson, Curt. "Activists Want Charles Taylor's Son Tried for War Crimes, Torture." *Associated Press*, 6 August 2006. *http://www.prosecutions.org/news/archives/002607.html*.

Anderson, Malcolm. *Policing the World: Interpol and the Politics of International Police Co-operation*. Oxford, UK: Clarendon Press, 1989.

Andreas, Peter, and Ethan Nadelmann. *Policing the Globe*. London: Oxford University Press, 2006.

Arquilla, John, and David Ronfeldt. *Networks and NetWars: The Future of Terror, Crime, and Militancy*. Washington, DC: RAND Corporation, 2001.

Arquilla, John. "It Takes a Network." *Los Angeles Times*, 25 August 2002.

Associated Press. "Al Qaeda Deploys Cell Phone Video Downloads." 6 January 2008. *http://www,msnbc.msn.com/id/22526746/*.

BIBLIOGRAPHY (Continued)

Balzer, Anthony J. "International Police Cooperation: Opportunities and Obstacles." In *Policing in Central Asia and Eastern Europe: Comparing Firsthand Knowledge with Experience from the West.* Slovenia: College of Police and Security Studies, 1995. *http://www.ncjrs.gov/policing/int63.htm.*

Balzer, Anthony J. "International Police Cooperation: Opportunities and Obstacles." In *Policing in Central Asia and Eastern Europe: Comparing Firsthand Knowledge with Experience from the West.* Last accessed 27 June 2009, Slovenia: College of Police and Security Studies, 1996. *http://www.ncjrs.gov/policing/int63.htm.*

Baram, Marcus. "Start Snitching: Inside the Witness Protection Program." *ABC News,* 26 October 2007. *http://abcnews.go.com/TheLaw/Story?id=3781361&page=1.*

Bayer, Mike. "Commentary," in *Improving the Law Enforcement-Intelligence Community Relationship: Can't We All Just Get Along?* June 2007, viii. *http://www.ndic.edu/press/5463.htm.*

Bayer, Michael. "Operation Global Pursuit: In Pursuit of the World's Most Dangerous Fugitives and Terrorists," *Police Chief Magazine,* 72, no. 8 (August 2008), 35-37.

BBC. "Profile: India's Fugitive Gangster." BBC News, 12 September 2006. *http://www.bbc.co.uk/2/hi/south_asia/4775531.stm.*

Best Jr., Richard A. *Intelligence and Law Enforcement: Countering Transnational Threats to the U.S.,* CRS Report for Congress RL30252 (Washington, DC: The Library of Congress, 16 January 2001.

Bergen, Peter. "Commentary: WMD Fears are Overblown," *CNN.com,* 5 December 2008, *http://www.cnn.com/2008/POLITICS/12/05/bergen.wmd/index.html#cnnSTCText.*

Bergen, Peter L. *Holy War, Inc.: Inside the Secret World of Osama bin Laden.* New York: The Free Press, 2001.

Berkely, Bill. "Code of Betrayal, Not Silence, Shines Light on Russian Mob." *New York Times,* 19 August 2002.

Berkowitz, Bruce. *The New Face of War: How War Will Be Fought in the 21st Century.* New York: The Free Press, 2003.

BIBLIOGRAPHY (Continued)

Block, Ludo. "Terrorism-OC Links: A Contemporary Issue?" *ECPR Standing Group On Organised Crime Newsletter*, Volume 5, Issue 2, May 2006.

Boukars, Anour. "The Challenge of Radical Islam in Mauritania." In *Unmasking Terror: A Global Review of Terrorist Activities*, Volume III (Washington, DC: The Jamestown Foundation, 2007), 243-247.

Bowden, Mark. *Killing Pablo: The Hunt for the World's Greatest Outlaw.* New York: Atlantic Monthly Press, 2001.

Brisco, Darren. "The New Face of Witness Protection." *Newsweek*, 2 May 2005. *http://www.newsweek.com/id/51906.*

Burton, Fred. "The Boom and Bust Cycle in Counterterrorism Spending." *Stratfor*, 28 March 2007. *http://www.stratfor.com/ boom_and_bust_cycle_counterterrorism_spending.*

Carter, Ashton, John Deutch, and Phillip Zelikow. "Catastrophic Terrorism: Tackling the New Danger." *Foreign Affairs* (November/December 1998), 82.

CBC News. "Canadian Gets 6 Years in Scam that Netted Millions and a Yacht." 28 August 2007. *http://www.cbc.ca/world/story/2007/08/28/ offshore.scam.html.*

CBS News. "Trucker: I'm no Hero." 25 October 2002. *http://www.cbsnews. com/stories/2002/10/25/earlyshow/main526939.shtml.*

Clarke, Richard A. "Plans of Attack." *Washington Post*, 7 December 2008, B01.

Clay, Nolan. "Lawman who caught Timothy McVeigh speaks of arrest." *The Oklahoman*, 29 August 2008. *http://newsok.com/article/3290630/.*

CNN. "France Postpones Extradition of U.S. Fugitive." *CNN.com*, 12 July 2001.*http://archives.cnn.com/2001/WORLD/europe/07/12/einhorn. france/index.html*

CNN. "India Police: Pakistan Spy Agency Behind Mumbai Bombings." *CNN.com*, 1 October 2006. *http://www.cnn.com/2006/WORLD/ asiapcf/09/30/india.bombs/idex.html?section=cnn_world#.*

CNN. "Terrorists Could Exploit Visa Program, Intelligence Chief Warns." *CNN.com*, 25 September 2007. *http://www.cnn.com/2007/ US/09/25/dni.alqaeda.threat/index.html.*

BIBLIOGRAPHY (Continued)

Coll, Steve. *The Taliban-Pakistan Alliance. http://www.pbs.org/wgbh/pages/ frontline/taliban/interviews/coll.html*, posted 3 October 2006.

Conetta, Carl. "A Prisoner to Primacy." Project on Defense Alternatives, Briefing Memo #43, 5 February 2008.

Connors, Timothy. "Putting the 'L' into Intelligence-Led Policing: How Police Leaders Can Leverage Intelligence Capability," *International Journal of Intelligence and CounterIntelligence* 22, no. 2 (Summer 2009), 237-245.

Cordesman, Anthony. "The Lessons of International Cooperation in Counterterrorism." Address to the RUSI Conference on Transnational Terrorism, A Global Approach, 18 January 2006.

Culver, Jeffrey W. "Stronger Partners: Program Celebrates 25 Years of Fighting Terrorism." *State Magazine*, December 2008, 14.

Daily, Dell (General). U.S. State Department Coordinator for Counterterrorism. Interview by author, 31 July 2008.

den Boer, Monica. "Law Enforcement Cooperation and Transnational Organized Crime in Europe." In *Transnational Organized Crime & International* Security, edited by Mats Berdal and Monica Serrano. Boulder, CO: Lynne Rienner, 2002.

Deflem, Mathieu. "Bureaucratization and Social Control: Historical Foundations of International Police Cooperation." *Law and Society Review* 34, no. 3 (2000), 616. *http://www.cas.sc.edu/socy/faculty/ deflem/zinsoco.htm*.

Deflem, Mathieu, "Europol and the Policing of International Terrorism: Counter-Terrorism in a Global Perspective." *Justice Quarterly*, (New York: Routledge, 2006), vol. 23, no. 3, 338-339.

Deflem, Mathieu. "Global Rule of Law or Global Rule of Law Enforcement? International Police Cooperation and Counter-Terrorism." *The Annals of the American Academy of Political and Social Science*, vol. 603, 240-252.

Deflem, Mathieu. "International Policing." *The Encyclopedia of Police Science*, Third Edition, Jack R. Greene, ed., New York: Routledge, 701-705, 2007.

BIBLIOGRAPHY (Continued)

Deflem, Mathieu. "Police and Counter-Terrorism: A Sociological Theory of International Cooperation." Paper presented at Bilkent University, Ankara, Turkey, 6-8 December 2007, 13, forthcoming as a chapter in a volume on intelligence sharing.

Deflem, Mathieu. *Policing World Society: Historical Foundations of International Police Cooperation.* New York: Oxford University Press, Inc., 2002.

Dershowitz, Alan M. *Why Terrorism Works: Understanding the Threat, Responding to the Challenge.* New Haven, CT: Yale University Press, 2002.

DeYoung, Karen, and Joby Warrick. "Pakistan and U.S. Have Tacit Deal on Airstrikes." *Washington Post*, 16 November 2008, A01.

Douglass R. Burgess, Jr. "Piracy is Terrorism." *International Herald Tribune*, 6-7 December 2008.

Dow Jones. "Al-Qaeda Link to Mumbai Blasts." 11 July 2006. *http://www. news24.com/News/0,,2-10-1462_1966228,00.html.*

Dwyer, Johnny. "The All-American Warlord." *The Observer*, 23 November 2008. *http://www.guardian.co.uk/world/2008/nov/23/liberia-war-crimes-chucky-taylor.*

Eggen, Dan. "Justice Dept. Database Stirs Privacy Fears." *Washington Post*, 26 December 2006.

Ericson, Timothy L. "Building Our Own 'Iron Curtain': The Emergence of Secrecy in American Government." *American Archivist* 68 (Spring/ Summer 2005), 18-52. *http://www.archivists.org/governance/ presidential/ericson.asp.*

Falconer, Bruce. "Victor Bout's Last Deal: How an Elite DEA Unit Brought Down the World's Most Notorious Arms Dealer." *Mother Jones*, 18 March 2008. *http://www.motherjones.com/news/feature/2008/03/ viktor-bout.html.*

"FBI Arrests Former Granada Bank President." *Caribbean Net News*, 2 June 2004. *http://www.caribbeannetnews.com/2004/06/02brink.htm.*

BIBLIOGRAPHY (Continued)

Federal Bureau of Investigation. *http://www.fbi.gov/congress01/ansir040301. html*.

Federal Bureau of Investigation. *FBI Strategic Plan 2004-2009.* Washington, DC: FBI, 2004. *http://www.fbi.gov/publications/strategicplan/ strategicplantext.htm.*

Federal Bureau of Investigation. National Security Branch. *http://www.fbi. gov/hq/nsb/nsb_integrating.htm.*

Federal Bureau of Investigation. *Integrating Intelligence and Operations. http://www.fbi.gov/hq/nsb/nsb_integrating.html.*

Fine, Glen A. Office of the Inspector General (OIG). *A Review of the FBI's Performance in Deterring, Detecting, and Investigating the Espionage Activities of Robert Philip Hanssen,* 14 August 2003. *http://www.fas. org/irp/agency/doj/oig/hanssen.html.*

Flournoy, Michele, and Shawn Brimley. "U.S. Strategy and Capabilities for Winning the Long War." In *Five Years after 9/11: An Assessment of America's War on Terror,* edited by Julianne Smith and Thomas Sanderson, 43-49, Washington, DC: The CSIS Press, 2006.

Foreign Affairs Handbook. Surveillance Detection Program (SDP) Training, 12 FAH-7, H-351, Introduction.

Foreign Affairs Manual, 12 FAM 540, SENSITIVE BUT UNCLASSIFIED INFORMATION (SBU), 12FAM 541 Scope.

Foreign Affairs Manual, 12 FAM 516 STANDARDS, 12 FAM 516.1.

Fox News. "Chertoff: Hezbollah Makes al-Qaeda Look Like a Minor-League Team." 29 May 2008. *http://www.foxnews.com/story/0,2933,359594,00. html.*

Frazier, Joseph B. "2 Plead Guilty in Grenada Bank Scam." *FOXNews.com,* 28 March 2007.

Freund, Gloria. "Unmasking Networks: Drug Enforcement Administration Tradecraft for the Intelligence Community." In *Improving the Law Enforcement-Intelligence Community Relationship: Can't We All Just Get Along?* edited by Timothy Christenson. Washington, DC: NDIC Press, 2007. *http://www.ndic.edu/press/5463.htm.*

BIBLIOGRAPHY (Continued)

Frieden, Terry. CNN, *http://www.cnn.com/2008/POLITICS/04/01/fbi. counterterrorism/index.html*. 1 April 2008.

Gehl, A.R. (Rod). "Multiagency Teams: A Leadership Challenge." *Police Chief* 71, no. 10 (October 2004), 142. *http://www.policechiemagazine org/magazine/index.cfm?fuseaction+display_arch&article_id+ 1395&issue_id+102004.*

Geisler, Daniel F. "Statement of Mr. Daniel F. Geisler, President, American Foreign Service Association, to the House Appropriations Subcommittee on Commerce, Justice, State, and the Judiciary," 15 April 1999. *http://www.afsa.org/congress/041599testimony.cfm*. Last accessed 27 June 2009.

Glazer, Jamie. "Symposium: The Death of a Traitor." *Front Page Magazine. com*, 29 February 2008. *http://frontpagemagazine.com/Articles/ Read.asp.aspx.*

Godson, Roy, et. al., eds. *U.S. Intelligence at a Crossroads*. Washington, DC: Brassey's, 1995.

Gompert, David C., and John Gordon IV. *War by Other Means: Complete and Balanced Capabilities for Counterinsurgency*. Washington, DC: RAND Corporation, 2008. *http://www.rand.org/pubs/monographs/ MG595.2/.*

Goodman, Melvin A. *Failure of Intelligence: The Decline and Fall of the CIA*. Lanham, MD: Rowman and Littlefield, 2008.

Griffin, Richard J. "Operation Triple X: Hitting Hard at Illegal Document Trade." *The Police Chief* 74, no. 10, October 2007. *http://www.policechiefmagazine.org/magazine/index. cfm?fuseaction=display_arch&article_id=1295&issue_id=102007.*

Gul, Ayaz. "Pakistan Offers to Help Investigate Mumbai Terror Attack." *VOANews.com*, 2 December 2008. *http://www.voanews.com/ english.2008-12-02-voa31.cfm.*

Gunaratna, Rohan. *Inside Al Qaeda: Global Network of Terror*. New York: Columbia University Press, 2002.

Hamilton, Hon. Lee H. "Government Secrecy after the Cold War." *Congressional Record*, E912 (1 April 1992). *http://fas.org/irp/ congress/1992_cr/h920401-spy.html.*

BIBLIOGRAPHY (Continued)

Harkeader, Erik. "Murder Suspect in Court." *The Sentinel*, 1 December 2005. *http://www.cumberlink.com/articles/2005/12/01/news/news01.txt*

Hayden, Michael V., Director, Central Intelligence Agency. "Statement for the Record to the Senate Select Committee on Intelligence." 11 January 2007. *https://www.cia.gov/news-information/speeches-testimony/2007/statement_011107.htm.*

Heil, Klaus, and Stephen Krause. German Embassy BKA Liaison Representatives. Interview by author. Washington, DC, 31 July 2007.

Herman, Michael. *Intelligence Power in Peace and War*. Cambridge, UK: University Press, 1996.

Herman, Michael. *Intelligence Services in the Information Age*. London: Taylor and Francis, 2001.

Heymann, Phillip B. *Terrorism, Freedom and Security: Winning without War*. Cambridge, MA: The MIT Press, 2003.

Hoffman, Bruce. "Commentary: Al Qaeda Isn't Dead Yet." *CNN.com*, 9 September 2008. *http://www.cnn.com/2008/POLITICS/09/09/hoffman.alqaeda/index.html#cnnSTCText.*

Hoffman, Bruce. *Inside Terrorism*. New York: Columbia University Press, 2006.

Houston, Robert "Sam." DEA-France Country Attache. Interview by author. Paris, France, 12 September 2008.

Houston, Robert "Sam." DEA-France Country Attache. Interview by author. Paris, France, 18 September 2008.

Hsu, Spencer R., and Joby Warrick. "Obama's Battle Against Terrorism to Go Beyond Bombs and Bullets," *Washington Post*, 6 August 2009, A1.

Ignatius, David. "A Quiet Deal with Pakistan." *Washington Post*, 4 November 2008, A17.

Ijaz, Mansoor. "Zardari and Mumbai." *Forbes.com*, 6 December 2008. *http://www.forbes.com/2008/12/05/zardari-mumbai-laskar-oped-cx_mi_1206ijaz.html.*

Inman, Bobby Ray (Admiral). Interview, *NewsHour* with Jim Lehrer transcript: "Searching for Answers." PBS *Online NewsHour*, 10 August 1998. *http://www.pbs.org/newshour/bb/africa/july-dec98/bomb_8-10.html.*

International Association of Chiefs of Police. *Criminal Intelligence Sharing: A National Plan for Intelligence-Led Policing At the Local, State and Federal Levels.* Alexandria, VA: IACP, 2002.

ISE Program Manager. *Feasibility Report for the Congress of the United States.* March 2008. *http://www.fas.org/irp/agency/ise/feasibility.pdf* and *http://www.dtic.mil/cgi-bin/GetTRDoc?AD=ADA484227&Locatio n=U2&doc=GetTRDoc.pdf.*

Isikoff, Michael. "The Fed Who Blew the Whistle: Is he a hero or a criminal?" *Newsweek*, 22 December 2008. *http://www.newsweek.com/id/174601.*

Jacobs, James B., Coleen Freil, and Robert Raddick. *Gotham Unbound: How New York City Was Liberated from the Grip of Organized Crime.* New York: NYU Press, 2001.

Jacobs, James B., Christopher Panarella, and Jay Worthington. *Busting the Mob.* New York: NYU Press, 1996.

Jehl, Douglas. "Abundance of Caution and Years of Budget Cuts are Seen to Limit CIA," *New York Times*, 11 May 2004.

Jenkins, Brian Michael. *Unconquerable Nation: Knowing Our Enemy, Strengthening Ourselves.* Santa Monica, CA: RAND Corporation, 2006. Original source: Donald Rumsfeld. "War in the Information Age." *Los Angeles Times*, 23 February 2006.

Johnson, Carrie. "Rule Changes Would Give FBI Agents Extensive New Powers." *Washington Post*, 12 September 2008, A02. *http://www.washingtonpost.com/wp/content/article/2008/09/11/AR200891103306_pf.html.*

Jones, Seth, and Martin Libicki. *How Terrorist Groups End: Lessons for Countering al Qa'ida.* Washington, DC: RAND Corporation, 2008.

Kaplan, David. "Paying For Terror." *US News and World Report*, 5 December 2005. *http://www.usnews.com/usnews/articles/051205/5terrror.htm.*

BIBLIOGRAPHY (Continued)

Kaplan, David E., and Kevin Whitelaw. "Remaking the U.S. Intelligence Community: Playing Defense." *U.S. News and World Report*, 13 November 2006. *http://www.usnews.com/usnews/news/articles/061103/3dni.intro.htm.*

Keyes, Charley. "U.S. Enemies Eating Our Lunch Online." *CNN.com*, 30 January 2008. *http://www.cnn.com/2008/POLITICS/01/30/internet.pr.failure/index.html.*

Kingsbury, Alex. "Lessons from the Near-defeat." *U.S. News & World Report*, 28 October 2008. *http://www.usnews.com/articles/news/world/2008/10/28/lessons-from-the-near-defeat-of-a-once-feared-al-qaeda-affiliate-in-indonesia.html.*

Kirschke, Joseph. "The Coke Coast: Cocaine and Failed States in West Africa." *World Politics Review*, 9 September 2008. *http://www.worldpoliticsreview.com/article.aspx?id=2629.*

Levitt, Stephen D., and Stephen J. Dubner. *Freakanomics: A Rogue Economist Explores the Hidden Side of Everything.* New York: Harper Collins, 2006.

Lewis, Bernard. *What Went Wrong: Western Impact and Middle Eastern Response.* New York and London: Oxford University Press, 2001.

Lia, Brynjar. *Globalisation and the Future of Terrorism: Patterns and Predictions.* New York: Routledge, 2005.

Lichtblau, Eric. "Terror Plan Would Give F.B.I. More Power." *New York Times*, 13 September 2008. *http://www.nytimes.com/2008/09/13/justice.html?ref=us.*

Locher III, James, et. al. *Project On National Security Reform: Forging a New Shield.* Arlington, VA: Project on National Security Reform, November 2008.

Mackinlay, John and Alison al-Baddawy, *Rethinking Counterinsurgency—A British Perspective: RAND Counterinsurgency StudyPaper 5* (Santa Monica, CA: RAND Corporation, OP-177-OSD, forthcoming).

Main, Frank. "Tunisia Returns Longtime Fugitive in Sex Abuse Case." *Chicago Sun-Times*, 25 January 2004, 3A.

BIBLIOGRAPHY (Continued)

Makarenko, Tamara. "The Crime – Terror Continuum: Tracing the Interplay between Transnational Organised Crime and Terrorism." *Global Crime* 6, No. 1 (February 2004), 130.

Marchetti, Victor, and John D. Marks. *The CIA and the Cult of Intelligence.* New York: Alfred A. Knopf, 1974.

Marchetti, Victor. *CIA and the Cult of Intelligence.* New York: Dell, 1989.

Markle Foundation Task Force on National Security in the Information Age, The. *Nation At Risk: Policy Makers Need Better Information to Protect the Country.* The Markle Foundation, March 2009.

Mason, Michael A. Executive Assistant Director for Criminal, Cyber Response and Services Branch, FBI. *2007 Worldwide Personnel Recovery Conference.* PowerPoint presentation, 10 January 2007. *http://proceedings.ndia.org/7040/12%20brief%by%20Mason.pdf.*

Mazzetti, Mark, and David Rohde. "Amid U.S. Policy Disputes, Qaeda Grows in Pakistan." *New York Times,* 30 June 2008. *http://www.nytimes.com/2008/06/30/washington/30tribal. html?pagewanted=1&_r=1&ref=todayspaper.*

Mazzetti, Mark, and Eric Schmitt. "A Wild Frontier." *The Economist,* 20 September 2008, 55.

Mazzetti, Mark. "Behind Analyst's Cool Demeanor, Deep Anxiety Over American Policy." *New York Times,* 26 December 2008. *http://www.nytimes.com/2008/12/27/washington/27reidel. html?_r=1&ref=todayspaper.*

Mazzetti, Mark. "When Spies Don't Play Well With Their Allies." *New York Times,* 20 July 2008.

McKusker, Rob. "Organised Crime and Terrorism: Convergence or Separation?" *ECPR Standing Group On Organised Crime Newsletter* 5, Issue 2 (May 2006), 3.

McShane, Larry. "Italian Mobsters in Widespread Decline." *USA Today,* 25 October 2007. *http://www.usatoday.com/news/nation/2007-10-25-2782988282_x.html.*

BIBLIOGRAPHY (Continued)

McShane, Larry. "Reputed Mobsters Rounded Up in U.S. Italy." *CNN.com*, 7 February 2008. *http://www.cnn.com/2008/CRIME/02/07/gambino. arrests.ap/index.html.*

Meyers, Lisa. "Foiling Millennium Attack was Mostly Luck." *MSNBC*, 29 April 2004. *http://www.msnbc.msn.com/id/4864792.*

Miller, John, et. al. *The Cell: Inside the 9/11 Plot, and Why the FBI and CIA Failed to Stop It.* New York: Hyperion, 2002.

Miller, Matt. "Husband Sentenced in 'Jane Doe' Murder." *The Patriot-News*, 4 January 2008. *http://www.pennlive.com/midstate/index. ssf/2008/01/_if_olga_shugar_has.html.*

Moloney, Anastasia. "Colombia's Uribe at Six Years: A Positive but Fragile Legacy." *World Politics Review*, 21 August 2008. *http://www. worldpoliticsreview.com/article.aspx?id=2589.*

Moreau, Ron, and Mark Hosenball. "Pakistan's Dangerous Double Game." *Newsweek*, 22 September 2008.

Nadelmann, Ethan, and Peter Andreas. *Policing the Globe: Criminalization and Crime Control in International Relations.* New York: Oxford University Press, 2006.

Nakashima, Ellen. "FBI Prepares Vast Database of Biometrics." *Washington Post*, 22 December 2007.

National Defense Intelligence College. *Improving the Law Enforcement-Intelligence Community Relationship: Can't We All Just Get Along?* edited by Timothy Christenson. Washington, DC: NDIC Press, 2007.

National Center for Missing and Exploited Children (NCMEC). "NCMEC applauds U.S. Marshals and ICE for Capture of Nation's Most Wanted Accused Child Pornographer." *http:// www.missingkids.com/missingkids/servlet/PageServlet? LanguageCountry=en_US&PageId=3155.*

National Strategy for Combating Terrorism (Washington, DC: White House, 2003), 16-17. *https://www.cia.gov/news-information/cia-the-war-on-terrorism/Counter_Terrorism_Strategy.pdf*

BIBLIOGRAPHY (Continued)

NationMaster. "1993 Mumbai Bombings." *NationMaster.com*, last accessed 27 June 2009. *http://www.nationmaster.com/encyclopedia/1993-Mumbai-bombings.*

9/11 Commission. *The 9/11 Commission Report.* Washington, DC: 2004.

Nussbaum, Brian. "Protecting Global Cities: New York, London, and the Internationalization of Municipal Policing for Counter-Terrorism." *Global Crime* 8, no. 3 (August 2007).

O'Connor, Matt. "Fugitive in Sex Case Brought Back to City." *Chicago Tribune*, 25 January 2004, Sec. 4, 3.

Office of the Director of National Intelligence. "National Intelligence Estimate: The Terrorist Threat to the U.S. Homeland." *National Intelligence Council.* Washington, DC, 17 July 2007. *http://dni.gov/press_releases/20070717_release.pdf.*

O'Neil, Siobhan. "Terrorist Precursor Crimes: Issues and Options for Congress." *CRS Report for Congress*, RL34014. Washington, DC: Congressional Research Service, 24 May 2007. *http://www.fas.org/sgp/crs/terror/RL34014.pdf.*

Ormerod, H.A. *Piracy in the Ancient World.* Liverpool, UK: University of Liverpool Press, 1978.

Osborne, Deborah. *Out of Bounds: Innovation and Change in Law Enforcement Intelligence Analysis.* Washington, DC: Joint Military Intelligence College, 2006. *http://www.ndic.edu/press/2201.htm.*

Pakkala, Tiffany. "'Jane Doe' Suspect Nabbed." *The Sentinel*, 4 December 2004. *http://www.cumberlink.com/articles/2004/12/04/news/news01.prt*

Pearl, Mariane. *A Mighty Heart.* New York: Scribner, 2003.

Perez, Emile. Commissionaire, French National Police. Interview by author. Paris, France. 7 March 2008.

Pillar, Paul. *Terrorism and Foreign Policy.* Washington, DC: Brookings, 2003.

Pincus, Walter. "Experts' Report Urges Changes in National Security System." *Washington Post*, 4 December 2008, A06. *http://www.washingtonpost.com/wp-dyn/content/article/2008/12/03/AR2008120303382.html.*

BIBLIOGRAPHY (Continued)

Posner, Richard A. *Uncertain Shield: The U.S. Intelligence System in the Throes of Reform.* Lanham, MD: Rowan & Littlefield Publishers, Inc., 2006.

Presidential Executive Order (EO) 12598, *Classified National Security Information* (as amended), 17 April 1995.

Priest, Dana. "Bush's War on Terror Comes to a Sudden End." *Washington Post*, 23 January 2009, A1. *http://www.washingtonpost.com/wp-dyn/content/article/2009/01/22/AR2009012203929_pf.html.*

Ransom, Harry Howe. "The Politicization of Intelligence." In *Intelligence and Intelligence Policy in a Democratic Society*, edited by Stephen J. Cimbala. Transnational Publishers, Inc., 1987.

Raustalia, Kal. "The Architecture of International Cooperation: Transgovernmental Networks and the Future of International Law." *Virginia Journal of International Law* 43, no. 1 (Fall 2002), 9, 63-64.

Rayman, Graham. "Stripped of Their Dignity." *Newsday*, 21 March 1999.

Reed, Donald. "Why Strategy Matters." *Homeland Security Affairs* 2, no. 3 (October 2006), 6. *http://www.hsaj.org/?article=2.3.10.*

Rewards for Justice. http://www.rewardsforjustice.net/index.cfm?page=success_stories&language=english.

Richelson, Jeffrey T. *The U.S. Intelligence Community.* 5th ed. Boulder, CO: Westview Press, 2008.

Riebling, Mark. *Wedge: From Pearl Harbor to 9/11: How the Secret War between the FBI and CIA has Endangered National Security.* New York: Alfred A. Knopf, 1994.

Riebling, Mark. *Wedge: The Secret War between the FBI and CIA.* New York: Alfred A. Knopf, 1994.

Risen, James. *State of War: The Secret History of the CIA and the Bush Administration.* New York: The Free Press, 2006.

Roberts, Mark J. "Pakistan's Inter-Services Intelligence Directorate: A State within a State?" *Joint Force Quarterly*, 48 (2008), 104-110.

BIBLIOGRAPHY (Continued)

Rotella, Sebastian, of the *Los Angeles Times*, in a question and answer seminar held at the U.S. Embassy in Paris, 22 April 2008.

Roy, Olivier. Globalized Islam: *The Search for a New Ummah*. New York: Columbia University Press, 2006.

Sanderson, Thomas, and Mary Beth Nikitin. "International Cooperation." In *Five Years After 9/11: An Assessment of America's War on Terror*, edited by Julianne Smith and Thomas Sanderson. Washington, DC: The CSIS Press, 2006.

Sanger, David E. "Obama's Advisers to Back Soft Power." *International Herald Tribune*, 1 December 2008. *http://www.iht.com/articles/2008/12/01/america/obama.php#top.*

Sheptycki, James. "Transnational Policing and the Makings of a Postmodern State." *British Journal of Criminology*, Vol. 35, no. 4 (Autumn 1995), 629-630.

Scheuer, Michael. *Imperial Hubris: Why the West is Losing the War on Terror*. Washington, DC: Brassey's Inc., 2004.

Scolino, Elaine, and Eric Schmitt. "A Not Very Private Feud Over Terrorism." *New York Times*, 8 June 2008. *http://www.nytimes.com/2008/06/08/weekinreview/08sciolino.html.*

Scowcroft, Brent (Lt Gen, USAF, Ret). Interview by author. 10 July 2007.

Shapiro, Al. "Lewis 'Scooter' Libby Found Guilty of Lying." *All Things Considered*, National Public Radio (NPR), 6 March 2007. *http://www.npr.org/templates/story/story.php?storyid=7738465.*

Shelly, Louise. "Organized Crime, Terrorism and Cybercrime." In *Security Sector Reform: Institutions, Society and Good Governance*, edited by Alan Bryden and Phillip Fluri. Baden Baden, Germany: Nomos Verlagsgeleelschaft, 2003.

Shelly, Louise, John Picarelli, et. al. *Methods and Motives: Exploring Links between Transnational Organized Crime & International Terrorism*. Washington, DC: National Institute of Justice, Office of Justice Programs, U.S. Department of Justice, 23 June 2007.

BIBLIOGRAPHY (Continued)

Sheptycki, James. "Policing, Intelligence Theory and the New Human Security Paradigm: Some Lessons From the Field," *Intelligence Theory: Key Questions and Debates*, Peter Gill, Stephen Marrin, and Mark Pythian, eds., 166-185, London and New York: Routledge, 2009.

Sheptycki, James. "Transnational Policing and the Makings of a Postmodern State." *British Journal of Criminology* 35, no. 4 (Autumn 1995). 629-630.

"Sicilian Mafia 'Decapitated' by Mass Arrests, Say Police." *CNN.com/* Europe, 16 December 2008. *http://www.cnn.com/2008/WORLD/ europe/12/16/mafia.raid.italy/index.html.*

Simmons, Greg. "NSA Spy Story Could Lead to New Leak Probe." *Fox News.com*, 29 December 2005. *http://www.foxnews.com/ story/0,2933,180149,00.html.*

Sims, Jennifer. "Understanding Ourselves." In *Transforming U.S. Intelligence*, 32-62. Washington, DC: Georgetown University Press, 2005.

Slaughter, Anne-Marie. "Breaking Out: The Proliferation of Actors in the International System." In *Global Prescriptions: The Production, Exploration, and Importation of a New State Orthodoxy*, edited by Yves Dezalay and Bryant G. Garth, 12-36. Ann Arbor: University of Michigan Press, 2002.

Slaughter, Anne-Marie. "Governing the Global Economy through Government Networks," in *Role of Law in International Politics*, edited by Michael Byers, 177-205, Oxford, UK: Oxford University Press, 2000.

Slaughter, Anne-Marie. "Government Networks: The heart of the liberal democratic order." In *Democratic Governance and International Law,* edited by Gregory H. Fox and Brad R. Roth, 199-235. Cambridge, UK: Cambridge University Press, 2000.

Slaughter, Anne-Marie. "Sovereignty and Power in a Networked World Order." *Stanford Journal of International Law* 40 (2004), 283-327.

Slaughter, Anne-Marie, and David Zaring. "Networking Goes International: An Update." In *Annual Review of Law and Social Science* 2 (December 2006), 211-229. *http://arjournals.annualreviews.org.*

BIBLIOGRAPHY (Continued)

Smith, R. Jeffrey, and Dafina Linzer. "CIA Officer's Job Made Any Leaks More Delicate." *Washington Post*, 23 April 2006, A01.

Spy Museum, The International. "Aldrich Ames—Dozens Exposed." *www.spymuseum.com/pages/agent-ames-aldrich-html*.

Steinberg, James B. *Erasing the Seams: An Integrated, International Strategy to Combat Terrorism.* Washington, DC: Brookings Institution, 3 May 2006. *http://www.brookings.edu/papers/2006/0503terrorism_steinberg.aspx*.

Steinberg, James B., Mary Graham, and Andrew Eggars. *Building Intelligence to Fight Terrorism—Policy Brief 125.* Washington DC: The Brookings Institution, September 2003. *http://www.brookings.edu/comm/policybriefs/pb125.htm*.

Sullivan, Jim. U.S. Marshal. Telephone interview by author. U.S. Virgin Islands, 23 May 2008.

"Suspect in Parental Kidnapping Returned from Cuba." *http://www.state.gov/m/ds/rls/75281.htm*.

Tavernise, Sabrina, "Organized Crime in Pakistan Feeds Taliban," *New York Times*, 28 August 2009. Available at: *http://www.nytimes.com/2009/08/29/world/asia/29karachi.html?pagewanted=1&_r=1&ref=global-home*.

Tayler, Letta, and Colby Itkowitz. "Names Put to Video Faces," *Newsday*, 26 July 2005.

Townsend, Frances Fragos. Interview by author. Washington, DC, 7 June 2007.

Turner, Michael A. *Why Secret Intelligence Fails.* Washington, DC: Potomac Books, Inc., 2006.

Tyson, Ann Scott. "Gates Urges Increased Funding for Diplomacy." *Washington Post*, 27 November 2007, A2.

Urbancic, Frank. Deputy Coordinator for Counterterrorism (S/CT), U.S. Department of State. Interview by the author. Washington, DC, 13 June 2007.

BIBLIOGRAPHY (Continued)

U.S. Department of Justice. Bureau of Justice Assistance (in collaboration with the Global Justice Information Sharing Initiative). *The National Criminal Intelligence Sharing Plan*. Washington, DC: Bureau of Justice Assistance, revised June 2005.

U.S. Department of Justice. Bureau of Justice Statistics. *World Factbook of Criminal Justice Systems*. *http://www.ojp.usdoj.gov/bjs/abstract/ wfcj.htm*.

U.S. Department of Justice. *Overview of the Law Enforcement Strategy to Combat International Organized Crime*. Washington, DC: DOJ, April 2008.

U.S. Department of State. Fact Sheet, "U.S.-Cuba Relations." *www.state. gov/p/wha/rls/fs/2001/2558.htm*.

U.S. Department of State. *Protection for State Department Buildings Abroad*. *http://www.state.gov/m/ds/rls/50892.htm*.

U.S. Government Accountability Office. *Combating Terrorism: Interagency Framework and Agency Programs to Address the Overseas Threat for Combating Terrorism*. Washington, DC: GAO, May 2003.

U.S. Government Accountability Office. *Combating Terrorism, Law Enforcement Agencies Lack Directives to Assist Foreign Nations to Identify, Disrupt, and Prosecute Terrorists*. GAO Highlights, May 2007.

U.S. Government Accountability Office. *Combating Terrorism: Law Enforcement Agencies Lack Directives to Assist Foreign Nations to Identify, Disrupt and Prosecute Terrorists*. GAO-07-697, 4 October 2007. *http://www.gao.gov/new.items/d08144t.pdf*.

U.S. Government Accountability Office. *Information Sharing: The Federal Government Needs to Establish Policies and Processes for Sharing Terrorism-Related and Sensitive but Unclassified Information*. Washington, DC: GAO, 2 March 2006.

U.S. Government Accountability Office. Report to Congressional Requesters. *COMBATING TERRORISM: Interagency Framework and Agency Programs to Address the Overseas Threat*. Washington, DC: May 2003, 55-56, 58-60.

BIBLIOGRAPHY (Continued)

U.S. Marshals Service. "America's Star: U.S. Marshals Service Talks WitSec to the World." *America's Star: FYI*, vol. 1, no. 1, August 2006. *http://www.marshals.gov/witsec/index.html.*

U.S. Marshals Service. "Former Lawman and Accused Child Rapist Returned to Washington State to Face Charges." *www.state.gov/m/ds/rls/93721.htm.*

Warrick, Joby. "U.S. Officials: Pakistani Agents Helped Plan Kabul Bombing." *Washington Post*, 1 August 2008, A1.

Whaley, Kevin. DEA Director of International Operations. Interview by author. DEA Headquarters, Arlington, VA, 7 June 2007.

White House, The. *Executive Memorandum: Steps to Combat Violence Against Women and Trafficking in Women and Girls.* The American President Project, 11 March 1998. *http://www.presidency.ucsb.edu/ws/indx.php?pid=55607.*

White House, The. *Executive Order Further Amendment to Executive Order 12958, as Amended, Classified National Security Information. http://www.archives.gov/isoo/policy-documents/eo-12958-amendment. html.*

Whitelaw, Kevin. "DS Gets Its Man," *Foreign Service Journal* (September 2005), 40. *http://www.afsa.org/fsj/sept05/whitelaw.pdf.*

Whitelaw, Kevin. "Inside Colombia's War on Kidnapping." *U.S. News & World Report*, 27 February 2008. *http://www.usnews.com/articles/news/world/2008/02/27/inside-colombias-war-on-kidnapping.html.*

Whitlock, Craig. "After a Decade at War With West, Al-Qaeda Still Impervious to Spies." *Washington Post*, 20 March 2008, A01.

Whitlock, Craig. "Al Qaeda's Growing Online Offensive." *Washington Post,* 24 June 2008, sec. A01.

Whitlock, Craig. "Extradition of Terror Suspects Founders." *Washington Post*, 21 December 2008, sec. A01. *http://www.washingtonpost. com/wpdyn/content/article/2008/12/20/AR2008122002096. html?hpid%3Dtopnews&sub=AR.*

Wiener, Tim. "Betrayer's Tale: A special report; A Decade as a Turncoat: Aldrich Ames's Own Story." *New York Times*, 28 July 1994.

BIBLIOGRAPHY (Continued)

Wight, Thomas. Deputy Assistant/Director, Witness Security Division, United States Marshals Service. Telephone interview by author, 5 December 2008.

Williams, Phil. Organized crime scholar at the University of Pittsburgh. Interview by author. Pittsburgh, PA, 22 March 2007.

Wilson, James Q. *Bureaucracy: What Government Agencies Do and Why They Do It*. Basic Books, 1989.

Wilson, Scott, and Al Kamen. "Global War on Terror is Given New Name," *Washington Post*, 25 March 2009, A4.

Wise, Jeff. "Civilian UAVs: No Pilot, No Problem." *Popular Mechanics*, April 2007.

Zegart, Amy. *Spying Blind*. Princeton, NJ: Princeton University Press, 2008.

Zimmett, Nora. "Bolivia Becoming a Hotbed of Islamic Extremist Report Concludes," *Fox News*, 16 June 2009. Available at *http://www.foxnews.com/story/0,2933.526753,00.html*.

INDEX

A

Agee, Phillip 58
Air Force Office of Special Investigations (AFOSI) 87
Al-Khafaji, Khardr 66
Al-Muhammed, Khamis Sirhan 66
Al-Zawahiri, Ayman 36, 153
Alcohol, Tobacco, and Firearms (ATF) 65
"America's Most Wanted" 57, 104, 134, 181
Ames, Aldrich 58, 169, 171
Andreas, Peter 22, 30, 91, 93, 94, 112, 123, 153, 164
Army Criminal Investigation Division (CID) 87
Australian Institute of Criminology 70
Azzam, Abdullah 36

B

Bergen, Peter 26, 75, 154
Bertillonage system 30
Bin Laden, Osama 26, 27, 36, 43, 44, 55, 115, 154
BKA (German Bundeskrimalimt) 18, 160
Block, Ludo ix, 69, 155
Bout, Victor 99, 100, 106, 157
Brink, Van A. (see Gilbert Zeigler) 128
Brown, Tina 27

C

Cage, Nicolas 99
Cartels—Colombia 60, 61, 65, 129
"Can-do attitude" 43, 44, 71
Central Intelligence Agency 3, 4, 7, 8, 9, 16, 25, 27, 44, 45, 47, 48, 49, 54, 55, 58, 59, 62, 65, 74, 75, 77, 78, 84, 136, 159, 160, 161, 163, 164, 166, 169
Chertoff, Michael 137, 158
Chirac, Jacques 78
Clarke, Richard 44, 75, 155
Classification (Top Secret, Secret, Confidential) 50, 51, 59, 78
"Connecting the dots" 109
Corruption, corrupt police xvi, 21, 79, 87, 108, 127, 128
Cover 78
Credit card fraud ix, 26, 76, 143

INDEX (Continued)

INDEX (Continued)

INDEX (Continued)

INDEX (Continued)

INDEX (Continued)

INDEX (Continued)

Z

ABOUT THE AUTHOR

Michael D. Bayer is a 22-year veteran of the U.S. Foreign Service and the federal law enforcement system. As a Special Agent for the U.S. Department of State's Diplomatic Security Service, he has served as a regional security officer at American embassies overseas, as chief of a transnational criminal investigative section, as a criminal investigator, and as a bodyguard for former Secretary of State James Baker.

Throughout his long career in security and law enforcement, Mike has worked extensively and intimately with all elements of the U.S. national security structure—to include U.S. (and foreign) intelligence agencies, the international diplomatic corps, U.S. military and Department of Defense elements, and international police and law enforcement entities. In 1999 he won national acclaim as a criminal investigator for having taken down an international organized crime ring, for which his work has been featured on the television series "America's Most Wanted." Mike was further recognized that year by the Federal Law Enforcement Officers Association (FLEOA) as a criminal investigator of the year—with an award for investigative excellence. As Chief of Diplomatic Security's Criminal Investigative Liaison Branch (CIL) from 2003 to 2006, he directed the location, apprehension, and return to the United States of over 300 (often notorious) American fugitives from overseas. He has served multi-year tours in Bogota, Colombia; Istanbul, Turkey; and most recently Paris, France. His next assignment will be Special Agent in Charge of the Denver Field Office beginning in the summer of 2010. Through the years, Mike has worked all over the world on various duty assignments and investigations.

In 2006 the author was nominated as a Research Fellow to the National Defense Intelligence College (NDIC), working in its Center for Strategic Intelligence Research (CSIR). This book is a product of that fellowship. In August 2005 Mike authored an article, "Operation Global Pursuit: In Pursuit of the World's Most Dangerous Fugitives and Terrorists," for *The Police Chief* magazine.

The author holds bachelor's and master's degrees from Duquesne University in Pittsburgh, Pennsylvania, and is presently pursuing a Ph.D. in law and transnational terrorism on a scholarship from the University of Wollongong in Australia.

Mike is a native of Pittsburgh. He and his wife Suzanne have two children, Ingrid and Gus, and a sweet Border Collie named Gracie. All are avid Pittsburgh Steelers football fans.